OXFORD READING

ETHICAL THEORY 2

ETHICAL THEORY 2
Theories About How We Should Live

Edited by

JAMES RACHELS

OXFORD UNIVERSITY PRESS

This book has been printed digitally and produced in a standard specification
in order to ensure its continuing availability

OXFORD
UNIVERSITY PRESS

Great Clarendon Street, Oxford OX2 6DP

Oxford University Press is a department of the University of Oxford.
It furthers the University's objective of excellence in research, scholarship,
and education by publishing worldwide in

Oxford New York

Auckland   Cape Town Dar es Salaam Hong Kong   Karachi
Kuala Lumpur Madrid Melbourne Mexico City   Nairobi
New Delhi Shanghai Taipei Toronto
With offices in
Argentina Austria Brazil Chile Czech Republic France Greece
Guatemala Hungary Italy Japan South Korea Poland Portugal
Singapore Switzerland Thailand Turkey Ukraine Vietnam

Oxford is a registered trade mark of Oxford University Press
in the UK and in certain other countries

Published in the United States
by Oxford University Press Inc., New York

Oxford is a registered trade mark of Oxford University Press
in the UK and in certain other countries

Published in the United States
by Oxford University Press Inc., New York

Introduction and selection © Oxford University Press 1998

The moral rights of the author have been asserted

Database right Oxford University Press (maker)

Reprinted 2004

ISBN 0-19-875186-9

CONTENTS

INTRODUCTION

JAMES RACHELS

Today no single theory dominates moral philosophy. For a long time, utilitarianism held centre-stage. Almost every moral philosopher in the twentieth century began by reacting to it in one way or another, some declaring their allegiance to utilitarianism and worrying over how best to formulate its doctrines, with others arguing that it is unsound and proposing alternatives. The result is that there are now a number of competing research programmes, each being pursued by a loose coalition of thinkers. The chapters collected in this book discuss the issues and ideas that animate these rival approaches.

I

In the year of the French Revolution Jeremy Bentham declared that all moral duties are derived from one ultimate principle, the principle of utility. Whenever we must choose what to do or what social policy to adopt, he said, we should survey the alternatives and ask which would have the best overall consequences for everyone concerned. Nothing else matters. Put simply, we should always strive to promote 'the greatest happiness of the greatest number'. In the nineteenth century John Stuart Mill and Henry Sidgwick developed and extended this idea, and utilitarianism became the leading option in moral philosophy.

But utilitarianism was not merely an academic theory; it became the basis of a popular movement. It seemed to be an enlightened ethic that set aside the superstitions and irrationalities of the past. It dismissed as mere 'rule worship' the idea that virtue consists in blindly following moral rules, and it grounded morality firmly in the practical necessities of this world rather than deferring to demands imposed from some supernatural realm. Utilitarian reformers set out to end slavery, secure property rights for women, end child labour, and make prisons less brutal. They championed a revolutionary ethical outlook that would have enormous influence in law, economics, and philosophy, as well as affecting how ordinary people think.

Its partisans believed that utilitarianism was the merest common sense. But, as the theory was examined more closely, it turned out to have implications that were not commonsensical at all. On the contrary, utilitarianism seemed to contradict common sense at every turn.

1. First, utilitarianism seems unable to account for *backward-looking reasons*. Suppose you promised to meet someone this afternoon. But when the time comes, you don't want to do it—you prefer to stay home and work instead. What should you do? If we take utility as our guide, we would ask which course would have the best overall outcome, and if the utility of getting your work done outweighs your friend's disappointment, we should conclude that it is right to break the promise. However, that does not seem correct. The fact that you promised creates an obligation that you cannot escape so easily. Of course, if the advantage of breaking the promise were great—if, for example, there was an emergency and you needed to rush someone to the hospital—you would be justified in breaking it. But a small gain in utility cannot overcome the obligation imposed by the fact that you promised. If promising does not create a real commitment, what's the point of it? Thus utilitarianism, which says that only consequences matter, seems mistaken.

Why is utilitarianism vulnerable to this sort of criticism? It is because the only kinds of consideration that the theory holds relevant to determining the rightness of actions are considerations having to do with the future. Utilitarianism has us confine our attention to what will happen as a result of our actions. However, we normally think that considerations about the past are also important. 'You promised' is a fact about the past.

Once we understand this, other examples of backward-looking reasons come easily to mind. The fact that someone did not commit a crime is a good reason why he should not be punished. The fact that someone once did you a favour may be a good reason for now doing him a favour. The fact that you did something to hurt someone may be a reason you should now make it up to her. These are all facts about the past that are relevant to determining our obligations. But utilitarianism makes the past irrelevant, and so it seems deficient.

2. A different sort of objection is that utilitarianism is *too demanding*. Suppose you are on your way to the theatre when someone points out that the money you are about to spend could be used to provide food for starving people or inoculations for Third World children. Surely, those people need food and medicine more than you need to see a play. So you

forgo your entertainment and give the money to a charitable agency. But that is not the end of it. By the same reasoning, you cannot buy new clothes, a car, a computer, or a camera. Probably you should move into a cheaper apartment; after all, what is more important—your having a nice apartment or children having food? In fact, faithful adherence to the utilitarian standard would require you to give away your resources until you have lowered your own standard of living to the level of the neediest people you could help. We might admire people who do this, but we do not regard them as doing simply what duty requires. Instead, we regard them as saintly people whose generosity goes far beyond what duty requires. We distinguish between *obligatory* actions, which are morally required, and *supererogatory* actions, which are praiseworthy but not strictly required. Utilitarianism seems to eliminate this distinction.

But the problem is not only that we would be required to give up most of our material resources. More importantly, abiding by utilitarianism's mandates would make it impossible for us to carry on our individual lives. Each of our lives includes projects and activities that give it character and meaning; these are what make our lives worth living. But an ethic that requires the subordination of everything to the impartial promotion of the general welfare would require us to abandon those projects and activities. Suppose you are a cabinet-maker, not getting rich but making a comfortable living; you have two children that you love; and on weekends you like to perform with an amateur theatre group. In addition you are interested in history and you read a lot. How could there be anything wrong with this? But judged by the utilitarian standard, you are probably leading a morally unacceptable life. After all, you could be doing a great deal more good if you spent your time in other ways. (On these issues, see Chapter XII of this volume.)

3. Utilitarianism also has startling implications for our *personal relationships*. One of the central components of utilitarianism is the idea of impartiality—the idea that each person's life and interests are equally important. In the words of John Stuart Mill, when we are weighing the interests of different people, we should be 'as strictly impartial as a disinterested and benevolent spectator'.[1] This sounds appealing in theory, but in practice none of us would be willing to adopt such a stance, for it would require that we abandon our special relationships with friends and family. We are all deeply partial where our friends and family are concerned. We love them and we would go to great lengths to help them. To us, they are not just members of the great crowd of humanity—they are special. The

[1] John Stuart Mill, *Utilitarianism* (1861; Indianapolis: Bobbs-Merrill, 1957), 22.

idea that we should be no more concerned for their welfare than for anyone else's seems absurd. As John Cottingham puts it, 'A parent who leaves his child to burn, on the ground that the building contains someone else whose future contribution to the general welfare promises to be greater, is not a hero; he is (rightly) an object of moral contempt, a moral leper.'[2]

4. Additional problems are connected with the closely related notions of *rights* and *justice*. It seems that pursuing the 'greatest good of the greatest number' can bring one directly into conflict with these values. One familiar (if fanciful) example concerns a hospital ward full of patients who need transplants: one needs a heart, another a kidney, another a liver, and so on. Now suppose we could provide life-saving transplants for five of them by kidnapping one healthy man and distributing his organs. From the point of view of utility, this would be a bargain—one man would die but five would be saved. Yet plainly this would be unacceptable, for it violates the rights of the man who is killed. Or, to take a different sort of example: a Peeping Tom creeps around people's houses, watching them through their bedroom windows. Suppose he is never caught, so that the only consequence of his spying is an increase in his own happiness. From the point of view of utility, there seem to be no grounds for objecting to what he does, even though it is a clear violation of the rights of his victims. (Chapter VII in this volume discusses the possibility of taking individual rights as the central notion of moral theory.)

The subject of justice is traditionally divided into two parts: retributive justice, which deals with rewards and punishments; and distributive justice, which is concerned with the way in which goods are spread out among individuals. Critics of utilitarianism have argued that it cannot account for either type of justice. As for retributive justice, here is H. J. McCloskey's famous example:

Suppose a utilitarian were visiting an area in which there was racial strife, and that, during his visit, a Negro rapes a white woman, and that race riots occur as a result of the crime, white mobs, with the connivance of the police, bashing and killing Negroes, etc. Suppose too that our utilitarian is in the area of the crime when it is committed such that his testimony would bring about the conviction of a particular Negro. If he knows that a quick arrest will stop the riots and lynchings, surely, as a utilitarian, he must conclude that he has a duty to bear false witness in order to bring about the punishment of an innocent person.[3]

Moreover, although utilitarianism mandates that we maximize well-being, it provides no guidance concerning how well-being should be dis-

---

[2] John Cottingham, 'Partialism, Favouritism and Morality', *Philosophical Quarterly*, 36 (1986), 357.
[3] H. J. McCloskey, 'A Non-Utilitarian Approach to Punishment', *Inquiry* 8 (1965), 240.

tributed. Should we, for example, prefer a situation in which one person is fabulously rich while everyone else is poor over a situation in which everyone is moderately well off? You might think not, but suppose the fortunate individual is rich enough that his extra wealth more than compensates for the deprivations of the poor? We may represent levels of welfare by numbers, where anything over zero is a life worth living. The comparison is between:

(A) one person at 200, nineteen people at 1;
(B) twenty people at 10.

If we are out to maximize *total* utility, (A) is preferable to (B). But many people would think this absurd. It will not help to switch our criterion to *average* utility, since the average welfare per person in (A) is also higher than in (B). Nor will it do any good to say that we want a distribution that is as equal as possible, for then we would have to prefer (C) over (D):

(C) twenty people at 10;
(D) ten people at 10, ten people at 20.

There may be reasons for preferring (C) to (D), but on its face it is hard to see how it can be objectionable, other things being equal, to make some people better off if no one else is made worse off.[4]

5. Finally, utilitarianism has been faulted on very different grounds, having to do with *character*. What would a person be like if he or she were willing to make all decisions on the basis of maximizing utility? A thoroughgoing utilitarian could hardly be a loyal friend, for he would have no special concern for friends beyond the concern he has for all people. She would not be a loving mother, for she would have no special concern for her children. Or consider this example, suggested by Michael Stocker:[5]

You are in the hospital recovering from a long illness. You are bored and restless, and so you are delighted when Smith arrives to visit. You have a good time chatting with him; his visit is just the tonic you needed. After a while you tell Smith how much you appreciate his coming: he really is a fine fellow and a good friend to take the trouble to come all the way across town to see you. But Smith demurs; he protests that he is merely doing his duty. At first you think Smith is only being modest, but the more you talk, the clearer it becomes that he is speaking the literal truth. He is not visiting

---

[4] The question of how to choose between distributions of welfare across whole populations is a central theme of Derek Parfit, *Reasons and Persons* (Oxford: Oxford University Press, 1984). Current discussion on the subject centres on problems discovered by Parfit.

[5] Michael Stocker, 'The Schizophrenia of Modern Ethical Theories', *Journal of Philosophy*, 73 (1976), 453–66.

you because he wants to, or because he likes you, but only because he thinks it is his duty to 'do the right thing', and on this occasion he has decided it is his duty to visit you—perhaps because he knows of no one else who is more in need of cheering up or no one easier to get to. Stocker comments that surely you would be very disappointed to learn Smith's motive; now his visit seems cold and calculating and it loses all value to you. You thought he was your friend, but now you learn otherwise. Stocker says about Smith's behaviour: 'Surely there is something lacking here—and lacking in moral merit or value.'

Thus, it is said, moral character consists of a great deal more than a capacity for utilitarian calculation. Indeed, the ability to make such calculations might turn out to be no more than a small, relatively insignificant part of what makes one a morally good person. (Chapters IV and IX in this volume take up questions of character.)

All of this adds up to an impressive case against utilitarianism. It is not surprising, then, that a great many contemporary moral philosophers reject this theory altogether. They do not, of course, reject its core value of beneficence—no one denies that we should, in general, try to make people better off. But they hold that there is much more to morality than merely this. Reviewing its deficiencies, Bernard Williams wrote that 'the simple-mindedness of utilitarianism disqualifies it totally', and he predicted that 'The day cannot be too far off in which we hear no more of it.'[6]

II

If utilitarianism is no good, what sort of view should replace it? During the middle decades of the twentieth century, utilitarianism's chief rival was the intuitionism of W. D. Ross. As early as 1930, in his book *The Right and the Good*, Ross had pointed out that utilitarianism leads to conclusions that seem plainly wrong. His diagnosis of the problem was that

[Utilitarianism] says, in effect, that the only morally significant relation in which my neighbours stand to me is that to being possible beneficiaries by my action. They do stand in this relation to me, and this relation is morally significant. But they may also stand to me in the relation of promisee to promiser, of creditor to debtor, of wife to husband, of child to parent, of friend to friend, of fellow countryman to fellow countryman, and the like; and each of these relations is the foundation of a prima-facie duty, which is more or less incumbent on me according to the circumstances of the case.[7]

---

[6] J. J. C. Smart and Bernard Williams, *Utilitarianism, For and Against* (Cambridge: Cambridge University Press, 1973), 150.

[7] W. D. Ross, *The Right and the Good* (Oxford: Oxford University Press, 1930), 19 (Ch. I, pp. 19–20 of this volume).

Ross argued that we have an indefinite number of these prima-facie duties, including at least the following: (1) duties resting on some previous act of our own, such as the duty to keep our promises and the duty to make restitution for wrongs we have done; (2) the duty of gratitude, to return favours others have done for us; (3) the duty of justice, to distribute goods fairly; (4) the duty of self-improvement, to develop our own talents and abilities; (5) the duty of beneficence, to act so as to benefit others; and (6) the duty of non-maleficence, not to injure others.

These duties, according to Ross, are independent of one another—they are not reducible to one another, nor are they reducible to any more general principle such as the principle of utility. Moreover, it is impossible to rank these duties in order of importance. Thus, when they come into conflict, there is no formula to tell us which duties override which others. Is it more important to keep one's promises, or to avoid injuring others? There is no general answer. In each particular case, we must make a judgement about what should be done in light of the circumstances at hand. (Ross's position is developed in Chapter I in this volume.)

Ross's intuitionism had the great advantage of conforming to common sense. Indeed, its critics sometimes charged that it was too closely tied to common sense—it seemed to be little more than a systematic description of what 'sensible people' happen to think. None the less, it was a natural reaction to utilitarianism, which was so frequently faulted for failing to match common sense closely enough.

Meanwhile, however, many philosophers believed that utilitarianism could be brought closer to common sense, by casting it into a new and improved form. One of the main strategies was to distinguish *act*-utilitarianism from *rule*-utilitarianism. The former is the idea that the principle of utility is to be applied to each individual action, one by one. So, to determine whether you ought to keep a promise, you would ask whether a particular act of promise-keeping would lead to the best possible outcome for everyone concerned. This is the method of classical utilitarianism, and it generated the difficulties that we have noted.

Rule-utilitarianism, however, suggests a more complicated approach. First, the principle of utility is used to select a set of rules that would be good to follow. We would all be better off, for example, if such rules as 'Keep your promises', 'Tell the truth', and 'Respect one another's privacy' were generally followed. Then, to determine whether a particular action is mandatory—such as keeping a particular promise you have made—we refer to this set of rules. The key point is that the principle of utility is not applied directly to particular actions; it is used only to identify which general rules are to be followed. Rule-utilitarianism, it was said, did not lead to the difficulties we have noted. Indeed, all of Ross's prima-facie duties could be understood as rules that are themselves ultimately validated by appeal to the principle of utility.

The distinction between act- and rule-utilitarianism made possible a host of subtle variations on the basic utilitarian idea. (Chapter II in this volume discusses this distinction.) There has been one other development of comparable importance for utilitarian theory, namely, the identification of *motive-utilitarianism* as a distinct approach. Motive-utilitarianism begins with the paradoxical observation that if we want to achieve 'the greatest happiness of the greatest number', we should not consciously aim to promote that goal; nor should we encourage other people to do so. Sidgwick observed that 'from the universal point of view no less than from that of the individual, it seems true that Happiness is likely to be better attained if the extent to which we set ourselves consciously to aim at it be carefully restricted'.[8] Thus, if we forget about utilitarian calculating, and instead concentrate on being loving parents and loyal friends, working at our jobs, supporting the local Little Theatre Company, and so on, we will likely end up doing more good than if we are constantly calculating—even though we will sometimes do things that would not be approved from the calculating point of view. Our motives in all this will be specific to the people and things we value—love of our children and friends; love of the theatre; and so on—rather than simply a desire to increase the general welfare. But that is all right, for the best way to increase welfare may be precisely to adopt such attitudes and to encourage others to do so as well. Sidgwick again:

And thus we may conclude that the pursuit of the ideal objectives before mentioned, Virtue, Truth, Freedom, Beauty, etc., for their own sakes, is indirectly and secondarily, though not primarily and absolutely, rational; on account not only of the happiness that will result from their attainment, but also of that which springs from their disinterested pursuit. While yet if we ask for a final criterion of the comparative value of the different objects of men's enthusiastic pursuit, and of the limits within which each may legitimately engross the attention of mankind, we shall none the less conceive it to depend upon the degree in which they respectively conduce to Happiness.[9]

We might therefore understand right action to be action that springs from the overall set of motives that best promotes the general welfare; and these motives might very well include the honesty, loyalty, faithfulness, and love of justice that have figured so prominently in the objections to simpler forms of utilitarian theory. (A detailed discussion of motive-utilitarianism is given in Chapter III.)

[8] Henry Sidgwick, *The Methods of Ethics* (1874; 7th edn. London: Macmillan, 1907), 405.
[9] Ibid. 405–6.

III

In 1967, introducing the first Oxford Readings volume on ethical theory, Philippa Foot explained that the book would include essays on 'the part played by social utility in determining right and wrong'.[10] That was the only issue of substantive moral theory covered in that book, and naturally so: although other sorts of theories were sometimes discussed, utilitarianism and intuitionism dominated the field. This changed with the publication of John Rawls's *A Theory of Justice* in 1971. Rarely has a single work had such impact. Rawls had published a series of articles beginning in the 1950s outlining his ideas; but when his book was published those ideas became the leading topic of debate among moral philosophers. (The most important of Rawls's original articles is included here as Chapter V.) Rawls sought to construct a general theory describing how moral judgements—in particular, judgements about the justice of social institutions—might be made and justified.

Rawls had two ideas about the justification of moral judgements. First was the method of 'reflective equilibrium'. Moral theory, he said, is 'the attempt to describe our moral capacity', just as a linguistic theory is an attempt to describe our capacity for language. Native speakers are able to distinguish well-formed from ill-formed sentences, even without a theory for guidance. The task of linguistic theory is to formulate 'clearly expressed principles which make the same discriminations as the native speaker', so that we can understand the speaker's capacity as if it were guided by those principles. Similarly, we are able to judge intuitively that some actions are right, and others wrong; and the task of moral theory is to formulate principles that explain and justify those judgements: 'what is required is a formulation of a set of principles which, when conjoined to our beliefs and knowledge of the circumstances, would lead us to make these judgements with their supporting reasons were we to apply these principles conscientiously and intelligently . . . These principles can serve as part of the premises of an argument which arrives at the matching judgements.'[11] An obvious problem with this is that commonly held moral beliefs can be incorrect; they might be the result of prejudice or selfishness, or they might be left over from discarded religious or metaphysical systems. The principles of a moral theory that remains faithful to our 'intuitions' will only enshrine our rationality. Rawls is sensitive to this obvious point, and he tries to meet it by stipulating that a moral theory

---

[10] Philippa Foot (ed.), *Theories of Ethics* (Oxford: Oxford University Press, 1967), 1.
[11] All the quotations in this paragraph are from John Rawls, *A Theory of Justice* (Cambridge, Mass.: Harvard University Press, 1971), ch. 1, sect. 9.

need not respect every intuitive judgement. Only 'considered judgements' need be taken into account: 'we can discard those judgements made with hesitation, or in which we have little confidence. Similarly, those given when we are frightened, or when we stand to gain one way or the other can be left aside. All these judgements are likely to be erroneous . . .'. Moreover, we may want to revise some of our judgements in the light of the theory, just as we may adjust our theory to accommodate some of the judgements. The process of give and take continues until the judgements and the theory are in a state of 'reflective equilibrium'. Then we have achieved a satisfactory theory together with an enlightened and defensible collection of moral judgements.

Rawls's second idea about justification placed his theory within the social contract tradition. He proposed that the rules of justice be conceived as whatever rules we would accept in special circumstances called 'the original position'. The original position is an imaginary situation in which we are negotiating with other people about how the basic institutions of society are to be structured. But the negotiation takes place under special constraints: everyone is ignorant of his or her own personal qualities and social position. No one knows whether they are male or female, black or white, talented or clumsy, smart or stupid, rich or poor. This influences how the negotiations will go. Because we lack this information, we cannot press for social arrangements that will favour ourselves or people like us. Instead we will be motivated to seek an arrangement in which everyone is as well-off as possible, so that we will have a maximum chance of flourishing regardless of who we turn out to be when the 'veil of ignorance' is lifted.

What would be the result of negotiating under such constraints? Rawls argues that we would agree on two general principles: first, that everyone should have the most extensive liberty compatible with a similar liberty for others; and secondly, that social or economic inequalities should not be permitted unless they work to everyone's advantage and are attached to positions open to everyone. These are the basic principles of justice: social institutions are acceptable, from the point of view of justice, only if they satisfy these conditions. These institutions would obviously be egalitarian and democratic.

By reviving the social contract tradition, Rawls introduced a fresh set of ideas into the philosophical debate about ethics. There was now a third major alternative, alongside utilitarianism and intuitionism. But Rawls himself became increasingly reluctant to view his theory as such an alternative. Initially, he had suggested that it might be interpreted as a general theory covering all of morality. However, as time passed Rawls claimed less for his theory, until it finally came to be presented as a theory about only one part of morality (the justice of basic social institutions) in only one kind of society (a constitutional democracy). Nevertheless, others have taken up the idea of the social contract as a general theory of ethics.

In its pure form, the social contract view is that morality is a set of rules that rational people will agree to adopt to further their own interests. It is obvious, for example, that each of us will be better off if we are able to live in a society in which murder, assault, and theft are prohibited. Therefore, we have good reason to accept such rules, and others like them, provided that other people will accept them as well. It is a simple and elegant conception, and it provides plausible answers to questions that have long puzzled philosophers. How are moral rules justified? By showing that they are necessary if we are to co-operate for our mutual benefit. Why is it reasonable for us to follow these rules? We agree to follow the moral rules because it is to our own advantage to live in a society in which the rules are accepted, and our own steady compliance is the reasonable price we pay in order to secure the steady compliance of others.

Finally, are there moral 'facts'? Does morality have an objective basis? For utilitarians, intuitionists, and other theorists, this is a difficult and complicated issue. But with the social contract conception at hand, no long explanation is needed. Morality is a rational enterprise. It really is true—independently of what anyone thinks or how anyone feels—that certain goods cannot be obtained without social co-operation, and that, therefore, rational self-interested people will have reason to co-operate with one another to obtain those goods. It is further true that this co-operation will involve accepting rules that constrain behaviour. If this is what moral rules are like, then it is easy to explain their rationality and objectivity without resorting to any strange or mystifying conception of 'objective values'.

IV

A fundamental question is why we should accede to the demands of morality—why should a rational person accept 'moral' constraints on his behaviour, rather than simply doing what he wants, or what he thinks best for himself, at any given time? One answer appeals to our emotions: each of us has 'benevolent sentiments', as Hume put it, that make us care about the welfare of other people as well as our own. Utilitarians have usually favoured this sort of answer, and it is hard to imagine what other answer they could give. Contract theorists, however, count it as an advantage of their approach that it does not require benevolent sentiments. On their view, even entirely self-interested people would have reason to accept moral constraints, as part of a bargain aimed at securing the benefits of social living.

Neither of these answers seems altogether satisfactory. The appeal to 'benevolent sentiments' fails to capture the stringency of moral requirements, the feeling that there are some things that one *must* or *must not* do, whatever one's feelings may be. The social contract theory likewise fails to account for the absolute character of moral obligation. Is it wrong for me to murder you *only* because we have made a deal that forbids it? And what of individuals who cannot participate in such agreements, such as animals and mentally defective humans?

Such thoughts have led some contemporary philosophers to reconsider ideas developed by Immanuel Kant in the late eighteenth century. These thinkers have produced a literature that is partly interpretation of Kant, whose own writings are notoriously obscure, and partly a defence of his approach as the soundest available understanding of morality. The source of morality, according to this approach, is not in the emotions or in social agreements. It is, instead, in the will of the rational, autonomous agent— the agent who gives himself or herself directives about what is to be done. Among the constraints on the will of the rational agent is consistency: he must not act for reasons that he would not be willing to acknowledge on other occasions, nor may he act for reasons that he would be unwilling to have guide the actions of others. As Kant put it, the autonomous agent must act only on principles that he would be willing to have everyone follow 'as a universal law'.[12]

Inevitably, this view appeals to more obscure metaphysical ideas than do other theories. On Kant's view, the rational will is not only the source of normativity; it is also the source of value. Rational agents—human persons—are the beings who value things; thus, if the world contained no persons, nothing would be valuable. Moreover, because their existence is a pre-condition for anything's having value, rational agents are themselves the only things in the world whose value is absolute. The obscurity of such ideas is one problem that the New Kantians have sought to overcome; another is Kant's own insistence that consistency in action requires that one accept absolute rules. On Kant's view, the rule against lying, for example, admits no exceptions—one may never lie, under any circumstances. Not many thinkers today are willing to accept such a rigoristic ethics. Thus, those sympathetic with Kant's approach have sought a way to

---

[12] Immanuel Kant, *Foundations of the Metaphysics of Morals* (1785), tr. Lewis White Beck (Indianapolis: Bobbs-Merrill, 1959), 39.

interpret the Kantian demand for consistency that does not lead to this conclusion. (These issues are discussed in Chapters XIII and XIV in this volume.)

V

The debate between utilitarian, contractarian, and Kantian approaches has dominated moral philosophy for two centuries, and still there is no prospect of a resolution. What is to be made of this? One possibility is that the lack of agreement signals something fundamentally wrong—that the whole subject is flawed in some deep way. In 1958 G. E. M. Anscombe suggested exactly this. 'Modern moral philosophy', she said, has been debating the wrong question. Modern moral philosophy conceives of its subject-matter as the evaluation of actions, and so it begins by asking *What ought we to do?* This leads to the development of theories about moral obligation and the difference between right and wrong action. But there is a different starting-point available. Aristotle and others in the ancient world took the primary questions of moral philosophy to concern character rather than action. They approached the subject by asking *What traits of character make one a good person?* and as a result they went on to develop theories of virtue rather than of rightness and obligation. According to Anscombe, we should return to the older way of thinking: 'The concepts of obligation, and duty—*moral* obligation and *moral* duty, that is to say—and of what is *morally* right and wrong, and of the *moral* sense of "ought," ought to be jettisoned . . . It would be a great improvement if, instead of "morally wrong," one always named a genus such as "untruthful," "unchaste," "unjust." '[13] To understand ethics, therefore, we must understand first and foremost what makes someone a virtuous person. Today this approach is enormously popular. 'Virtue theory' is one of the most vigorously pursued options in moral philosophy. (See Chapters X and XI in this volume.)

A theory of virtue should do several things. First there should be an explanation of what a virtue is. It may be said, for example, that a virtue is a trait of character, manifested in habitual action, that it is good for a person to have. Secondly, there should be some specification of which character traits are virtues—courage, perhaps, and compassion, generosity, loyalty, tolerance, prudence, and more. Thirdly, there should be an explanation of what these virtues consist in. What is courage? What

---

[13] G. E. M. Anscombe, 'Modern Moral Philosophy', *Philosophy*, 33 (1958), 1–18; repr. in *Ethics, Religion, and Politics, Collected Papers*, iii (Minneapolis: University of Minnesota Press, 1981), 26, 33.

exactly does tolerance require? There are innumerable questions of this type that might be investigated; here is a research project to last a lifetime. Fourthly, there should be an explanation of why these qualities are good ones for a person to have. The explanations might vary with the different virtues: courage might be valuable because life is full of dangers and without courage we would be unable to cope with them; whereas honesty might be needed because without it relations between people would go wrong in all sorts of ways. However, it might be possible, as Aristotle thought, to give a more general explanation of why the virtues are important: Aristotle believed that the virtues are the qualities of character that we need if we are to flourish as human beings, living in the kinds of societies it is natural for us to form.

Virtue theory is popular among philosophers today because it seems to provide a natural way of understanding the moral life that does not land one in the various problems endemic to the other theories. But it is not just a return to ancient forms of thought. It also connects, in an interesting way, with ideas as modern as feminism. Feminists have argued that modern moral philosophy incorporates a subtle male bias. In the modern world men have typically been responsible for public life, for business and politics, whereas women's roles have been conceived in connection with home and hearth. With this in mind, think about the theories of 'right action' that have dominated modern moral philosophy—theories produced by male philosophers whose sensibilities were shaped by their own distinctive sorts of experience. The influence of that experience is plain. Their theories emphasize impersonal duty, contracts, the harmonization of competing interests, and the calculation of costs and benefits. The values that govern human relationships on the small scale—loving, nurturing, caring for friends and family—are almost wholly absent. The theory of virtue may be seen as a corrective to this imbalance. It can make a place for the virtues of private life as well as the rather different virtues that are required by public life. Feminist philosophers are among those who are keenest on the ethics of virtue.

But is the theory of virtue to be understood as a supplement to a theory of right action, or as a self-sufficient replacement for theories of right action? One way of proceeding would be to develop a theory that combines the best features of the right-action approach with insights drawn from the virtues approach—we might try to improve utilitarianism, Kantianism, and the like by adding to them a better account of moral character. Our total theory would then include an account of the virtues, but that account would be offered as a supplement to a theory of right action. This sounds sensible, and if such a project could be carried out successfully, there would obviously be much to be said in its favour.

Some virtue theorists, however, have argued that the ethics of virtue should be considered as an alternative to the other sorts of theories—as an independent theory of ethics that is complete in itself. Whether this is possible is one of the principal problems for virtue theory. The problem is that, standing alone, virtue theory seems incomplete. Consider a typical virtue, such as honesty. Suppose a person is tempted to lie, perhaps because lying offers some advantage in a particular situation. The reason he or she should not lie, according to the virtue ethics approach, is simply because doing so would be dishonest. This sounds plausible enough. But what does it mean to be honest? Is an honest person simply one who follows such rules as 'Do not lie'? It is hard to see what honesty consists in if it is not the disposition to follow such rules.

But we cannot avoid asking why such rules are important. Why shouldn't a person lie, especially when there is some advantage to be gained from it? Plainly we need an answer that goes beyond the simple observation that doing so would be incompatible with having a particular character trait; we need an explanation of why it is better to have this trait than its opposite. Candidate answers might be that a policy of truth-telling promotes the general welfare; or that it is needed by people who must live together relying on one another. The first explanation looks suspiciously utilitarian, while the second recalls contractarian ways of thinking. And in any case, giving any explanation at all seems to take us beyond the limits of unsupplemented virtue theory.

Secondly, it is difficult to see how unsupplemented virtue theory could handle cases of moral conflict. Suppose it would be dishonest but kind to do A, and honest but unkind to B. (An example might be telling the truth in circumstances that would be hurtful to someone.) Honesty and kindness are both virtues, and so there are reasons both for and against each alternative. But you must do one or the other—you must either tell the truth, and be unkind, or not tell the truth, and be dishonest. So which should you do? The admonition to act virtuously does not, by itself, offer much help. It only leaves you wondering which virtue takes precedence. It seems that we need general guidance of a kind that unsupplemented virtue theory cannot offer.

VI

Does the lack of agreement among contemporary moral philosophers mean, as some critics suggest, that the whole subject is flawed in some deep way? Virtue theorists are not the only thinkers who suspect that this may be so. The final essay in this collection, by Thomas Nagel, argues that morality is too complicated a business, drawing on too many disparate sources, to be summed up and encompassed in any unified theory. Paradoxically, the option of having no theory at all is one of the major alternatives in current theory. This would mean, in the end, that we would be left with something like Rossian intuitionism, which, in one important sense, is not a 'theory' at all, because it provides no way of ordering the moral rules. Yet there are other possible explanations of why philosophical disagreement about ethics is so persistent. Derek Parfit has suggested that non-religious ethics is still a young subject that has a long way to go. It might be added that the subject-matter of ethics, which is difficult enough to begin with, engages people's emotions in a way that makes dispassionate thinking hard to attain. It is, after all, about how we should live. This is a complication that theorists of other subjects do not have to contend with, and it might counsel patience here.

I

WHAT MAKES RIGHT ACTS RIGHT?

W. D. ROSS

The real point at issue between hedonism and utilitarianism on the one hand and their opponents on the other is not whether 'right' means 'productive of so-and-so'; for it cannot with any plausibility be maintained that it does. The point at issue is that to which we now pass, viz. whether there is any general character which makes right acts right, and if so, what it is. Among the main historical attempts to state a single characteristic of all right actions which is the foundation of their rightness are those made by egoism and utilitarianism. But I do not propose to discuss these, not because the subject is unimportant, but because it has been dealt with so often and so well already, and because there has come to be so much agreement among moral philosophers that neither of these theories is satisfactory. A much more attractive theory has been put forward by Professor Moore: that what makes actions right is that they are productive of more *good* than could have been produced by any other action open to the agent.[1]

This theory is in fact the culmination of all the attempts to base rightness on productivity of some sort of result. The first form this attempt takes is the attempt to base rightness on conduciveness to the advantage or pleasure of the agent. This theory comes to grief over the fact, which stares us in the face, that a great part of duty consists in an observance of the rights and a furtherance of the interests of others, whatever the cost to ourselves may be. Plato and others may be right in holding that a regard for the rights of others never in the long run involves a loss of happiness for the agent, that 'the just life profits a man'. But this, even if true, is irrelevant to the rightness of the act. As soon as a man does an action *because* he thinks he

From W. D. Ross, *The Right and the Good* (Oxford: Oxford University Press, 1930), 16–41. Reprinted by permission of Oxford University Press.

[1] I take the theory which, as I have tried to show, seems to be put forward in *Ethics* (Oxford: Oxford University Press, 1912) rather than the earlier and less plausible theory put forward in *Principia Ethica* (1903). For the difference, cf. *The Right and the Good*, 8–11.

will promote his own interests thereby, he is acting not form a sense of its rightness but from self-interest.

To the egoistic theory hedonistic utilitarianism supplies a much-needed amendment. It points our correctly that the fact that a certain pleasure will be enjoyed by the agent is no reason why he *ought* to bring it into being rather than an equal or greater pleasure to be enjoyed by another, though, human nature being what it is, it makes it not unlikely that he *will* try to bring it into being. But hedonistic utilitarianism in its turn needs a correction. On reflection it seems clear that pleasure is not the only thing in life that we think good in itself, that for instance we think the possession of a good character, or an intelligent understanding of the world, as good or better. A great advance is made by the substitution of 'productive of the greatest good' for 'productive of the greatest pleasure'.

Not only is this theory more attractive than hedonistic utilitarianism, but its logical relation to that theory is such that the latter could not be true unless *it* were true, while it might be true though hedonistic utilitarianism were not. It is in fact one of the logical bases of hedonistic utilitarianism. For the view that what produces the maximum pleasure is right has for its bases the views (1) that what produces the maximum good is right, and (2) that pleasure is the only thing good in itself. If they were not assuming that what produces the maximum *good* is right, the utilitarians' attempt to show that pleasure is the only thing good in itself, which is in fact the point they take most pains to establish, would have been quite irrelevant to their attempt to prove that only what produces the maximum *pleasure* is right. If, therefore, it can be shown that productivity of the maximum good is not what makes all right actions right, we shall *a fortiori* have refuted hedonistic utilitarianism.

When a plain man fulfils a promise because he thinks he ought to do so, it seems clear that he does so with no thought of its total consequences, still less with any opinion that these are likely to be the best possible. He thinks in fact much more of the past than of the future. What makes him think it right to act in a certain way is the fact that he has promised to do so—that and, usually, nothing more. That his act will produce the best possible consequences is not his reason for calling it right. What lends colour to the theory we are examining, then, is not the actions (which form probably a great majority of our actions) in which some such reflection as 'I have promised' is the only reason we give ourselves for thinking a certain action right, but the exceptional cases in which the consequences of fulfilling a promise (for instance) would be so disastrous to others that we judge it right not to do so. It must of course be admitted that such cases exist. If I have promised to meet a friend at a particular time for some trivial purpose, I should certainly think myself justified in breaking my engagement if by doing so I could prevent a serious accident or bring relief to the victims of one. And the supporters of the view we are examining hold that my thinking so is due to my thinking that I shall bring more good into existence by the one action than by the other. A different account may, however, be given of the matter, an account which will, I believe, show itself to be the true one. It may be said that besides the duty of fulfilling promises I have and recognize a duty of relieving distress,[2] and that when I think it right to do the latter at the cost of not doing the former, it is not because I think I shall produce more good thereby but because I think it the duty which is in the circumstances more of a duty. This account surely corresponds much more closely with what we really think in such a situation. If, so far as I can see, I could bring equal amounts of good into being by fulfilling my promise and by helping some one to whom I had made no promise, I should not hesitate to regard the former as my duty. Yet on the view that what is right is right because it is productive of the most good I should not so regard it.

There are two theories, each in its way simple, that offer a solution of such cases of conscience. One is the view of Kant, that there are certain duties of perfect obligation, such as those of fulfilling promises, of paying debts, of telling the truth, which admit of no exception whatever in favour of duties of imperfect obligation, such as that of relieving distress. The other is the view of, for instance, Professor Moore and Dr Rashdall, that there is only the duty of producing good, and that all 'conflicts of duties' should be resolved by asking 'by which action will most good be produced?' But it is more important that our theory fit the facts than that it be simple, and the account we have given above corresponds (it seems to me) better than either of the simpler theories with what we really think, viz. that normally promise-keeping, for example, should come before benevolence, but that when and only when the good to be produced by the benevolent act is very great and the promise comparatively trivial, the act of benevolence becomes our duty.

In fact the theory of 'ideal utilitarianism', if I may for brevity refer so to the theory of Professor Moore, seems to simplify unduly our relations to our fellows. It says, in effect, that the only morally significant relation in which my neighbours stand to me is that of being possible beneficiaries by my action.[3] They do stand in this relation to me, and this relation is morally significant. But they may also stand to me in the relation of promisee to

---

[2] These are not strictly speaking duties, but things that tend to be our duty, or prima-facie duties. Cf. pp. 20–1 of this volume.

[3] Some will think it, apart from other considerations, a sufficient refutation of this view to point out that I also stand in that relation to myself, so that for this view the distinction of oneself from others is morally insignificant.

promiser, of creditor to debtor, of wife to husband, of child to parent, of friend to friend, of fellow countryman to fellow countryman, and the like; and each of these relations is the foundation of a prima-facie duty, which is more or less incumbent on me according to the circumstances of the case. When I am in a situation, as perhaps I always am, in which more than one of these prima-facie duties is incumbent on me, what I have to do is to study the situation as fully as I can until I form the considered opinion (it is never more) that in the circumstances one of them is more incumbent than any other; then I am bound to think that to do this prima-facie duty is my duty *sans phrase* in the situation.

I suggest 'prima-facie duty' or 'conditional duty' as brief way of referring to the characteristic (quite distinct from that of being a duty proper) which an act has, in virtue of being of a certain kind (e.g. the keeping of a promise), of being an act which would be a duty proper if it were not at the same time of another kind which is morally significant. Whether an act is a duty proper of actual duty depends on *all* the morally significant kinds it is an instance of. The phrase 'prima-facie duty' must be apologized for, since (1) it suggests that what we are speaking of is a certain kind of duty, whereas it is in fact not a duty, but something related in a special way to duty. Strictly speaking, we want not a phrase in which duty is qualified by an adjective, but a separate noun. (2) 'Prima' facie suggests that one is speaking only of an appearance which a moral situation presents at first sight, and which may turn out to be illusory; whereas what I am speaking of is an objective fact involved in the nature of the situation, or more strictly in an element of its nature, though not, as duty proper does, arising from its *whole* nature. I can, however, think of no term which fully meets the case. 'Claim' has been suggested by Professor Prichard. The word' claim' has the advantage of being quite a familiar one in this connection, and it seems to cover much of the ground. It would be quite natural to say, 'a person to whom I have made a promise has a claim on me', and also, 'a person whose distress I could relieve (at the cost of breaking the promise) has a claim on me'. But (1) while 'claim' is appropriate from *their* point of view, we want a word to express the corresponding fact from the agent's point of view—the fact of his being subject to claims that can be made against him; and ordinary language provides us with no such correlative to 'claim'. And (2) (what is more important) 'claim' seems inevitably to suggest two persons, one of whom might make a claim on the other; and while this covers the ground of social duty, it is inappropriate in the case of that important part of duty which is the duty of cultivating a certain kind of character in oneself. It would be artificial, I think, and at any rate metaphorical, to say that one's character has a claim on oneself.

There is nothing arbitrary about these prima-facie duties. Each rests on a definite circumstance which cannot seriously be held to be without moral significance. Of prima-facie duties I suggest, without claiming completeness or finality for it, the following division.[4]

(1) Some duties rest on previous acts of my own. These duties seem to include two kinds, (a) those resting on a promise or what may fairly be called an implicit promise, such as the implicit undertaking not to tell lies which seems to be implied in the act of entering into conversation (at any rate by civilized men), or of writing books that purport to be history and not fiction. These may be called the duties of fidelity. (b) Those resting on a previous wrongful act. These may be called the duties of reparation. (2) Some rest on previous acts of other men, i.e. services done by them to me. These may be loosely described as the duties of gratitude.[5] (3) Some rest on the fact or possibility of a distribution of pleasure or happiness (or of the means thereto) which is not in accordance with the merit of the persons concerned; in such cases there arises a duty to upset or prevent such a distribution. These are the duties of justice. (4) Some rest on the mere fact that there are other beings in the world whose condition we can make better in respect of virtue, or of intelligence, or of pleasure. These are the duties of beneficence. (5) Some rest on the fact that we can improve our own condition in respect of virtue or of intelligence. These are the duties of self-improvement. (6) I think that we should distinguish from (4) the duties that may be summed up under the title of 'not injuring others'. No doubt to injure others is incidentally to fail to do them good; but it seems to me clear that non-maleficence is apprehended as a duty distinct from that of beneficence, and as a duty of a more stringent character. It will be noticed that this alone among the types of duty has been stated in a negative way. An attempt might no doubt be made to state this duty, like the others, in a positive way. It might be said that it is really the duty to prevent ourselves from acting either form an inclination to harm others or from an inclination to seek our own pleasure, in doing which we should

---

[4] I should make it plain at this stage that I am *assuming* the correctness of some of our main convictions as to prima-facie duties, or, more strictly, am claiming that we *know* them to be true. To me it seems as self-evident as anything could be, that to make a promise, for instance, is to create a moral claim on us in someone else. Many readers will perhaps say that they do *not* know this to be true. If so, I certainly cannot prove it to them; I can only ask them to reflect again, in the hope that they will ultimately agree that they also know it to be true. The main moral convictions of the plain man seem to me to be, not opinions which it is for philosophy to prove or disprove, but knowledge from the start; and in my own case I seem to find little difficulty in distinguishing these essential convictions from other moral convictions which I also have, which are merely fallible opinions based on an imperfect study of the working for good or evil of certain institutions or types of action.

[5] For a needed correction of this statement, cf. pp. 22–3.

incidentally harm them. But on reflection it seems clear that the primary duty here is the duty not to harm others, this being a duty whether or not we have an inclination that if followed would lead to our harming them; and that when we have such an inclination the primary duty not to harm others gives rise to a consequential duty to resist the inclination. The recognition of this duty of non-maleficence is the first step on the way to the recognition of the duty of beneficence; and that accounts for the prominence of the commands 'thou shalt not kill', 'thou shalt not commit adultery', 'thou shalt not steal', 'thou shalt not bear false witness', in so early a code as the Decalogue. But even when we have come to recognize the duty of beneficence, it appears to me that the duty of non-maleficence is recognized as a distinct one, and as prima facie more binding. We should not in general consider it justifiable to kill one person in order to keep another alive, or to steal from one in order to give alms to another.

The essential defect of the 'ideal utilitarian' theory is that it ignores, or at least does not do full justice to, the highly personal character of duty. If the only duty is to produce the maximum of good, the question who is to have the good—whether it is myself, or my benefactor, or a person to whom I have made a promise to confer that good on him, or a mere fellow man to whom I stand in no such special relation—should make no difference to my having a duty to produce that good. But we are all in fact sure that it makes a vast difference.

One or two other comments must be made on this provisional list of the divisions of duty.

1. The nomenclature is not strictly correct. For by 'fidelity' or 'gratitude' we mean, strictly, certain states of motivation; and, as I have urged, it is not our duty to have certain motives, but to do certain acts. By 'fidelity', for instance, is meant, strictly, the disposition to fulfil promises and implicit promises *because we have made them*. We have no general word to cover the actual fulfilment of promises and implicit promises *irrespective of motive*; and I use 'fidelity', loosely but perhaps conveniently, to fill this gap. So too I use 'gratitude' for the returning of services, irrespective of motive. The term 'justice' is not so much confined, in ordinary usage, to a certain state of motivation, for we should often talk of a man as acting justly even when we did not think his motive was the wish to do what was just simply for the sake of doing so. Less apology is therefore needed for our use of 'justice' in this sense. And I have used the word 'beneficence' rather than 'benevolence', in order to emphasize the fact that it is our duty to do certain things, and not to do them from certain motives.

2. If the objection be made, that this catalogue of the main types of duty

is an unsystematic one resting on no logical principle, it may be replied, first, that it makes no claim to being ultimate. It is a prima-facie classification of the duties which reflection on our moral convictions seems actually to reveal. And if these convictions are, as I would claim that they are, of the nature of knowledge, and if I have not misstated them, the list will be a list of authentic conditional duties, correct as far as it goes though not necessarily complete. The list of *goods* put forward by the rival theory is reached by exactly the same method—the only sound one in the circumstances—viz. that of direct reflection on what we really think. Loyalty to the facts is worth more than a symmetrical architectonic or a hastily reached simplicity. If further reflection discovers a perfect logical basis for this or for a better classification, so much the better.

3. It may, again, be objected that our theory that there are these various and often conflicting types of prima-facie duty leaves us with no principle upon which to discern what is our actual duty in particular circumstances. But this objection is not one which the rival theory is in a position to bring forward. For when we have to choose between the production of two heterogeneous goods, say knowledge and pleasure, the 'ideal utilitarian' theory can only fall back on an opinion, for which no logical basis can be offered, that one of the goods is the greater; and this is no better than a similar opinion that one of two duties is the more urgent. And again, when we consider the infinite variety of the effects of our actions in the way of pleasure, it must surely be admitted that the claim which *hedonism* sometimes makes, that it offers a readily applicable criterion of right conduct, is quite illusory.

I am unwilling, however, to content myself with an *argumentum ad hominem*, and I would contend that in principle there is no reason to anticipate that every act that is our duty is so for one and the same reason. Why should two sets of circumstances, or one set of circumstances, *not* posses different characteristics, any one of which makes a certain act our prima-facie duty? When I ask what it is that makes me in certain cases sure that I have a prima-facie duty to do so-and-so, I find that it lies in the fact that I have made a promise; when I ask the same question in another case, I find the answer lies in the fact that I have done a wrong. And if on reflection I find (as I think I do) that neither of these reasons is reducible to the other, I must not on any a priori ground assume that such a reduction is possible.

An attempt may be made to arrange in a more systematic way the main types of duty which we have indicated. In the first place it seems self-evident that if there are things that are intrinsically good, it is prima facie a duty to bring them into existence rather than not to do so, and to bring as much of them into existence as possible. It will be argued elsewhere that there are three main things that are intrinsically good—virtue, knowledge, and, with certain limitations, pleasure. And since a given virtuous disposition, for instance, is equally good whether it is realized in myself or in another, it seems to be my duty to bring it into existence whether in myself or in another. So too with a given piece of knowledge.

The case of pleasure is difficult; for while we clearly recognize a duty to produce pleasure for others, it is by no means so clear that we recognize a duty to produce pleasure for ourselves. This appears to arise from the following facts. The thought of an act as our duty is one that presupposes a certain amount of reflection about the act; and for that reason does not normally arise in connection with acts towards which we are already impelled by another strong impulse. So far, the cause of our not thinking of the promotion of our own pleasure as a duty is analogous to the cause which usually prevents a highly sympathetic person from thinking of the promotion of the pleasure of others as a duty. He is impelled so strongly by direct interest in the well-being of others towards promoting their pleasure that he does not stop to ask whether it is his duty to promote it; and we are all impelled so strongly towards the promotion of our own pleasure that we do not stop to ask whether it is a duty or not. But here is a further reason why even when we stop to think about the matter it does not usually present itself as a duty: viz. that, since the performance of most of our duties involves the giving up of some pleasure that we desire, the doing of duty and the getting of pleasure for ourselves come by a natural association of ideas to be thought of as incompatible things. This association of ideas is in the main salutary in its operation, since it puts a check on what but for it would be much too strong, the tendency to pursue one's own pleasure without thought of other considerations. Yet if pleasure is good, it seems in the long run clear that it is right to get it for ourselves as well as to produce it for others, when this does not involve the failure to discharge some more stringent prima-facie duty. The question is a very difficult one, but it seems that this conclusion can be denied only on one or other of three grounds: (1) that pleasure is not prima-facie good (i.e. good when it is neither the actualization of a bad disposition nor undeserved), (2) that there is no prima-facie duty to produce as much that is good as we can, or (3) that though there is a prima-facie duty to produce other things that are good, there is no prima-facie duty to produce pleasure which will be enjoyed by ourselves. I give reasons elsewhere[6] for not accepting the first

---

[6] Ross, *The Right and the Good*, 135–8

contention. The second hardly admits of argument but seems to me plainly false. The third seems plausible only if we hold that an act that is pleasant or brings pleasure to ourselves must for that reason not be a duty; and this would lead to paradoxical consequences, such as that if a man enjoys giving pleasure to others or working for their moral improvement, it cannot be his duty to do so. Yet it seems to be a very stubborn fact, that in our ordinary consciousness we are not aware of a duty to get pleasure for ourselves; and by way of partial explanation of this I may add that though, as I think, one's own pleasure is a good and there is a duty to produce it, it is only if we *think* of our own pleasure not as simply our own pleasure, but as an objective good, something that an impartial spectator would approve, that we can think of the getting it as duty; and we do not habitually think of it in this way.

If these contentions are right, what we have called the duty of beneficence and the duty of self-improvement rest on the same ground. No different principles of duty are involved in the two cases. If we feel a special responsibility for improving our own character rather than that of others, it is not because a special principle is involved, but because we are aware that the one is more under our control than the other. It was on this ground that Kant expressed the practical law of duty in the form 'seek to make yourself good and other people happy'. He was so persuaded of the internality of virtue that he regarded any attempt by one person to produce virtue in another as bound to produce, at most, only a counterfeit of virtue, the doing of externally right acts not from the true principle of virtuous action but out of regard to another person. It must be admitted that one man cannot compel another to be virtuous; compulsory virtue would just not be virtue. But experience clearly shows that Kant overshoots the mark when he contends that one man cannot do anything to *promote* virtue in another, to bring such influences to bear upon him that his own response to them is more likely to be virtuous than his response to other influences would have been. And our duty to do this is not different in kind from our duty to improve our own characters.

It is equally clear, and clear at an earlier stage of moral development, that if there are things that are bad in themselves we ought, prima facie, not to bring them upon others; and on this fact rests the duty of nonmaleficence.

The duty of justice is particularly complicated, and the word is used to cover things which are really very different—things such as the payment of debts, the reparation of injuries done by oneself to another, and the bringing about of a distribution of happiness between other people in proportion to merit. I use the word to denote only the last of these three.

I try to show elsewhere[7] that besides the three (comparatively) simple goods, virtue, knowledge, and pleasure, there is a more complex good, not reducible to these, consisting in the proportionment of happiness to virtue. The bringing of this about is a duty which we owe to all men alike, though it may be reinforced by special responsibilities that we have undertaken to particular men. This, therefore, with beneficence and self-improvement, comes under the general principle that we should produce as much good as possible, though the good there involved is different in kind from any other.

But besides this general obligation, there are special obligations. These may arise, in the first place, incidentally, from acts which were not essentially meant to create such an obligation, but which nevertheless create it. From the nature of the case such acts may be of two kinds—the infliction of injuries on others, and the acceptance of benefits from them. It seems clear that these put us under a special obligation to other men, and that only these acts can do so incidentally. From these arise the twin duties of reparation and gratitude.

And finally there are special obligations arising from acts the very intention of which, when they were done, was to put us under such an obligation. The name for such acts is 'promises'; the name is wide enough if we are willing to include under it implicit promises, i.e. modes of behaviour in which without explicit verbal promise we intentionally create an expectation that we can be counted on to behave in a certain way in the interest of another person.

These seem to be, in principle, all the ways in which prima-facie duties arise. In actual experience they are compounded together in highly complex ways. Thus, for example, the duty of obeying the laws of one's country arises partly (as Socrates contends in the *Crito*) from the duty of gratitude for the benefits one has received form it; partly from the implicit promise to obey which seems to be involved in permanent residence in a country whose laws we know we are *expected* to obey, and still more clearly involved when we ourselves invoke the protection of its laws (this is the truth underlying the doctrine of the social contract); and partly (if we are fortunate in our country) from the fact that its laws are potent instruments for the general good.

Or again, the sense of a general obligation to bring about (so far as we can) a just apportionment of happiness to merit is often greatly reinforced by the fact that many of the existing injustices are due to a social and economic system which we have, not indeed created, but taken part in

[7] Ross, *The Right and the Good*, ch. 5.

and assented to; the duty of justice is then reinforced by the duty of reparation.

It is necessary to say something by way of clearing up the relation between prima-facie duties and the actual or absolute duty to do one particular act in particular circumstances. If, as almost all moralists except Kant are agreed, and as most plain men think, it is sometimes right to tell a lie or to break a promise, it must be maintained that there is a difference between prima-facie duty and actual or absolute duty. When we think ourselves justified in breaking, and indeed morally obliged to break, a promise in order to relieve some one's distress, we do not for a moment cease to recognize a prima-facie duty to keep our promise, and this leads us to feel, not indeed shame or repentance, but certainly compunction, for behaving as we do; we recognize, further, that it is our duty to make up somehow to the promisee for the breaking of the promise. We have to distinguish from the characteristic of being our duty that of tending to be our duty. Any act that we do contains various elements in virtue of which it falls under various categories. In virtue of being the breaking of a promise, for instance, it tends to be wrong; in virtue of being an instance of relieving distress it tends to be right. Tendency to be one's duty may be called a parti-resultant attribute, i.e. one which belongs to an act in virtue of some one component in its nature. *Being* one's duty is a toti-resultant attribute, one which belongs to an act in virtue of its whole nature and of nothing less than this.[8] This distinction between parti-resultant and toti-resultant attributes is one which we shall meet in another context also.[9]

Another instance of the same distinction may be found in the operation of natural laws. *Qua* subject to the force of gravitation towards some other body, each body tends to move in a particular direction with a particular velocity; but its actual movement depends on *all* the forces to which it is subject. It is only by recognizing this distinction that we can preserve the absoluteness of laws of nature, and only by recognizing a corresponding distinction that we can preserve the absoluteness of the general principles of morality. But an important difference between the two cases must be pointed out. When we say that in virtue of gravitation a body tends to move in a certain way, we are referring to a causal influence actually exercised on it by another body or other bodies. When we say that in virtue of being deliberately untrue a certain remark tends to be wrong, we are referring to no causal relation, to no relation that involves succession in time, but to such a relation as connects the various attributes of a

---

[8] But cf. the qualification in n. 11.
[9] Cf. Ross, *The Right and the Good*, 122–3.

mathematical figure. And if the word 'tendency' is thought to suggest too much a causal relation, it is better to talk of certain types of act as being prima facie right or wrong (or of different persons as having different and possibly conflicting claims upon us), than of their tending to be right or wrong.

Something should be said of the relation between our apprehension of the prima-facie rightness of certain types of act and our mental attitude towards particular acts. It is proper to use the word 'apprehension' in the former case and not in the latter. That an act, *qua* fulfilling a promise, or *qua* effecting a just distribution of good, or *qua* returning services rendered, or *qua* promoting the good of others, or *qua* promoting the virtue or insight of the agent, is prima facie right, is self-evident; not in the sense that it is evident from the beginning of our lives, or as soon as we attend to the proposition for the first time, but in the sense that when we have reached sufficient mental maturity and have given sufficient attention to the proposition it is evident without any need of proof, or of evidence beyond itself. It is self-evident just as a mathematical axiom, or the validity of a form of inference, is evident. The moral order expressed in these propositions is just as much part of the fundamental nature of the universe (and, we may add, of any possible universe in which there were moral agents at all) as is the spatial or numerical structure expressed in the axioms of geometry or arithmetic. In our confidence that these propositions are true there is involved the same trust in our reason that is involved in our confidence in mathematics; and we should have no justification for trusting it in the latter sphere and distrusting it in the former. In both cases we are dealing with propositions that cannot be proved, but that just as certainly need no proof.

Some of these general principles of prima-facie duty may appear to be open to criticism. It may be thought, for example, that the principle of returning good for good is a falling off from the Christian principle, generally and rightly recognized as expressing the highest morality, of returning good for evil. To this it may be replied that I do not suggest that there is a principle commanding us to return good for good and forbidding us to return good for evil, and that I do suggest that there is a positive duty to seek the good of all men. What I maintain is that an act in which good is returned for good is recognized as *specially* binding on us just because it is of that character, and that *ceteris paribus* any one would think it his duty to help his benefactors rather than his enemies, if he could not do both; just as it is generally recognized that *ceteris paribus* we should pay our debts rather than give our money in charity, when we cannot do both. A benefactor is not only a man, calling for our effort on his behalf on that ground, but also our benefactor, calling for our *special* effort on *that* ground.

Our judgements about our actual duty in concrete situations have none of the certainty that attaches to our recognition of the general principles of duty. A statement is certain, i.e. is an expression of knowledge, only in one or other of two cases: when it is either self-evident, or a valid conclusion from self-evident premises. And our judgements about our particular duties have neither of these characters. (1) They are not self-evident. Where a possible act is seen to have two characteristics, in virtue of one of which it is prima facie right, and in virtue of the other prima facie wrong, we are (I think) well aware that we are not certain whether we ought or ought not to do it; that whether we do it or not, we are taking a moral risk. We come in the long run, after consideration, to think one duty more pressing than the other, but we do not feel certain that it is so. And though we do not always recognize that a possible act has two such characteristics, and though there *may* be cases in which it has not, we are never certain that any particular possible act has not, and therefore never certain that it is right, nor certain that it is wrong. For, to go no further in the analysis, it is enough to point out that any particular act will in all probability in the course of time contribute to the bringing about of good or of evil for many human beings, and thus have a prima-facie rightness or wrongness of which we know nothing. (2) Again, our judgements about our particular duties are not logical conclusions from self-evident premises. The only possible premises would be the general principles stating their prima-facie rightness or wrongness *qua* having the different characteristics they do have; and even if we could (as we cannot) apprehend the extent to which an act will tend on the one hand, for example, to bring about advantages for our benefactors, and on the other hand to bring about disadvantages for fellow men who are not our benefactors, there is no principle by which we can draw the conclusion that it is on the whole right or on the whole wrong. In this respect the judgement as to the rightness of a particular act is just like judgement as to the beauty of a particular natural object or work of art. A poem is, for instance, in respect of certain qualities beautiful and in respect of certain others not beautiful; and our judgement as to the degree of beauty it possesses on the whole is never reached by logical reasoning from the apprehension of its particular beauties or particular defects. Both in this and in the moral case we have more or less probable opinions which are not logically justified conclusions from the general principles that are recognized as self-evident.

There is therefore much truth in the description of the right act as a fortunate act. If we cannot be certain that it is right, it is our good fortune if the act we do is the right act. This consideration does not, however, make the doing of our duty a mere matter of chance. There is a parallel here between the doing of duty and the doing of what will be to our personal advantage. We never *know* what act will in the long run be to our advantage. Yet it is certain that we are more likely in general to secure our advantage if we estimate to the best of our ability the probable tendencies of our actions in this respect, than if we act on caprice. And similarly we are more likely to do our duty if we reflect to the best of our ability on the prima-facie rightness or wrongness of various possible acts in virtue of the characteristics we perceive them to have, than if we act without reflection. With this greater likelihood we must be content.

Many people would be inclined to say that the right act for me is not that whose general nature I have been describing, viz. that which if I were omniscient I should see to be my duty, but that which on all the evidence available to me I should think to be my duty. But suppose that from the state of partial knowledge in which I think act *A* to be my duty, I could pass to a state of perfect knowledge in which I saw act *B* to be my duty, should I not say 'act *B* was the right act for me to do'? I should no doubt add 'though I am not to be blamed for doing act *A*'. But in adding this, am I not passing from the question 'what is right' to the question 'what is morally good'? At the same time I am not making the *full* passage from the one notion to the other; for in order that the act should be morally good, or an act I am not to be blamed for doing, it must not merely be the act which it is reasonable for me to think my duty; it must also be done for that reason, or from some other morally good motive. Thus the conception of the right act as the act which it is reasonable for me to think my duty is an unsatisfactory compromise between the true notion of the right act and the notion of the morally good action.

The general principles of duty are obviously not self-evident from the beginning or our lives. How do they come to be so? The answer is, that they come to be self-evident to us just as mathematical axioms do. We find by experience that this couple of matches and that couple make four matches, that this couple of balls on a wire and that couple make four balls: and by reflection on these and similar discoveries we come to see that it is of the nature of two and two to make four. In a precisely similar way, we see the prima-facie rightness of an act which would be the fulfilment of a particular promise, and of another which would be the fulfilment of another promise, and when we have reached sufficient maturity to think in general terms, we apprehend prima-facie rightness to belong to the nature of any fulfilment of promise. What comes first in time is the apprehension of the self-evident prima-facie rightness of an individual act of a particular type. From this we come by reflection to apprehend the self-evident general principle of prima-facie duty. From this, too, perhaps along with the apprehension of the self-evident prima-facie rightness of the same act in virtue of its having another characteristic as well, and perhaps in spite of the apprehension of its prima-facie wrongness in virtue of its having some third characteristic, we come to believe something not self-evident at all, but an object of probable opinion, viz. that this particular act is (not prima facie but) actually right.

In this respect there is an important difference between rightness and mathematical properties. A triangle which is isosceles necessarily has two of its angles equal, whatever other characteristics the triangle may have—whatever, for instance, be its area, or the size of its third angle. The equality of the two angles is a parti-resultant attribute.[10] And the same is true of all mathematical attributes. It is true, I may add, of prima-facie rightness. But no act is ever, in virtue of falling under some general description, necessarily actually right; its rightness depends on its whole nature[11] and not on any element in it. The reason is that no mathematical object (no figure, for instance, or angle) ever has two characteristics that tend to give it opposite resultant characteristics, while moral acts often (as every one knows) and indeed always (as on reflection we must admit) have different characteristics that tend to make them at the same time prima-facie right and prima-facie wrong; there is probably no act, for instance, which does good to any one without doing harm to some one else, and vice versa.

Supposing it to be agreed, as I think on reflection it must, that no one *means* by 'right' just 'productive of the best possible consequences', or 'optimific', the attributes 'right' and 'optimific' might stand in either of two kinds of relation to each other. (1) They might be so related that we could apprehend a priori, either immediately or deductively, that any act that is optimific is right and any act that is right is optimific, as we can apprehend that any triangle that is equilateral is equiangular and vice versa. Professor Moore's view is, I think, that the coextensiveness of 'right' and 'optimific' is apprehended immediately.[12] He rejects the possibility of any proof of it.

[10] Cf. p. 26; and Ross, *The Right and the Good*, 122–3.
[11] To avoid complicating unduly the statement of the general view I am putting forward, I have here rather overstated it. Any act is the origination of a great variety of things many of which make no difference to its rightness or wrongness. But there are always many elements in its nature (i.e. in what it is the origination of) that make a difference to its rightness or wrongness, and no element in its nature can be dismissed without consideration as indifferent.
[12] *Ethics*, 181.

Or (2) the two attributes might be such that the question whether they are invariably connected had to be answered by means of an inductive inquiry. Now at first sight it might seem as if the constant connection of the two attributes could be immediately apprehended. It might seem absurd to suggest that it could be right for any one to do an act which would produce consequences less good than those which would be produced by some other act in his power. Yet a little though will convince us that this is not absurd. The type of case in which it is easiest to see that this is so is, perhaps, that in which one has made a promise. In such a case we all think that prima facie it is our duty to fulfil the promise irrespective of the precise goodness of the total consequences. And though we do not think it is necessarily our actual or absolute duty to do so, we are far from thinking that any, even the slightest, gain in the value of the total consequences will necessarily justify us in doing something else instead. Suppose, to simplify the case by abstraction, that the fulfilment of a promise to A would produce 1,000 units of good[13] for him, but that by doing some other act I could produce 1,001 units of good for B, to whom I have made no promise, the other consequences of the two acts being of equal value; should we really think it self-evident that it was our duty to do the second act and not the first? I think not. We should, I fancy, hold that only a much greater disparity of value between the total consequences would justify us in failing to discharge our prima-facie duty to A. After all, a promise is a promise, and is not to be treated so lightly as the theory we are examining would imply. What, exactly, a promise is, is not so easy to determine, but we are surely agreed that it constitutes a serious moral limitation to our freedom of action. To produce the 1,001 units of good for B rather than fulfil our promise to A would be to take, not perhaps our duty as philanthropists too seriously, but certainly our duty as makers of promises too lightly.

Or consider another phase of the same problem. If I have promised to confer on A a particular benefit containing 1,000 units of good, is it self-evident that if by doing some different act I could produce 1,001 units of good for A himself (the other consequences of the two acts being supposed equal in value), it would be right for me to do so? Again, I think not. Apart from my general prima-facie duty to do A what good I can, I have another prima-facie duty to do him the particular service I have promised to do him, and this is not to be set aside in consequence of a disparity of good of

---

[13] I am assuming that good is objectively quantitative (cf. Ross, *The Right and the Good*, 142–4), but not that we can accurately assign an exact quantitative measure to it. Since it is of a definite amount, we can make the *supposition* that its amount is so-and-so, though we cannot with any confidence *assert* that it is.

the order of 1,001 to 1,000 though a much greater disparity might justify me in so doing.

Or again, suppose that *A* is a very good and *B* a very bad man, should I then, even when I have made no promise, think it self-evidently right to produce 1,001 units of good for *B* rather than 1,000 for *A*? Surely not. I should be sensible of prima-facie duty of justice, i.e. of producing a distribution of goods in proportion to merit, which is not outweighed by such a slight disparity in the total goods to be produced.

Such instances—and they might easily be added to—make it clear that there is no self-evident connection between the attributes 'right' and 'optimific'. The theory we are examining has a certain attractiveness when applied to our decision that a particular act is our duty (though I have tried to show that it does not agree with our actual moral judgements even here). But it is not even plausible when applied to our recognition of prima-facie duty. For if it were self-evident that the right coincides with the optimific, it should be self-evident that what is prima facie right is prima facie optimific. But whereas we are certain that keeping a promise is prima facie right, we are not certain that it is prima facie optimific (though we are perhaps certain that it is prima facie bonific). Our certainty that it is prima facie right depends not on its consequences but on its being the fulfilment of a promise. The theory we are examining involves too much difference between the evident ground of our conviction about prima-facie duty and the alleged ground of our conviction about actual duty.

The coextensiveness of the right and the optimific is, then, not self-evident. And I can see no way of proving it deductively; nor, so far as I know, has any one tried to do so. There remains the question whether it can be established inductively. Such an inquiry, to be conclusive, would have to be very thorough and extensive. We should have to take a large variety of the acts which we, to the best of our ability, judge to be right. We should have to trace as far as possible their consequences, not only for the persons directly affected but also for those indirectly affected, and to these no limit can be set. To make our inquiry thoroughly conclusive, we should have to do what we cannot do, viz. trace these consequences into an unending future. And even to make it reasonably conclusive, we should have to trace them far into the future. It is clear that the most we could possibly say is that a large variety of typical acts that are judged right appear, so far as we can trace their consequences, to produce more good than any other acts possible to the agents in the circumstances. And such a result falls far short of proving the constant connection of the two attributes. But it is surely clear that no inductive inquiry justifying even this result has ever been carried through. The advocates of utilitarian systems have been so much persuaded either of the identity or of the self-evident connection of the attributes 'right' and 'optimific' (or 'felicific') that they have not attempted even such an inductive inquiry as is possible. And in view of the enormous complexity of the task and the inevitable inconclusiveness of the result, it is worth no one's while to make the attempt. What, after all, would be gained by it?" If, as I have tried to show, for an act to be right and to be optimific are not the same thing, and an act's being optimific is not even the ground of its being right, then if we could ask ourselves (though the question is really unmeaning) which we ought to do, right acts because they are right or optimific acts because they are optimific, our answer must be 'the former'. If they are optimific as well as right, that is interesting but not morally important; if not, we still ought to do them (which is only another way of saying that they *are* the right acts), and the question whether they are optimific has no importance for moral theory.

There is one direction in which a fairly serious attempt has been made to show the connection of the attributes 'right' and 'optimific'. One of the most evident facts of our moral consciousness is the sense which we have of the sanctity of promises, a sense which does not, on the face of it, involve the thought that one will be bringing more good into existence by fulfilling the promise than by breaking it. It is plain, I think, that in our normal thought we consider that the fact that we have made a promise is in itself sufficient to create a duty of keeping it, the sense of duty resting on remembrance of the past promise and not on thoughts of the future consequences of its fulfilment. Utilitarianism tries to show that this is not so, that the sanctity of promises rests on the good consequences of the fulfilment of them and the bad consequences of their non-fulfilment. It does so in this way: it points out that when you break a promise you not only fail to confer a certain advantage on your promisee but you diminish his confidence, and indirectly the confidence of others, in the fulfilment of promises. You thus strike a blow at one of the devices that have been found most useful in the relations between man and man—the device on which, for example, the whole system of commercial credit rests—and you tend to bring about a state of things wherein each man, being entirely unable to rely on the keeping of promises by others, will have to do everything for himself, to the enormous impoverishment of human well-being.

To put the matter otherwise, utilitarians say that when a promise ought to be kept it is because the total good to be produced by keeping it is greater than the total good to be produced by breaking it, the former including as its main element the maintenance and strengthening of general mutual confidence, and the latter being greatly diminished by a weakening of this confidence. They say, in fact, that the case I put some pages back[14] never arises—the case in which by fulfilling a promise I shall bring into being 1,000 units of good for my promisee, and by breaking it 1,001 units of good for some one else, the other effects of the two acts being of equal value. The other effects, they say, never are of equal value. By keeping my promise I am helping to strengthen the system of mutual confidence; by breaking it I am helping to weaken this; so that really the first act produces $1,000 + x$ units of good, and the second $1,001 - y$ units, and the difference between $+x$ and $-y$ is enough to outweigh the slight superiority in the *immediate* effects of the second act. In answer to this it may be pointed out that there must be *some* amount of good that exceeds the difference between $+x$ and $-y$ (i.e. exceeds $x + y$); say, $x + y + z$. Let us suppose the *immediate* good effects of the second act to be assessed not at 1,001 but at $1,000 + x + y + z$. Then its *net* good effects are $1,000 + x + z$, i.e. greater than those of the fulfilment of the promise; and the utilitarian is bound to say forthwith that the promise should be broken. Now, we may ask whether that is really the way we think about promises? Do we really think that the production of the slightest balance of good, no matter who will enjoy it, by the breach of a promise frees us from the obligation to keep our promise? We need not doubt that a system by which promises are made and kept is one that has great advantages for the general well-being. But that is not the whole truth. To make a promise is not merely to adapt an ingenious device for promoting the general well-being; it is to put oneself in a new relation to one person in particular, a relation which creates a specifically new prima-facie duty to him, not reducible to the duty of promoting the general well-being of society. By all means let us try to foresee the net good effects of keeping one's promise and the net good effects of breaking it, but even if we assess the first at $1,000 + x$ and the second at $1,000 + x + z$, the question still remains whether it is not our duty to fulfil the promise. It may be suspected, too, that the effect of a single keeping or breaking of a promise in strengthening or weakening the fabric of mutual confidence is greatly exaggerated by the theory we are examining. And if we suppose two men dying together alone, do we think that the duty of one to fulfil before he dies a promise he has made to the other would be extinguished by the fact that neither act would have any effect on the general confidence? Any one who holds this may be suspected of not having reflected on what a promise is.

I conclude that the attributes 'right' and 'optimific' are not identical, and that we do not know either by intuition, by deduction, or by induction that

---

[14] p 31

they coincide in their application, still less that the latter is the foundation of the former. It must be added, however, that if we are ever under no special obligation such as that of fidelity to a promisee or of gratitude to a benefactor, we ought to do what will produce most good; and that even when we are under a special obligation the tendency of acts to promote general good is one of the main factors in determining whether they are right.

In what has preceded, a good deal of use has been made of 'what we really think' about moral questions; a certain theory has been rejected because it does not agree with what we really think. It might be said that this is in principle wrong; that we should not be content to expound what our present moral consciousness tells us but should aim at a criticism of our existing moral consciousness in the light of theory. Now I do not doubt that the moral consciousness of men has in detail undergone a good deal of modification as regards the things we think right, at the hands of moral theory. But if we are told, for instance, that we should give up our view that there is a special obligatoriness attaching to the keeping of promises because it is self-evident that the only duty is to produce as much good as possible, we have to ask ourselves whether we really, when we reflect, *are* convinced that this is self-evident, and whether we really *can* get rid of our view that promise-keeping has a bindingness independent of productiveness of maximum good. In my own experience I find that I cannot, in spite of a very genuine attempt to do so; and I venture to think that most people will find the same, and that just because they cannot lose the sense of special obligation, they cannot accept as self-evident, or even as true, the theory which would require them to do so. In fact it seems, on reflection, self-evident that a promise, simply as such, is something that prima facie ought to be kept, and it does *not*, on reflection, seem self-evident that production of maximum good is the only thing that makes an act obligatory. And to ask us to given up at the bidding of a theory our actual apprehension of what is right and what is wrong seems like asking people to repudiate their actual experience of beauty, at the bidding of a theory which says 'only that which satisfies such and such conditions can be beautiful'. If what I have called our actual apprehension is (as I would maintain that it is) truly an apprehension, i.e. an instance of knowledge, the request is nothing less than absurd.

I would maintain, in fact, that what we are apt to describe as 'what we think' about moral questions contains a considerable amount that we do not think but know, and that this forms the standard by reference to which the truth of any moral theory has to be tested, instead of having itself to be tested by reference to any theory. I hope that I have in what precedes indicated what in my view these elements of knowledge are that are involved in our ordinary moral consciousness.

It would be a mistake to found a natural science on 'what we really think', i.e. on what reasonably thoughtful and well-educated people think about the subjects of the science before they have studied them scientifically. For such opinions are interpretations, and often misinterpretations, of sense-experience; and the man of science must appeal from these to sense-experience itself, which furnishes his real data. In ethics no such appeal is possible. We have no more direct way of access to the facts about rightness and goodness and about what things are right or good, than by thinking about them; the moral convictions of thoughtful and well-educated people are the data of ethics just as sense-perceptions are the data of a natural science. Just as some of the latter have to be rejected as illusory, so have some of the former; but as the latter are rejected only when they are in conflict with other more accurate sense-perceptions, the former are rejected only when they are in conflict with other convictions which stand better the test of reflection. The existing body of moral convictions of the best people is the cumulative product of the moral reflection of many generations, which has developed an extremely delicate power of appreciation of moral distinctions; and this the theorist cannot afford to treat with anything other than the greatest respect. The verdicts of the moral consciousness of the best people are the foundation on which he must build; though he must first compare them with one another and eliminate any contradictions they may contain.

II

EXTREME AND RESTRICTED
UTILITARIANISM

J. J. C. SMART

I

Utilitarianism is the doctrine that the rightness of actions is to be judged by their consequences. What do we mean by 'actions' here? Do we mean particular actions or do we mean classes of actions? According to which way we interpret the word 'actions' we get two different theories, both of which merit the appellation 'utilitarian'.

1. If by 'actions' we mean particular individual actions we get the sort of doctrine held by Bentham, Sidgwick, and Moore. According to this doctrine we test individual actions by their consequences, and general rules, like 'keep promises', are mere rules of thumb which we use only to avoid the necessity of estimating the probable consequences of our actions at every step. The rightness or wrongness of keeping a promise on a particular occasion depends only on the goodness or badness of the consequences of keeping or of breaking the promise on that particular occasion. Of course part of the consequences of breaking the promise, and a part to which we will normally ascribe decisive importance, will be the weakening of faith in the institution of promising. However, if the goodness of the consequences of breaking the rule is *in toto* greater than the goodness of the consequences of keeping it, then we must break the rule, irrespective of whether the goodness of the consequences of *everybody's* obeying the rule is or is not greater than the consequences of *everybody's* breaking it. To put it shortly, rules do not matter, save *per accidens* as rules of thumb and as *de facto*

From *Philosophical Quarterly*, 6 (1956), 344–54. Copyright © The Editors of the *Philosophical Quarterly* (1956). Reprinted, with emendation, by permission of the author and the *Philosophical Quarterly*.

Based on a paper read to the Victorian Branch of the Australasian Association of Psychology and Philosophy, Oct. 1955. [The article is discussed in H. J. McCloskey, 'An Examination of Restricted Utilitarianism', *Philosophical Review*, 66 (1957), 466–85; also by D. Lyons, *Forms and Limits of Utilitarianism* (Oxford: Clarendon Press, 1965). Ed.]

social institutions with which the utilitarian has to reckon when estimating consequences. I shall call this doctrine 'extreme utilitarianism'.

2. A more modest form of utilitarianism has recently become fashionable. The doctrine is to be found in Toulmin's book *The Place of Reason in Ethics*, in Nowell-Smith's *Ethics* (though I think Nowell-Smith has qualms), in John Austin's *Lectures on Jurisprudence* (Lecture II), and even in J. S. Mill, if Urmson's interpretation of him is correct.[1] Part of its charm is that it appears to resolve the dispute in moral philosophy between intuitionists and utilitarians in a way which is very neat. The above philosophers hold, or seem to hold, that moral rules are more than rules of thumb. In general the rightness of an action is *not* to be tested by evaluating its consequences but only by considering whether or not it falls under a certain rule. Whether the rule is to be considered an acceptable moral rule, is, however, to be decided by considering the consequences of adopting the rule. Broadly, then, actions are to be tested by rules and rules by consequences. The only cases in which we must test an individual action directly by its consequences are (*a*) when the action comes under two different rules, one of which enjoins it and one of which forbids it, and (*b*) when there is no rule whatever that governs the given case. I shall call this doctrine 'restricted utilitarianism'.

It should be noticed that the distinction I am making cuts across, and is quite different from, the distinction commonly made between hedonistic and ideal utilitarianism. Bentham was an extreme hedonistic utilitarian and Moore an extreme ideal utilitarian, and Toulmin (perhaps) could be classified as a restricted ideal utilitarian. A hedonistic utilitarian holds that the goodness of the consequences of an action is a function only of their pleasurableness and an ideal utilitarian, like Moore, holds that pleasurableness is not even a necessary condition of goodness. Mill seems, if we are to take his remarks about higher and lower pleasures seriously, to be neither a pure hedonistic nor a pure ideal utilitarian. He seems to hold that pleasurableness is a necessary condition for goodness, but that goodness is a function of other qualities of mind as well. Perhaps we can call him a quasi-ideal utilitarian. When we say that a state of mind is good I take it that we are expressing some sort of *rational preference*. When we say that it is pleasurable I take it that we are saying that it is enjoyable, and when we say that something is a higher pleasure I take it that we are saying that it is more truly, or more deeply, enjoyable. I am doubtful whether 'more

---

[1] S. E. Toulmin, *The Place of Reason in Ethics* (Cambridge: Cambridge University Press, 1950); p. 4. Nowell-Smith, *Ethics* (Harmondsworth: Penguin, 1954); John Austin, *Lectures on Jurisprudence* (London: Weidenfeld and Nicolson, 1954); J. O. Urmson, 'The Interpretation of the Moral Philosophy of J. S. Mill', *Philosophical Quarterly*, 3 (1953), 33–9.

deeply enjoyable' does not just mean 'more enjoyable, even though not more enjoyable on a first look', and so I am doubtful whether quasi-ideal utilitarianism, and possibly ideal utilitarianism too, would not collapse into hedonistic utilitarianism on a closer scrutiny of the logic of words like 'preference', 'pleasure', 'enjoy', 'deeply enjoy', and so on. However, it is beside the point of the present paper to go into these questions. I am here concerned only with the issue between extreme and restricted utilitarianism and am ready to concede that both forms of utilitarianism can be either hedonistic or non-hedonistic.

The issue between extreme and restricted utilitarianism can be illustrated by considering the remark 'But suppose everyone did the same'.[2] Stout distinguishes two forms of the universalization principle, the causal forms and the hypothetical form. To say that you ought not to do an action A because it would have bad results if everyone (or many people) did action A may be merely to point out that while the action A would otherwise be the optimific one, nevertheless when you take into account that doing A will probably cause other people to do A too, you can see that A is not, on a broad view, really optimific. If this causal influence could be avoided (as may happen in the case of a secret desert island promise) then we would disregard the universalization principle. This is the causal form of the principle. A person who accepted the universalization principle in its hypothetical form would be one who was concerned only with what would happen *if* everyone did the action A: he would be totally unconcerned with the question of whether in fact everyone would do the action A. That is, he might say that it would be wrong not to vote because it would have bad results if everyone took this attitude, and he would be totally unmoved by arguments purporting to show that my refusing to vote has no effect whatever on other people's propensity to vote. Making use of Stout's distinction, we can say that an extreme utilitarian would apply the universalization principle in the causal form, while a restricted utilitarian would apply it in the hypothetical form.

How are we to decide the issue between extreme and restricted utilitarianism? I wish to repudiate at the outset that milk and water approach which describes itself sometimes as 'investigating what is implicit in the common moral consciousness' and sometimes as 'investigating how people ordinarily talk about morality'. We have only to read the newspaper correspondence about capital punishment or about what should be done with Formosa to realize that the common moral consciousness is in part made up of superstitious elements, of morally bad elements, and of logically

[2] Cf. A. K. Stout's article 'But Suppose Everybody Did the Same', *The Australasian Journal of Philosophy*, 32 (1954), 1–29.

confused elements. I address myself to good-hearted and benevolent people and so I hope that if we rid ourselves of the logical confusion the superstitious and morally bad elements will largely fall away. For even among good hearted and benevolent people it is possible to find superstitious and morally bad reasons for moral beliefs. These superstitious and morally bad reasons hide behind the protective screen of logical confusion. With people who are not logically confused but who are openly superstitious or morally bad I can of course do nothing. That is, our ultimate pro-attitudes may be different. Nevertheless I propose to rely on *my own* moral consciousness and to appeal to *your* moral consciousness and to forget about what people ordinarily say. 'The obligation to obey a rule', says Nowell-Smith, 'does not, *in the opinion of ordinary men*, rest on the beneficial consequences of obeying it in a particular case.'[3] What does this prove? Surely it is more than likely that ordinary men are confused here. Philosophers should be able to examine the question more rationally.

II

For an extreme utilitarian moral rules are rules of thumb. In practice the extreme utilitarian will mostly guide his conduct by appealing to the rules ('do not lie', 'do not break promises', etc.) of common-sense morality. This is not because there is anything sacrosanct in the rules themselves but because he can argue that probably he will most often act in an extreme utilitarian way if he does not think as a utilitarian. For one thing, actions have frequently to be done in a hurry. Imagine a man seeing a person drowning. He jumps in and rescues him. There is not time to reason the matter out, but usually this will be the course of action which an extreme utilitarian would recommend if he did reason the matter out. If, however, the man drowning had been drowning in a river near Berchtesgaden in 1938, and if he had had the well-known black forelock and moustache of Adolf Hitler, an extreme utilitarian would, if he had time, work out the probability of the man's being the villainous dictator, and if the probability were high enough he would, on extreme utilitarian grounds, leave him to drown. The rescuer, however, has not time. He trusts to his instincts and dives in and rescues the man. And this trusting to instincts and to moral rules can be justified on extreme utilitarian grounds. Furthermore, an extreme utilitarian who knew that the drowning man was Hitler would nevertheless praise the rescuer, not condemn him. For by praising the man

---

[3] *Ethics*, 239 (my italics).

he is strengthening a courageous and benevolent disposition of mind, and in general this disposition has great positive utility. (Next time, perhaps, it will be Winston Churchill that the man saves!) We must never forget that an extreme utilitarian may praise actions which he knows to be wrong. Saving Hitler was wrong, but it was a member of a class of actions which are generally right, and the motive to do actions of this class is in general an optimific one. In considering questions of praise and blame it is not the expediency of the praised or blamed action that is at issue, but the expediency of the praise. It can be expedient to praise an inexpedient action and inexpedient to praise an expedient one.

Lack of time is not the only reason why an extreme utilitarian may, on extreme utilitarian principles, trust to rules of common-sense morality. He knows that in particular cases where his own interests are involved his calculations are likely to be biased in his own favour. Suppose that he is unhappily married and is deciding whether to get divorced. He will in all probability greatly exaggerate his own unhappiness (and possibly his wife's) and greatly underestimate the harm done to his children by the break-up of the family. He will probably also underestimate the likely harm done by the weakening of the general faith in marriage vows. So probably he will come to the correct extreme utilitarian conclusion if he does not in this instance think as an extreme utilitarian but trusts to common-sense morality.

There are many more and subtle points that could be made in connection with the relation between extreme utilitarianism and the morality of common sense. All those that I have just made and many more will be found in book IV, chapters 3–5 of Sidgwick's *Methods of Ethics*.[4] I think that this book is the best book ever written on ethics, and that these chapters are the best chapters of the book. As they occur so near the end of a very long book they are unduly neglected. I refer the reader, then, to Sidgwick for the classical exposition of the relation between (extreme) utilitarianism and the morality of common sense. One further point raised by Sidgwick in this connection is whether an (extreme) utilitarian ought on (extreme) utilitarian principles to propagate (extreme) utilitarianism among the public. As most people are not very philosophical and not good at empirical calculations, it is probable that they will most often act in an extreme utilitarian way if they do not try to think as extreme utilitarians. We have seen how easy it would be to misapply the extreme utilitarian criterion in the case of divorce. Sidgwick seems to think it quite probable that an extreme utilitarian should not propagate his doctrine too widely.

[4] (1874; 7th edn. New York: Dover, 1966.)

However, the great danger to humanity comes nowadays on the plane of public morality—not private morality. There is a greater danger to humanity from the hydrogen bomb than from an increase of the divorce rate, regrettable though that might be, and there seems no doubt that extreme utilitarianism makes for good sense in international relations. When France walked out of the United Nations because she did not wish Morocco discussed, she said that she was within her rights because Morocco and Algiers are part of her metropolitan territory and nothing to do with UN. This was clearly a legalistic if not superstitious argument. We should not be concerned with the so-called 'rights' of France or any other country but with whether the cause of humanity would best be served by discussing Morocco in UN. (I am not saying that the answer to this is 'Yes'. There are good grounds for supposing that more harm than good would come by such a discussion.) I myself have no hesitation in saying that on extreme utilitarian principles we ought to propagate extreme utilitarianism as widely as possible. But Sidgwick had respectable reasons for suspecting the opposite.

The extreme utilitarian, then, regards moral rules as rules of thumb and as sociological facts that have to be taken into account when deciding what to do, just as facts of any other sort have to be taken into account. But in themselves they do not justify any action.

III

The restricted utilitarian regards moral rules as more than rules of thumb for short-circuiting calculations of consequences. Generally, he argues, consequences are not relevant at all when we are deciding what to do in a particular case. In general, they are relevant only to deciding what rules are good reasons for acting in a certain way in particular cases. This doctrine is possibly a good account of how the modern unreflective twentieth-century Englishman often thinks about morality, but surely it is monstrous as an account of how it is most rational to think about morality. Suppose that there is a rule R and that in 99 per cent of cases the best possible results are obtained by acting in accordance with R. Then clearly R is a useful rule of thumb; if we have not time or are not impartial enough to assess the consequences of an action it is an extremely good bet that the thing to do is to act in accordance with R. But is it not monstrous to suppose that if we *have* worked out the consequences and if we have perfect faith in the impartiality of our calculations, and if we *know* that in this instance to break R will have better results than to keep it, we should nevertheless obey the rule? Is it not to erect R into a sort of idol if we keep it when breaking it will prevent, say, some avoidable misery? Is not this a form of superstitious rule-worship (easily explicable psychologically) and not the rational thought of a philosopher?

The point may be made more clearly if we consider Mill's comparison of moral rules to the tables in the nautical almanack.[5] This comparison of Mill's is adduced by Urmson as evidence that Mill was a restricted utilitarian, but I do not think that it will bear this interpretation at all. (Though I quite agree with Urmson that many other things said by Mill are in harmony with restricted rather than extreme utilitarianism. Probably Mill had never thought very much about the distinction and was arguing for utilitarianism, restricted or extreme, against other and quite non-utilitarian forms of moral argument.) Mill says: 'Nobody argues that the art of navigation is not founded on astronomy, because sailors cannot wait to calculate the Nautical Almanack. Being rational creatures, they go out upon the sea of life with their minds made up on the common questions of right and wrong, as well as on many of the far more difficult questions of wise and foolish. . . . Whatever we adopt as the fundamental principle of morality, we require subordinate principles to apply it by.' Notice that this is, as it stands, only an argument for subordinate principles as rules of thumb. The example of the Nautical Almanack is misleading because the information given in the almanack is in all cases the same as the information one would get if one made a long and laborious calculation from the original astronomical data on which the almanack is founded. Suppose, however, that astronomy were different. Suppose that the behaviour of the sun, moon, and planets was very nearly as it is now, but that on rare occasions there were peculiar irregularities and discontinuities, so that the almanack gave us rules of the form 'in 99 per cent of cases where the observations are such and such you can deduce that your position is so and so'. Furthermore, let us suppose that there were methods which enabled us, by direct and laborious calculation from the original astronomical data, not using the rough-and-ready tables of the almanack, to get our correct position in 100 per cent of cases. Seafarers might use the almanack because they never had time for the long calculations and they were content with a 99 per cent chance of success in calculating their positions. Would it not be absurd, however, if they *did* make the direct calculation, and finding that it disagreed with the almanack calculation, nevertheless they ignored it and stuck to the almanack conclusion? Of course the case would be altered if there were a high enough probability of making slips in the direct calculation:

---

[5] *Utilitarianism*, Everyman (London: Dent, 1910), 22–3.

then we might stick to the almanack result, liable to error though we knew it to be, simply because the direct calculation would be open to error for a different reason, the fallibility of the computer. This would be analogous to the case of the extreme utilitarian who abides by the conventional rule against the dictates of his utilitarian calculations simply because he thinks that his calculations are probably affected by personal bias. But if the navigator were sure of his direct calculations would he not be foolish to abide by his almanack? I conclude, then, that if we change our suppositions about astronomy and the almanack (to which there are no exceptions) to bring the case into line with that of morality (to whose rules there are exceptions), Mill's example loses its appearance of supporting the restricted form of utilitarianism. Let me say once more that I am not here concerned with how ordinary men think about morality but with how they ought to think. We could quite well imagine a race of sailors who acquired a superstitious reverence for their almanack, even though it was only right in 99 per cent of cases, and who indignantly threw overboard any man who mentioned the possibility of a direct calculation. But would this behaviour of the sailors be rational?

Let us consider a much discussed sort of case in which the extreme utilitarian might go against the conventional moral rule. I have promised to a friend, dying on a desert island from which I am subsequently rescued, that I will see that his fortune (over which I have control) is given to a jockey club. However, when I am rescued I decide that it would be better to give the money to a hospital, which can do more good with it. It may be argued that I am wrong to give the money to the hospital. But why? (a) The hospital can do more good with the money than the jockey club can. (b) The present case is unlike most cases of promising in that no one except me knows about the promise. In breaking the promise I am doing so with complete secrecy and am doing nothing to weaken the general faith in promises. That is, a factor, which would normally keep the extreme utilitarian from promise-breaking even in otherwise unoptimific cases, does not at present operate. (c) There is no doubt a slight weakening in my own character as a habitual promise-keeper, and moreover psychological tensions will be set up in me every time I am asked what the man made me promise him to do. For clearly I shall have to say that he made me promise to give the money to the hospital, and, since I am a habitual truth-teller, this will go very much against the grain with me. Indeed I am pretty sure that in practice I myself would keep the promise. But we are not discussing what my moral habits would probably make me do; we are discussing what I ought to do. Moreover, we must not forget that even if it would be most rational of me to give the money to the hospital it would also be most rational of you to punish or condemn me if you did, most improbably, find out the truth (e.g. by finding a note washed ashore in a bottle). Furthermore, I would agree that though it was most rational of me to give the money to the hospital it would be most rational of you to condemn me for it. We revert again to Sidgwick's distinction between the utility of the action and the utility of the praise of it.

Many such issues are discussed by A. K. Stout in the article to which I have already referred. I do not wish to go over the same ground again, especially as I think that Stout's arguments support my own point of view. It will be useful, however, to consider one other example that he gives. · Suppose that during hot weather there is an edict that no water must be used for watering gardens. I have a garden and I reason that most people are sure to obey the edict, and that as the amount of water that I use will be by itself negligible no harm will be done if I use the water secretly. So I do use the water, thus producing some lovely flowers which give happiness to various people. Still, you may say, though the action was perhaps optimific, it was unfair and wrong.

There are several matters to consider. Certainly my action should be condemned. We revert once more to Sidgwick's distinction. A right action may be rationally condemned. Furthermore, this sort of offence is normally found out. If I have a wonderful garden when everybody else's is dry and brown there is only one explanation. So if I water my garden I am weakening my respect for law and order, and as this leads to bad results an extreme utilitarian would agree that I was wrong to water the garden. Suppose now that the case is altered and that I can keep the thing secret: there is a secluded part of the garden where I grow flowers which I give away anonymously to a home for old ladies. Are you still so sure that I did the wrong thing by watering my garden? However, this is still a weaker case than that of the hospital and the jockey club. There will be tensions set up within myself: my secret knowledge that I have broken the rule will make it hard for me to exhort others to keep the rule. These psychological ill effects in myself may be not inconsiderable: directly and indirectly they may lead to harm which is at least of the same order as the happiness that the old ladies get from the flowers. You can see that on an extreme utilitarian view there are two sides to the question.

So far I have been considering the duty of an extreme utilitarian in a predominantly non-utilitarian society. The case is altered if we consider the extreme utilitarian who lives in a society every member, or most members, of which can be expected to reason as he does. Should he water his flowers now? (Granting, what is doubtful, that in the case already considered he would have been right to water his flowers.) As a first approximation, the answer is that he should not do so. For since the situation is a completely symmetrical one, what is rational for him is rational for others. Hence, by a *reductio ad absurdum* argument, it would seem that watering his garden would be rational for none. Nevertheless, a more refined analysis shows that the above argument is not quite correct, though it is correct enough for practical purposes. The argument considers each person as confronted with the choice either of watering his garden or of not watering it. However there is a third possibility, which is that each person should, with the aid of a suitable randomizing device, such as throwing dice, give himself a certain probability of watering his garden. This would be to adopt what in the theory of games is called 'a mixed strategy'. If we could give numerical values to the private benefit of garden-watering and to the public harm done by 1, 2, 3, etc., persons using the water in this way, we could work out a value of the probability of watering his garden that each extreme utilitarian should give himself. Let a be the value which each extreme utilitarian gets from watering his garden, and let $f(1), f(2), f(3)$, etc., be the public harm done by exactly 1, 2, 3, etc., persons respectively watering their gardens. Suppose that p is the probability that each person gives himself of watering his garden. Then we can easily calculate, as functions of p, the probabilities that exactly 1, 2, 3, etc.. persons will water their gardens. Let these probabilities be $p_1, p_2, \ldots p_n$. Then the total net probable benefit can be expressed as

$$V = p_1\big(a - f(1)\big) + p_2\big(2a - f(2)\big) + \ldots p_n\big(na - f(n)\big).$$

Then if we know the function $f(x)$ we can calculate the value of p for which $(dV/dp) = 0$. This gives the value of p which it would be rational for each extreme utilitarian to adopt. The present argument does not of course depend on a perhaps unjustified assumption that the values in question are measurable, and in a practical case such as that of the garden-watering we can doubtless assume that p will be so small that we can take it near enough as equal to zero. However the argument is of interest for the theoretical underpinning of extreme utilitarianism, since the possibility of a mixed strategy is usually neglected by critics of utilitarianism, who wrongly assume that the only relevant and symmetrical alternatives are of the form 'everybody does X' and 'nobody does X'.

I now pass on to a type of case which may be thought to be the trump card of restricted utilitarianism. Consider the rule of the road. It may be said that since all that matters is that everyone should do the same it is indifferent which rule we have, 'go on the left-hand side' or 'go on the right-hand side'. Hence the only *reason* for going on the left-hand side in

British countries is that this is the rule. Here the rule does seem to be a reason, in itself, for acting in a certain way. I wish to argue against this. The rule in itself is not a reason for our actions. We would be perfectly justified in going on the right-hand side if (a) we knew that the rule was to go on the left-hand side, and (b) we were in a country peopled by super-anarchists who always on principle did the opposite of what they were told. This shows that the rule does not give us a reason for acting so much as an indication of the probable actions of others, which helps us to find out what would be our own most rational course of action. If we are in a country not peopled by anarchists, but by non-anarchist extreme utilitarians, we expect, other things being equal that they will keep rules laid down for them. Knowledge of the rule enables us to predict their behaviour and to harmonize our own actions with theirs. The rule 'keep to the left-hand side', then, is not a logical *reason* for action but an anthropological datum for planning actions.

I conclude that in every case if there is a rule R the keeping of which is in general optimific, but such that in a special sort of circumstances the optimific behaviour is to break R, then in these circumstances we should break R. Of course we must consider all the less obvious effects of breaking R, such as reducing people's faith in the moral order, before coming to the conclusion that to break R is right: in fact we shall rarely come to such a conclusion. Moral rules, on the extreme utilitarian view, are rules of thumb only, but they are not bad rules of thumb. But if we *do* come to the conclusion that we should break the rule and if we have weighed in the balance our own fallibility and liability to personal bias, what good reason remains for keeping the rule? I can understand 'it is optimific' as a reason for action, but why should 'it is a member of a class of actions which are usually optimific' or 'it is a member of a class of actions which as a class are more optimific than any alternative general class' be a good reason? You might as well say that a person ought to be picked to play for Australia just because all his brothers have been, or that the Australian team should be composed entirely of the Harvey family because this would be better than composing it entirely of any other family. The extreme utilitarian does not appeal to artificial feelings, but only to our feelings of benevolence, and what better feelings can there be to appeal to? Admittedly we can have a pro-attitude to anything, even to rules, but such artificially begotten pro-attitudes smack of superstition. Let us get down to realities, human happiness and misery, and make these the objects of our pro-attitudes and anti-attitudes.

The restricted utilitarian might say that he is talking only of *morality*, not of such things as rules of the road. I am not sure how far this objection, if valid, would affect my argument, but in any case I would reply that as a philosopher I conceive of ethics as the study of how it would be *most rational* to act. If my opponent wishes to restrict the word 'morality' to a narrower use he can have the word. The fundamental question is the question of rationality of action *in general*. Similarly if the restricted utilitarian were to appeal to ordinary usage and say 'it might be most rational to leave Hitler to drown but it would surely not be *wrong* to rescue him', I should again let him have the words 'right' and 'wrong' and should stick to 'rational' and 'irrational'. We already saw that it would be rational to praise Hitler's rescuer, even though it would have been most rational not to have rescued Hitler. In ordinary language, no doubt, 'right' and 'wrong' have not only the meaning 'most rational to do' and 'not most rational to do' but also have the meaning 'praiseworthy' and 'not praiseworthy'. Usually to the utility of an action corresponds utility of praise of it, but as we saw, this is not always so. Moral language could thus do with tidying up, for example by reserving 'right' for 'most rational' and 'good' as an epithet of praise for the motive from which the action sprang. It would be more becoming in a philosopher to try to iron out illogicalities in moral language and to make suggestions for its reform than to use it as a court of appeal whereby to perpetuate confusions.

One last defence of restricted utilitarianism might be as follows. 'Act optimifically' might be regarded as itself one of the rules of our system (though it would be odd to say that this rule was justified by its optimificality). According to Toulmin[6] if 'keep promises', say, conflicts with another rule we are allowed to argue the case on its merits, as if we were extreme utilitarians. If 'act optimifically' is itself one of our rules then there will always be a conflict of rules whenever to keep a rule is not itself optimific. If this is so, restricted utilitarianism collapses into extreme utilitarianism. And no one could read Toulmin's book or Urmson's article on Mill without thinking that Toulmin and Urmson are of the opinion that they have thought of a doctrine which does *not* collapse into extreme utilitarianism, but which is, on the contrary, an improvement on it.

[6] *The Place of Reason in Ethics* 146–8.

III

MOTIVE UTILITARIANISM

ROBERT M. ADAMS

Philosophers have written much about the morality of traits of character, much more about the morality of actions, and much less about the morality of motives. (By 'motives' here I mean principally wants and desires, considered as giving rise, or tending to give rise to actions. A desire, if strong, stable, and for a fairly general object (e.g. the desire to get as much money as possible), may perhaps constitute a trait of character; but motives are not in general the same, and may not be as persistent, as traits of character.) Utilitarian theories form a good place to begin an investigation of the relation between the ethics of motives and the ethics of actions, because they have a clear structure and provide us with familiar and comprehensible, if not always plausible, grounds of argument. I believe that a study of possible treatments of motives in utilitarianism will also shed light on some of the difficulties surrounding the attempt to make the maximization of utility the guiding interest of ethical theory.

I

What would be the motives of a person morally perfect by utilitarian standards? It is natural to suppose that he or she would be completely controlled, if not exclusively moved, by the desire to maximize utility. Isn't this ideal of single-mindedly optimific motivation demanded by the principle of utility, if the principle, as Bentham puts it, 'states the greatest happiness of all those whose interest is in question, as being the right and proper, and only right and proper and universally desirable, end of human action'?[1]

From *Journal of Philosophy*, 73 (1976), 467–81. Reprinted by permission of the *Journal of Philosophy* and the author.

The largest part of my work on this paper was supported by a fellowship from the National Endowment for the Humanities. I am indebted to several, and especially to Gregory Kavka, Jan Narveson, and Derek Parfit, for helpful discussion and comments on earlier versions.

[1] Jeremy Bentham, *An Introduction to the Principles of Morals and Legislation* (1789; New York: Hafner, 1961) (referred to hereafter as *Introduction*, with page number), 1 n.

But there is a good utilitarian objection to such single-mindedness: it is not in general conducive to human happiness. As Sidgwick says, 'Happiness [general as well as individual] is likely to be better attained if the extent to which we set ourselves consciously to aim at it be carefully restricted.'[2] Suggestions of a utilitarian theory about motivation that accommodates this objection can be found in both Bentham and Sidgwick.

The test of utility is used in different theories to evaluate different objects. It is applied to acts in act-utilitarianism and to roles, practices, and types of action in the various forms of rule-utilitarianism. In the view about motives stated in the first paragraph above, the test is not applied at all: nothing is evaluated for its utility, but perfect motivation is identified with an all-controlling desire to maximize utility. The test of utility could be applied in various ways in the evaluation of motives.

It could be applied directly to the motives themselves, and is so applied by Bentham, when he says, 'If they [motives] are good or bad, it is only on account of their effects: good, on account of their tendency to produce pleasure, or avert pain: bad, on account of their tendency to produce pain, or avert pleasure' (*Introduction*, 102). Alternatively, we could apply the test directly to objects of desire and only indirectly to the desires, saying that the best motives are desires for the objects that have most utility. Sidgwick seems to take this line when he says, 'While yet if we ask for a final criterion of the comparative value of the different objects of men's enthusiastic pursuit, and of the limits within which each may legitimately engross the attention of mankind, we shall none the less conceive it to depend upon the degree in which they respectively conduce to Happiness' (*Methods*, 406). Or we could apply the test of utility to the acts to which motives give rise (or are likely to give rise) and, thence, indirectly to the motives; the best motives would be those productive of utility-maximizing acts.[3]

Another approach, also endorsed by Bentham, is to evaluate motives by the intentions to which they give rise: 'A motive is good, when the intention it gives birth to is a good one; bad, when the intention is a bad one' (*Introduction*, 120). The value of an intention to do an act, he regards as depending, in turn, on whether 'the consequences of the act, had they proved what to the agent they seemed likely to be, *would* have been of a beneficial nature' or the opposite (*Introduction*, 93). This approach seems

---

[2] Henry Sidgwick, *The Methods of Ethics* (1874; 7th edn. New York: Dover, 1966) (referred to hereafter as *Methods*, with page number), 405.

[3] This too may find some support in Sidgwick. Cf. *Methods*, 493, on the praise of motives conceived to prompt to felicific conduct.

inconsistent with Bentham's insistence that the test of utility must be applied to everything that is to be evaluated—that 'Strictly speaking, nothing can be said to be good or bad, but either in itself; which is the case only with pain or pleasure: or on account of its effects; which is the case only with things that are the causes or preventives of pain and pleasure' (*Introduction*, 87; cf. 102).

Bentham would presumably defend the evaluating of intentions by the utility of expected consequences of the intended act rather than the utility of the intentions themselves in the same way that he defends a similar method of evaluating dispositions. That is, he would appeal to the assumption 'that in the ordinary course of things the consequences of actions commonly turn out conformable to intentions' (*Introduction*, 133), so that there is no practical difference between the utility of the intention and the utility of the expected consequences of the intended action. This assumption is plausible as regards the short-term consequences of our actions, though even there it yields at best a very rough equivalence between utility of intentions and utility of expected consequences. It is wildly and implausibly optimistic as regards our ability to foresee the long-term consequences of our actions.[4]

Bentham similarly regards the evaluating of motives by the value of intentions arising from them as consistent with (or even practically equivalent to) a direct application of the test of utility to motives, on the ground that the intention resulting from a motive is responsible for 'the most material part of [the motive's] effects' (*Introduction*, 120). His position will still be inconsistent, however, unless he maintains (falsely, I believe) that the resulting intentions to act are responsible for *all* the relevant effects of having a motive.

If the moral point of view, the point of view from which moral evaluations are made, is dominated by concern for the maximization of human happiness, then it seems we must revert to the thesis that the test of utility is to be applied directly to everything, including motives. This is the conclusion toward which the following argument from Sidgwick tends:

Finally, the doctrine that Universal Happiness is the ultimate *standard* must not be understood to imply that Universal Benevolence is the only right or always best *motive* of action. For . . . if experience shows that the general happiness will be more satisfactorily attained if men frequently act from other motives than pure universal philanthropy, it is obvious that these other motives are reasonably to be preferred on Utilitarian principles. (*Methods*, 413)

[4] Also, as Gregory Kavka has pointed out to me, the utility of *having* an intention (e.g. to retaliate if attacked) may be quite different from the utility (actual or expected) of *acting* on it. I shall be making a similar point about motives, below.

Accordingly, the theory that will be my principal subject here is that one pattern of motivation is morally better than another to the extent that the former has more utility than the latter. The morally perfect person, on this view, would have the most useful desires, and have them in exactly the most useful strengths; he or she would have the most useful among the patterns of motivation that are causally possible for human beings.[5] Let us call this doctrine *motive utilitarianism*.

II

It is distinct, both theoretically and practically, from act-utilitarianism. It can be better, by motive-utilitarian standards, to have a pattern of motivation that will lead one to act wrongly, by act-utilitarian standards, than to have a motivation that would lead to right action. Even if there is no difference in external circumstances, the motivational pattern that leads to more useful actions is not necessarily the more useful of two motivational patterns, on the whole. For the consequences of any acts one is thereby led to perform are not always the only utility-bearing consequences of being influenced, to a given degree, by a motive.[6]

This can be seen in the following fictitious case. Jack is a lover of art who is visiting the cathedral at Chartres for the first time. He is greatly excited by it, enjoying it enormously, and acquiring memories which will give him pleasure for years to come. He is so excited that he is spending much more time at Chartres than he had planned, looking at the cathedral from as many interior and exterior angles, and examining as many of its details, as he can. In fact, he is spending too much time there, from a utilitarian point of view. He had planned to spend only the morning, but he is spending the whole day; and this is going to cause him considerable inconvenience and unpleasantness. He will miss his dinner, do several hours of night driving, which he hates, and have trouble finding a place to sleep. On the whole, he will count the day well spent, but some of the time spent in the cathedral will not produce as much utility as would have been produced by departing that much earlier. At the moment, for example, Jack is studying the sixteenth- to eighteenth-century sculpture on the stone choir screen. He is

[5] It is difficult to say what is meant by the question, whether a certain pattern of motivation is causally possible for human beings, and how one would answer it. I shall side-step these issues here, for I shall be making comparative evaluations of motives assumed to be possible, rather than trying to determine the most useful of all causally possible motivations.

[6] I am here denying, as applied to motives, what Bernard Williams rather obscurely calls the 'act-adequacy premise' ('A Critique of Utilitarianism', in J. J. C. Smart and Bernard Williams, *Utilitarianism, For and Against* (New York: Cambridge University Press, 1975), 119–30).

enjoying this less than other parts of the cathedral, and will not remember it very well. It is not completely unrewarding, but he would have more happiness on balance if he passed by these carvings and saved the time for an earlier departure. Jack knows all this, although it is knowledge to which he is not paying much attention. He brushes it aside and goes on looking at the choir screen because he is more strongly interested in seeing, as nearly as possible, everything in the cathedral than in maximizing utility. This action of his is therefore wrong by act-utilitarian standards, and in some measure intentionally so. And this is not the only such case. In the course of the day he knowingly does, for the same reason, several other things that have the same sort of act-utilitarian wrongness.

On the other hand, Jack would not have omitted these things unless he had been less interested in seeing everything in the cathedral than in maximizing utility. And it is plausible to suppose that if his motivation had been different in that respect, he would have enjoyed the cathedral much less. It may very well be that his caring more about seeing the cathedral than about maximizing utility has augmented utility, through enhancing his enjoyment, by more than it has diminished utility through leading him to spend too much time at Chartres. In this case his motivation is right by motive-utilitarian standards, even though it causes him to do several things that are wrong by act-utilitarian standards.

Perhaps it will be objected that the motive-utilitarian should say that Jack ought indeed to have been as interested in the cathedral as he was, but ought to have been even more interested in maximizing utility. Thus he would have had as much enjoyment from the more rewarding parts of the cathedral, according to the objector, but would not have spent too much time on the less rewarding parts. The weak point in this objection is the assumption that Jack's enjoyment of the things he would still have seen would not be diminished in these circumstances. I think, and I take it that Sidgwick thought too,[7] that a great concern to squeeze out the last drop of utility is likely to be a great impediment to the enjoyment of life. Therefore it seems plausible to suppose that from a motive-utilitarian point of view Jack ought not only to have been as strongly interested in seeing the cathedral as he was, but also to have been as weakly interested in maximizing utility as he was.

In describing this case I have been treating the maximization of utility as a unitary end which Jack might have pursued for its own sake. Perhaps it will be suggested that, although an all-controlling desire for that end would

---

[7] I believe this is the most natural reading of Sidgwick, but it may be barely possible to construe him as meaning only that the perpetual *consciousness* of such a concern would be an impediment. See *Methods*, 48–9.

have diminished utility by dulling Jack's enjoyment, he could have had undimmed enjoyment without wrong action if he had had the maximization of utility as an *inclusive end*—that is, if he had been moved by desire for more particular ends for their own sakes, but in exact proportion to their utility.[8] But this suggestion is not plausible. While he is in the cathedral Jack's desire to see everything in it is stronger, and his desire for the benefits of an early departure is weaker, than would be proportionate to the utility of those ends. And a stronger desire for an early departure would probably have interfered with his enjoyment just as much as a stronger desire for utility maximization as such. We are likely in general to enjoy life more if we are often more interested in the object of an enthusiastic pursuit, and less concerned about other ends, than would be proportionate to their utility. It follows that failing (to some extent) to have utility maximization as an inclusive end is often right by motive-utilitarian standards, and may be supposed to be so in Jack's case.

In order to justify the view that motive-utilitarianism implies something practically equivalent to act-utilitarianism one would have to show that the benefits that justify Jack's motivation by motive-utilitarian standards also justify his spending time on the choir screen by act-utilitarian standards. But they do not. For they are not consequences of his spending time there, but independent consequences of something that caused, or manifested itself in, his spending time there. It is not that deciding to devote only a cursory inspection to the choir screen would have put him in the wrong frame of mind for enjoying the visit. It is rather that, being in the right frame of mind for enjoying the visit, he could not bring himself to leave the choir screen as quickly as would have maximized utility.

III

The act-utilitarian may try to domesticate motive-utilitarianism, arguing (A) that motive-utilitarianism is merely a theorem of act utilitarianism, and denying (B) that behaviour like Jack's inspection of the choir screen, if resulting from obedience to the dictates of motive-utilitarianism, can properly be called wrong action.

(A) Since act-utilitarianism implies that one ought to do whatever has most utility, it implies that, other things equal, one ought to foster and

---

[8] The terminology of 'dominant' and 'inclusive' ends was developed by W. F. R. Hardie, 'The Final Good in Aristotle's Ethics', *Philosophy*, 40/154 (Oct. 1965), 277–95; Rawls makes use of it. J. S. Mill seems to treat the maximization of utility as an inclusive end in *Utilitarianism* (1861), ch. 4, sects. 5–8.

promote in oneself those motives which have most utility. And that, it may be claimed, is precisely what motive-utilitarianism teaches.

(B) Jack was once, let us suppose, an excessively conscientious act-utilitarian. Recognizing the duty of cultivating more useful motives in himself, he took a course of capriciousness training, with the result that he now stands, careless of utility, before the choir screen. It would be unfair, it may be argued, to regard what Jack is now doing as a wrong action by utilitarian standards. Rather, we must see it as only an inescapable part of a larger, right action, which began with his enrolling for capriciousness training—just as we do not say that a person rightly jumped from a burning building, saving his life, but wrongly struck the ground, breaking his leg. It is unreasonable, on this view, to separate, for moral evaluation, actions that are causally inseparable.

Both of these arguments are to be rejected. The second (B) involves deep issues about the individuation of actions and the relation between causal determination and moral responsibility. It seems clear enough, however, that Jack's staying at the choir screen is separable from his earlier efforts at character reform in a way that striking the ground is not separable from jumping out of a building. Once you have jumped, it is no longer in your power to refrain from striking the ground, even if you want to. If you are sane and well informed about the situation, you have only one choice to make: to jump or not to jump. There is no further choice about hitting the ground, and therefore it is inappropriate to separate the impact from the leap, as an object of moral evaluation. But even after Jack has taken capriciousness training, it is still in his power to leave the choir screen if he wants to; it is just that he does not want to. His choice to stay and examine it is a new choice, which he did not make, years ago, when he decided to reform. He did decide then to become such that he would sometimes make non-utilitarian choices, but it may not even have occurred to him then that he would ever be in Chartres. It seems perfectly appropriate to ask whether the choice that he now makes is morally right or wrong.

It is plausible, indeed, to say that Jack is not acting wrongly in acting on the motivation that he has rightly cultivated in himself. But I think that is because it is plausible to depart from act-utilitarianism at least so far as to allow the rightness or wrongness of Jack's action in this case to depend partly on the goodness or badness of his motive, and not solely on the utility of the act. It is noteworthy in this connection that it would be no less plausible to acquit Jack of wrongdoing if he had always been as easygoing as he now is about small increments of utility, even though there would not in that case be any larger action of character reform, of which Jack's present scrutiny of the choir screen could be regarded as an inescapable part.

A similar irrelevant emphasis on doing something about one's own motivational patterns also infects the attempt (A) to derive motive-utilitarianism from act-utilitarianism. Motive-utilitarianism is not a theorem of act-utilitarianism, for the simple reason that motive-utilitarianism is not about what motives one ought to foster and promote, or *try* to have, but about what motives one ought to *have*. There is a pre-conception to be overcome here which threatens to frustrate from the outset the development of any independent ethics of motives. I refer to the assumption that 'What should I (try to) do?' is *the* ethical question, and that we are engaged in substantive *ethical* thinking only in so far as we are considering *action*-guiding principles.[9] If we hold this assumption, we are almost bound to read 'What motives should I have?' as 'What motives should I try to develop and maintain in myself?'

There are other questions, however, that are as fundamental to ethics as 'What should I do?' It is characteristic of moral as opposed to pragmatic thinking that, for example, the question 'Have I lived well?' is of interest for its own sake. In pragmatic self-appraisal that question is of interest only in so far as the answer may guide me toward future successes. If I am personally concerned, in more than this instrumental way, and not just in curiosity, about whether I have lived well, my concern is not purely pragmatic, but involves at least a sense of style, if not of morality.

If the question is 'Have I lived well?' the motives I have *had* are relevant, and not just the motives I have *tried* to have. If I tried to have the right motive, but none the less had the wrong one—if I tried to love righteousness and my neighbours, but failed and did my duty out of fear of hell-fire for the most part—then I did not live as well as I would have lived if I had *had* the right motive.

Suppose, similarly, that Martha is an over-scrupulous utilitarian, completely dominated by the desire to maximize utility. She has acted rightly, by act-utilitarian standards, just as often as she could. Among her right actions (or attempts at right action) are many *attempts* to become strongly interested in particular objects—more strongly, indeed, than is proportionate to their utility. For she realizes that she and her acquaintances would be happier if she had such interests. But all these attempts have failed.

[9] Cf. Jan Narveson, *Morality and Utility* (Baltimore: Johns Hopkins University Press, 1967), 105: 'Let us begin by recalling the primary function of ethical principles: to tell us what to do, i.e., to guide action. Whatever else an ethical principle is supposed to do, it must do that, otherwise it could not (logically) be an ethical principle at all.'

Mary, on the other hand, has not had to work on herself to develop such non-utilitarian interests, but has always had them; and, largely because of them, her motivational patterns have had more utility, on the whole, than Martha's. The motive-utilitarian will take this as a reason (not necessarily decisive) for saying that Martha has *lived less well* than Mary. This censure of Martha's motives is not derivable from act-utilitarianism, for her actions have been the best that were causally possible for her. (If you are tempted to say that Martha's conscientiousness is better than Mary's more useful motives, you are experiencing a reluctance to apply the test of utility to motives.)

IV

I have argued that right action, by act-utilitarian standards, and right motivation, by motive-utilitarian standards, are incompatible in some cases. It does not immediately follow, but it may further be argued, that act-utilitarianism and motive-utilitarianism are incompatible theories.

One argument for this conclusion is suggested, in effect, by Bernard Williams. He does not formulate or discuss motive-utilitarianism, but he holds that it is inconsistent of J. J. C. Smart, following Sidgwick, 'to present direct [i.e. act-] utilitarianism as a doctrine merely about justification and not about motivation'. Williams's argument is, 'There is no distinctive place for *direct* utilitarianism unless it is, within fairly narrow limits, a doctrine about how one should decide what to do. This is because its distinctive doctrine is about what acts are right, and, especially for utilitarians, the only distinctive interest or point of the question what acts are right, relates to the situation of deciding to do them.'[10] The doctrine about motives that Williams believes to be implied by act-utilitarianism is presumably the doctrine, discarded at the beginning of my present essay, that one ought always to be controlled by the desire or purpose of maximizing utility. And this doctrine, if conjoined with plausible empirical beliefs illustrated in Section II above, is inconsistent with motive-utilitarianism.

There are two questionable points in Williams's argument. One is the claim that for utilitarians the only use of the question, What acts are right? is for guidance in deciding what to do. He defends this claim, arguing that 'utilitarians in fact are not very keen on people blaming themselves, which they see as an unproductive activity', and that they therefore will not be

[10] 'A Critique of Utilitarianism', 128.

interested in the question, 'Did he (or I) do the right thing?'[11] I am not convinced by this defence. Blame is a self-administered negative reinforcement which may perhaps cause desirable modifications of future behaviour. The retrospective question about the evaluation of one's action is a question in which one can hardly help taking an interest if one has a conscience; one who desires to act well will naturally desire to *have* acted well. And the desire to act well, at least in weighty matters, will surely be approved on motive-utilitarian grounds.

But suppose, for the sake of argument, we grant Williams that the point of act-utilitarian judgements, when they have a point, is to guide us in deciding what to do. His argument still rests on the assumption that the act-utilitarian is committed to the view that it is generally useful to ask what acts are right, and that one ought always or almost always to be interested in the question. Why should the act-utilitarian be committed to this view? If he is also a motive-utilitarian, he will have reason to say that, although it is indeed useful to be guided by utilitarian judgements in actions of great consequence, it is sometimes better to be relatively uninterested in considerations of utility (and so of morality). 'For everything there is a season and a time for every matter under heaven: . . . a time to kill, and a time to heal; a time to break down, and a time to build up,' said the Preacher (Ecclesiastes 3: 1, 3 RSV). The act-and-motive-utilitarian adds, 'There is a time to be moral, and a time to be amoral.' (The act-and-motive-utilitarian is one who holds both act- and motive-utilitarianism as *theories*. He does not, for he cannot, always satisfy the demands of both theories in his acts and motives.)

Perhaps it will be objected that this reply to Williams overlooks the utility of conscientiousness. Conscience is, in part, a motive: the desire to act or live in accordance with moral principles. If the moral principles are mainly sound, it is so useful a motive that it is important, from a motive-utilitarian standpoint, not to undermine it. This consideration might make a motive-utilitarian reluctant to approve the idea of 'a time to be amoral', lest such 'moral holidays' weaken a predominantly useful conscience.

The question facing the act-and-motive-utilitarian at this point is, what sort of conscience has greatest utility. We have seen reason to believe that an act-utilitarian conscience that is scrupulous about small increments of utility would have bad effects on human happiness, smothering many innocent enjoyments in a wet blanket of excessive earnestness. A more useful sort of conscience is probably available to the act-and-motive-

[11] Ibid.

utilitarian. It would incorporate a vigorous desire to *live well*, in terms of the overall utility of his life, but not necessarily to *act rightly* on every occasion. Having such a conscience, he would be strongly concerned (1) not to act in ways gravely detrimental to utility, and (2) not to be in a bad motivational state. If he performs a mildly unutilitarian action as an inevitable consequence of the most useful motivation that he can have, on the other hand, he is still living as well as possible, by his overall utilitarian standards; and there is no reason why such action should undermine his determination to live well. A conscience of this sort seems as possible, and at least as likely to be stable, as a conscience that insists on maximizing utility in every action. Thus the act-and-motive-utilitarian has good motive-utilitarian reasons for believing that he should sometimes be, in relation to his act-utilitarian principles, amoral.

V

But this conclusion may be taken, quite apart from Williams's argument, as grounds for thinking that act-utilitarianism and motive-utilitarianism are incompatible in the sense that holding the latter ought reasonably to prevent us from holding the former as a *moral* theory. The incompatibility has to do with moral seriousness. The problem is not just that one cannot *succeed* in living up to the ideals of both theories simultaneously. It is rather that the motive-utilitarian is led to the conclusion that it is morally better on many occasions to be so motivated that one will not even *try* to do what one ought, by act-utilitarian standards, to do. If the act-and-motive-utilitarian accepts this conclusion, however, we must wonder whether all his act-utilitarian judgements about what one ought to do are really judgements of *moral* obligation. For it is commonly made a criterion for a theory's being a theory of *moral* obligation, that it claim a special seriousness for its judgements of obligation. By this criterion, act-utilitarianism cannot really be a theory of moral obligation (as it purports to be) if it is conjoined with the view that some of its dictates should be taken as lightly as motive-utilitarianism would lead us to think they should be taken.

This argument depends on the triviality of any reasonable human interest in some of the obligations that act-utilitarianism would lay on us. And the triviality is due to the totalitarian character of act-utilitarianism, to its insistence that, as Sidgwick puts it, 'it is *always* wrong for a man knowingly to do *anything* other than what he believes to be most conducive to Universal Happiness' (*Methods*, 492, my italics).

Without this triviality a conflict between the ethics of actions and the ethics of motives need not destroy the seriousness of either. Maybe *no* plausible comprehensive ethical theory can avoid all such conflicts. Are there *some* circumstances in which it is best, for example, in the true morality of motives, to be unable to bring oneself to sacrifice the happiness of a friend when an important duty obliges one, in the true morality of actions, to do so? I don't know. But if there are, the interests involved, on both sides, are far from trivial, and the seriousness of both moralities can be maintained. If one fails to perform the important duty, one ought, seriously, to feel guilty; but one could not do one's duty in such a case without having a motivation of which one ought, seriously, to be ashamed. The situation presents a tragic inevitability of moral disgrace.

There are, accordingly, two ways in which the utilitarian might deal with the argument if he has been trying to combine act- and motive-utilitarianism and accepts the view I have urged on him about the kind of conscience it would be most useful to have. (A) He could simply acknowledge that he is operating with a modified conception of moral obligation, under which a special seriousness attaches to some but not all moral obligations.[12] He would claim that his use of 'morally ought' none the less has enough similarity, in other respects, to the traditional use, to be a reasonable extension of it.

(B) The other, to my mind more attractive, way is to modify the act-utilitarian principle, eliminating trivial obligations, and limiting the realm of duty to actions that would be of concern to a conscience of the most useful sort. Under such a limitation it would not be regarded as morally wrong, in general, to fail to maximize utility by a *small* margin. One's relatively uninfluential practical choices would be subject to moral judgement only indirectly, through the motive-utilitarian judgement on the motives on which one acted (and perhaps a character-utilitarian judgement on the traits of character manifested by the action). Some acts, however, such as shoplifting in a dime store or telling inconsequential lies, would still be regarded as wrong even if only slightly detrimental in the particular case, because it is clear that they would be opposed by the most useful sort of conscience. I leave unanswered here the question whether a conscience of the most useful kind would be offended by some acts that maximize utility—particularly by some utility-maximizing violations of such rules as those against stealing and lying. If the answer is affirmative, the position we are considering would have approximately the same

---

[12] It may be thought that Sidgwick has already begun this modification, by holding that good actions ought not to be praised, nor bad ones blamed, except in so far as it is useful to praise and blame them. See *Methods*, 428–9, 493.

practical consequences as are commonly expected from rule-utilitarianism. This position—that we have a *moral duty* to do an act, if and only if it would be demanded of us by the most useful kind of conscience we could have—may be called 'conscience-utilitarianism', and is a very natural position for a motive-utilitarian to take in the ethics of actions.

The moral point of view—the point of view from which moral judgements are made—cannot safely be defined as a point of view in which the test of utility is applied directly to all objects of moral evaluation. For it is doubtful that the most useful motives, and the most useful sort of conscience, are related to the most useful acts in the way that the motives, and especially the kind of conscience, regarded as right must be related to the acts regarded as right in anything that is to count as a morality. And therefore it is doubtful that direct application of the test of utility to everything results in a system that counts as a morality.

VI

Considered on its own merits, as a theory in the ethics of motives, which may or may not be combined with some other type of utilitarianism in the ethics of actions, how plausible is motive-utilitarianism? That is a question which we can hardly begin to explore in a brief paper, because of the variety of forms that the theory might assume, and the difficulty of stating some of them. The exploration might start with a distinction between individualistic and universalistic motive-utilitarianism, analogous to the distinction between act- and rule-utilitarianism.

Individualistic motive-utilitarianism holds that a person's motivation on any given occasion is better, the greater the utility of *his* having it on *that* occasion. This seemed to Bentham, on the whole, the least unsatisfactory view about the moral worth of motives: 'The only way, it should seem, in which a motive can with safety and propriety be styled good or bad, is with reference to its effects *in each individual instance*' (*Introduction*, 120, my italics). This doctrine seems liable to counter-examples similar to those which are commonly urged against act-utilitarianism. An industrialist's greed, a general's bloodthirstiness, may on some occasions have better consequences on the whole than kinder motives would, and even predictably so. But we want to say that they remain worse motives.

Universalistic motive-utilitarianism is supposed to let us say this, but is difficult to formulate. If we try to state it as the thesis that motives are better, the greater the utility of *everybody's* having them on *all* occasions, we implausibly ignore the utility of diversity in motives. A more satisfactory view might be that a motivation is better, the greater the average probable utility of *anyone's* having it on *any* occasion. This formulation gives rise to questions about averaging: do we weigh equally the utility of a motive on all the occasions when it could conceivably occur, or do we have some formula for weighing more heavily the occasions when it is more likely to occur? There are also difficult issues about the relevant description of the motive. One and the same concrete individual motive might be described correctly as a desire to protect Henry Franklin, a desire to protect (an individual whom one knows to be) one's spouse, a desire to protect (an individual whom one knows to be) the chief executive of one's government, and a desire to protect (an individual whom one knows to be) a betrayer of the public trust; these motive types surely have very different average utilities. If one makes the relevant description of the motive too full, of course, one risks making universalistic motive-utilitarianism equivalent to individualistic.[13] If the description is not full enough, it will be hard to get any determination of average utility at all. Bentham's principal effort, in his discussion of the ethics of motives, is to show, by a tiresome profusion of examples, that the application of the test of utility to sorts of motive yields no results, because 'there is no sort of motive but may give birth to any sort of action' (*Introduction*, 128); his argument depends on the use of very thin descriptions of sorts of motive.

The doctrine that a type of motive is better, the greater the utility of commending or fostering it in a system of moral education, might seem to be another version of universalistic motive-utilitarianism, but is not a form of motive-utilitarianism at all. For in it the test of utility is directly applied not to motives or types of motive, but to systems of moral education.

I am not convinced (nor even inclined to believe) that any purely utilitarian theory about the worth of motives is correct. But motive-utilitarian considerations will have some place in any sound theory of the ethics of motives, because utility, or conduciveness to human happiness (or more generally, to the good), is certainly a great advantage in motives (as in other things), even if it is not a morally decisive advantage.

---

[13] By a process similar to that by which David Lyons, in his *Forms and Limits of Utilitarianism* (New York: Oxford University Press, 1965), has tried to show that rule-utilitarianism is equivalent to act-utilitarianism.

IV

ON CONSEQUENTIALISM

JAMES CARGILE

> ... if someone really thinks, in advance, that it is open to question whether such an action as procuring the judicial execution of the innocent should be quite excluded from consideration—I do not want to argue with him; he shows a corrupt mind.
>
> (G. E. M. Anscombe)

I

In the above passage, Miss Anscombe is indicating that there is practically no modern moral philosopher she cares to argue with, at least on the topic mentioned. For she holds that most modern moral philosophers, even such deontologists as Ross, are consequentialists in the sense that they would hold that any given principle could be set aside in some cases by suitable considerations as to consequences. Anscombe is in sympathy with an ethic involving 'the prohibition of certain things simply in virtue of their description as such-and-such identifiable kinds of action, regardless of any further consequences'.[1] And she holds that 'every academic philosopher since Sidgwick has written in such a way as to exclude' such an ethic. She says:

It is noticeable that none of these philosophers displays any consciousness that there is such an ethic, which he is contradicting: it is pretty well taken for obvious among them all that a prohibition such as that on murder does not operate in face of some consequences. But of course the strictness of the prohibition has as its point *that you are not to be tempted by fear or hope of consequences.*

A notable exponent of the opposing view is Jonathan Bennett, who says that 'anyone who accepted *and really understood* the principle: "It would always be wrong to kill an innocent human, whatever the consequences of not doing so" ', would 'have delivered himself over to a moral authority

From *Analysis*, 29 (1969), 78–88. Reprinted by permission of the author.

I am grateful to the Wilson Fund for a summer grant enabling me to work on this paper.

[1] 'Modern Moral Philosophy', *Philosophy*, 33 (1958), 10.

and . . . opted out of moral thinking altogether' just as if he had sincerely and in his right mind adopted such principles as 'It would always be wrong to leave a bucket in the hallway, whatever the consequences of not doing so' or 'It would always be wrong to shout, whatever the consequences of not doing so'. And this discussion of the principle that it would always be wrong to kill an innocent human, whatever the consequences of not doing so, 'will tell equally against any principle of the form "It would always be wrong to . . . whatever the consequences of not doing so" '.[2]

This disagreement between Anscombe and Bennett is of fundamental importance for ethics. On the one hand we have the view that the essence of certain moral prohibitions is to exclude considerations about consequences. On the other hand we have the view that there are no moral prohibitions against any describable kind of action whatsoever which do not have exceptions at least in possible cases. It is an exciting question to ask which side is right, and even if we do not settle the matter we may hope to learn much of interest in attempting to do so. To begin, it may be well to set out the disagreement in more detail.

II

Anscombe does not say of those 'certain things' which should be prohibited 'simply in virtue of their description as such-and-such identifiable kinds of action, regardless of any further consequences', that it would always be wrong to do such things. And this latter does not follow logically from the former. Someone could consistently maintain that a certain sort of action ought to be prohibited absolutely while admitting that it is sometimes not really wrong to do such an action. This attitude might be questionable morally, but not logically.

Furthermore, Bennett does not say that someone who holds that it would always be wrong to do a certain kind of thing, regardless of consequences, is mistaken. He says rather that such a person has opted out of moral thinking to the same degree that a man would who sincerely and in his right mind adopts such a principle as 'It would always be wrong to shout, whatever the consequences of not doing so'. So there is not a flatly stated disagreement between Anscombe and Bennett in the passages quoted.

However, Bennett probably means moral thinking to include discussion of possible cases. So we shall assume that he regards it as generally false to say something of the form 'It would always be wrong to . . . whatever the

---

[2] 'Whatever the Consequences', *Analysis*, 26 (1966), 84–5.

consequences of not doing so', when possible cases are brought into consideration. And we shall assume that Anscombe would hold that something of this form is true, even when possible cases are brought in.

III

With these simplifying assumptions we may take Anscombe's example of 'procuring the judicial execution of the innocent' as an action which she would hold it would be wrong to do in any possible case. And then Bennett must hold that in some possible case, it would not be wrong to do such a thing. And the case must be clearly possible.

The sort of thing Bennett might advance is a case in which some dangerous political leader could be done away with by framing him on a murder charge, so that he will be executed. Suppose that the leader has never committed any crime but is campaigning for office on a platform which promises the virtual enslavement of a large minority group. He is a spellbinding orator and is winning so much public support that it is likely he will win election. He is essential to his movement and it would collapse without him. Suppose that he is known to have quarrelled with his wife and that his wife is murdered in circumstances that strongly implicate him. One man or perhaps a small group of men are in a position to conclusively clear the leader of the charge. On the other hand, by suppressing their evidence, they can get the leader convicted. They think as follows: 'If we get this man convicted of murder his vicious movement will be discredited and collapse. The case against him will be so convincing that his followers, mostly religious, will make no effort to save him. On the other hand, if we tell the truth he will be set free and will surely be elected. He will implement his oppressive policies and fighting will result in which many people will be killed and many more suffer. And all this will be his fault. We ought to suppress the evidence and bear false testimony.'

This is of course only a very skeletal account of one sort of case which might be advanced on Bennett's side. A whole novel could be devoted to the details. But it seems that the case could at least be filled out so that it is one that might really arise, not just an absurd fantasy, and one in which the consequences of procuring the judicial execution of an innocent man would be better than the consequences of not doing so. It would be easy to take the above skeletal account and fill it out into a novel designed to show the folly of suppressing the truth. The group might be caught and the political leader gain new strength as a result. But surely sufficient details could be provided so that we should have a case in which it is clear that the total consequences of procuring the judicial execution of an innocent man would be vastly better than the consequences of not doing so.

Perhaps Anscombe would not agree with this. The contention that it would always be wrong to procure the judicial execution of an innocent man might be based on the claim that such an action could never have vastly better total consequences than any of the alternatives. However, rather than attempt to resolve this question about possibilities, we shall assume that a case of the sort described above is possible and go on to see how Anscombe might yet hold that the action would be wrong.

For one philosopher, establishing that the consequences of procuring the judicial execution of the political leader despite his innocence would be better than the consequences of not doing so would automatically establish that the action would not be wrong. In *Ethics*, Moore has a whole chapter entitled 'Results the Test of Right and Wrong', in which he stresses that an action is right if it has the best consequences among the alternatives, and wrong otherwise. If this is right, then Bennett is right and Anscombe is wrong, if the above possibility is granted. So we should consider briefly whether Moore is right.

IV

Moore admits that on his view 'we are committed to the paradox that a man may really deserve the strongest moral condemnation for choosing an action, which *actually* is right'. This paradox can be illustrated forcefully as follows. Many people would accept as true the counterfactual conditional 'If Hitler had been murdered as an infant, the world would have been much better off'. If this is true, then if some vicious thief had murdered the 2-year-old Hitler in order to obtain a silver ring the child is wearing without the risk of having the child later identify him as the thief, Moore would have to say not only that the thief's action was not wrong, but that it was positively right. And yet, if the thief had murdered the 2-year-old Hitler, no one would ever have known that what he did was right. Not then, or ever. On Moore's view, then, we must say of even the most vicious child-murders, that while the murderer may deserve the harshest punishment and the strongest moral blame, it is possible that his action was not wrong. This is possible since the child might have grown up to do great harm, which the world was spared by the murder.

Moore's view is obviously not without a strong basis, like all his views. But it requires us to say such things as that some men deserve the harshest condemnation and punishment even though they have never done anything wrong. Perhaps Moore adequately sums up this situation by saying 'we are committed to a paradox', but we should avoid paradoxes where possible.

There are different ways of applying the word 'wrong' to actions. When we say 'That was the wrong course of action' or 'That was the wrong thing to do', Moore's definition of 'wrong' is not so bad, for we are often speaking of results alone when we say these things. But when we say 'What he did was wrong' ('terribly wrong') or 'He did wrong', or 'It was wrong of him to do that', we are not usually speaking of results alone. We will also regard motives as relevant, and the degree to which the agent could reasonably expect the results that did obtain, rather than some other, and the like. And we shall assume that it is in these latter ways of using 'wrong', for which Moore's definition is not adequate, that the disagreement between Anscombe and Bennett is couched.

On this assumption, Bennett's claim that all principles of the form 'It would always be wrong to . . . whatever the consequences of not doing so' are false, has to be slightly modified. For such a principle as 'It would always be wrong to kill an innocent human for no other reason than that you enjoyed doing so (or for no other reason than that you thereby obtain his money, etc.)' is true. It is just for this reason that we can call such an act as killing an innocent human prima-facie wrong, as opposed to such an act as shouting. When we hear that someone has killed an innocent human, we feel that an excuse or justification is in order; there have to be favourable considerations about consequences or the agent is in trouble. But when we hear that someone has shouted, it does not similarly follow that there must be considerations in favour of doing so if the agent is to escape blame.

Precisely how Bennett's claim is to be modified need not trouble us here. He obviously has in mind in his claim, that considerations about consequences can override general prohibitions. And it would not be fair to him to counter with prohibitions in which considerations about consequences have already been built in. We shall just assume that these cases are somehow excluded from the discussion.

Let us return, then, to the case of the dangerous political leader. It is not enough to show that the consequences of procuring his judicial execution are better than the consequences of not doing so. Even if we grant that, in a sense, this would make procuring the execution the right course, we are concerned rather with whether, for the person or persons in a position to incriminate the leader, it would be wrong for them to do so. And here we must ask if their knowledge of the likely consequences and their motivation are such that, for them, the action would not be wrong.

V

We are assuming that Anscombe would say that the action would be wrong. But she would also say that even considering this case as one in which it is open to question whether such an action would be wrong 'shows a corrupt mind'. That is, for a 'non-corrupt' mind, it would be out of the question to procure the judicial execution of an innocent man. However, Anscombe says 'in *advance*', and this may be a qualification. That is, she may mean that in advance of being confronted with a situation in which the actual choice arises, it would take a corrupt mind to consider procuring the judicial execution of an innocent man as a course of action, while not meaning to say anything about the man who considers such a course when he is actually faced with it.

However, it is more interesting to consider this view without the qualification. This is the view that for a 'non-corrupt' mind, some things are out of the question. This is quite different from saying that some things are always wrong. It is one thing to say that an action is wrong and another thing to say that a good man could not possibly do it. After all, it is possible for a good man to do something wrong.

Thus, besides the absolutism which holds that some kinds of action are always wrong, we have the absolutism which says that some kinds of actions could not be performed by a good man. Such actions would be physically within the power of a human body. But any agent who could bring himself to perform them would not be good.

In what follows I shall discuss the question as to how this latter sort of absolutism stands against Bennett's consequentialism. This is to set aside the earlier sort of absolutism which was put in terms of 'wrong', but not to set aside Bennett's consequentialism, which is put in such terms. I think that this new sort of absolutism is a stronger opponent to Bennett's view.

A consequentialist could just ignore our absolutism on the grounds that he has said nothing about whether there are actions which no good man could perform, but only that there are no actions which it would always be wrong to perform. But to admit that an action could not be performed by a good man makes saying that it would not be wrong to perform it hollow. It involves going back to using 'wrong' to mean merely 'did not have the best total consequences among the alternatives', without any reference to motives and the like. This reply to absolutism is not interesting. The reply that is interesting is the denial that there are any actions which no good man could perform.

So far, this version of absolutism (and consequently the denial of it), is very skeletal, since nothing has been said about what constitutes being a bad man. This could be filled in a great variety of ways. For example, a bad man might be defined as one able to pass Old Glory while voluntarily refraining from saluting. It is only in connection with some plausible theory of badness that we have anything worth discussing.

Furthermore, consequentialism is also skeletal in the same way. What needs filling in is the notion of good or bad consequences. And this too can be done in a great variety of ways.

We shall henceforth assume that this filling in is carried out in a manner suggested by utilitarianism. We shall assume that the consequentialist under consideration reckons the goodness or badness of consequences in terms of human pleasure and pain, and that our absolutist reckons the goodness or badness of a man in terms of his disposition to act in ways conducive to human pleasure or pain, respectively.

Utilitarianism is sometimes thought of as a form of consequentialism. However, the Utilitarians came before Sidgwick, and thus do not fall under Anscombe's generalization about English philosophers. We shall now try to determine whether the utilitarian can consistently side with the absolutist against the consequentialist.

VI

In taking the good man to be one disposed to act in ways conducive to human pleasure we of course do not mean to include the persistently bumbling fiend who, in operating a fun house, thinks he is running a torture chamber. Nor should we seek to rule out this case by speaking of a disposition to consciously seek to promote the happiness of others, since a good man may do this unconsciously, without reflecting on what he is doing. What we want, roughly, is that the man is impressed by considerations as to human happiness and that he is concerned with increasing it, whether this concern is conscious or purely natural.

Taking human suffering as the basic evil, and human happiness as the basic good, invites a famous question. Do we count happiness at the misery of others and misery at the happiness of others as on a par with the more common sorts of happiness and misery? It is worth noting that the utilitarian has an answer for this, for the answer is an essential qualification to the otherwise hopelessly vague injunction to seek the greatest good for the greatest number. It is sometimes suggested that this injunction makes it impossible for the utilitarian to adequately justify forbidding the persecution of minorities in cases where this gives pleasure to the majority. It appears that if publicly torturing someone will give great pleasure to the crowd, the torturer can claim to be a humanitarian, exhibiting a disposition to want to increase the happiness of his fellow men.

Now human happiness is not always good, in cases where it is happiness at the misery of others. However, human misery is always bad, even when it is misery at the happiness of others. When we regret that someone is happy at another's suffering, we regret both that other person's suffering and that someone should be in such an awful condition that he rejoices at suffering. When we regret that someone is miserable at someone else's happiness, we do not regret the happiness, but only that someone should be in such a state that he is made miserable by human happiness. A good man cannot be happy in contemplating a fiend who is suffering because others are happy. He may rejoice at the happiness, but he can only feel sorry for the fiend and horrified at the prospect of a man so disordered. A good man can never rejoice at anyone's misery, be he a fiend or otherwise. On the other hand, a good man may be miserable in contemplating another's happiness, if it is happiness at the suffering of others.

For a utilitarian, sympathy, that is, feeling for humanity, is the basis of human moral goodness. There are two kinds of sympathy, namely, sympathetic happiness at the happiness of others, and sympathetic misery at the misery of others. The above considerations suggest that it is this latter which is most fundamental, and which should take precedence. This is helpful in a case in which a majority will take pleasure in someone's suffering. The majority may not be happy without it, but it is unlikely that it will be miserable without it, especially on a scale similar to the suffering of the victim, unless we imagine some absurdly different species of men.

In fact, there should be nothing to prevent a utilitarian from distinguishing one degree of suffering from another and holding that the one takes absolute precedence. It is better that one person be hit on the toe with a hammer than that one person be murdered. It is better that twenty persons be hit on the toe. It would be better even if all the men in the world were hit on the toe than that one person should be murdered. The two sorts of suffering are not comparable. And there is nothing to prevent a utilitarian from recognizing this.

In fitting our absolutism into utilitarianism, there is a crucial ambiguity in the principle that 'An action is right if it had the best consequences and the agent was motivated by this consideration' which remains to be resolved. It is in 'motivated'. For our absolutist there are some actions such that no one capable of performing one is capable of fellow feeling, that is, of being motivated to his performance *in any morally redeeming way* by considerations as to consequences. He may claim to have considered consequences as the utilitarian requires, and we may even be able to show that he would not have done what he did had there not been the favourable consequences. But if the utilitarian settles for this, he cannot agree with the absolutist. Just any concern for consequences will not do, since this might lead to counting some scrupulous psychopath as a good man. The concern must spring from a feeling for humanity which a psychopath does not have.

This requirement is compatible with utilitarianism. For it does not involve any change in what a utilitarian enjoins people to do. It merely involves distinguishing between a good man and one who happens to be a producer of good consequences. And this is easy enough if we remember that one may happen to produce good consequences even over a long period without having a disposition to do so. A psychopath who always acts for the general good must have some reason for doing so other than concern for the general good. Otherwise he would not be a psychopath.

If we credit our absolutist with the point that there are certain actions which are absolutely bad in the sense that no good man could perform them, we should still be careful not to be misled into taking him to have thus found some absolute prohibitions. We must distinguish between condemning someone's action because it reveals a bad character and condemning it on the less specific grounds that it was a bad thing to do. In the former case, prohibitions seem rather pointless, since they will be wasted on someone with the sort of character which permits him to do the thing, and superfluous with someone who does not have that sort of character. It is the absolute condemnation which is important and not the prohibition.

There is no reason for considering this sort of absolutism incompatible with utilitarianism. Suppose that a wise utilitarian ruler is informed that one of his subjects is being confronted with a choice between doing or not doing some hideous thing which only a bad man could bring himself to do, on pain of something awful happening to the whole country. (We assume that some higher power is posing the choice.) Then the ruler may very well hope that the subject confronted with the choice happens to be a bad man, and in hoping for this, be hoping for the best under the circumstances. And when the deed is done, he may well condemn the man, even though he did not prohibit the action and may even have encouraged it. And if the subject cannot perform the action, the wise ruler may greet him as a comrade as they go to meet their common fate, understanding and fully sympathizing with his inability while regretting it none the less.

In a case like this, the question 'Was the subject acting wrongly?' is rather confusing. Our absolutist has a basis for answering yes. Does a utilitarian? Well, the subject did what under the circumstances had the best possible consequences. The utilitarian has only one question left. Did the subject consider the consequences and have good reason for thinking the alternatives were what they were? Here our absolutist says that the subject can't have cared in any morally redeeming way about consequences, that only a man who had no feeling for others could do what he did. And there is no reason why a utilitarian could not consistently adopt this view. It makes for a confusing situation, because we may be urging someone to do something for the sake of the country which we hold that only a bad man could do. In such a case asking if the action is wrong is confusing. But we only need keep the details in mind. It is consistent to urge people to do things if they can, to try to do things, which we know that no good man could do.

It may be said that a utilitarian cannot consistently deny that a man who fails to act to produce the best consequences when it is in his power to do so is acting wrongly. But a utilitarian can recognize a disposition to produce good consequences, that is, a disposition to increase happiness and eliminate misery, as good, and there is no reason why he cannot count such a disposition as a limitation on a good man's power to act in some cases. That is, the utilitarian can recognize, besides physical limitations, genuine moral limitations on a person's power to act for the best consequences in particular cases.

It may also be said that a ruler who can urge a man to do something and then condemn him for it is guilty of hypocrisy. But this is entirely dependent upon the details of the case. Sometimes it would be true, sometimes not. And of course urging someone to do what you then condemn him for doing is not being endorsed in a blanket way.

It may be asked whether present absolutist theory should not be extended. The theory holds that there are certain actions such that no good man could perform one no matter how high the preponderance of good consequences on the side of doing the action. But perhaps there are also actions such that while there are preponderances of consequences in favour of the action which are sufficiently high that a good man could be brought, in view of such a preponderance, to do the action, there would be other preponderances of consequences which, while coming out on balance in favour of the action, would not be sufficiently high that any good man could bring himself to do the action with only such a preponderance to motivate him. This is a complicated matter which will not be discussed here.

While a utilitarian may accept the present absolutist view, he also may not. These hold-outs may be divided into two classes according to whether or not they accept the absolutist claim that there are actions which someone possessing the dispositions characteristic of a good man could not possibly perform in any circumstances.

The utilitarian who accepts this absolutist claim and yet continues to hold to consequentialism is in a position already criticized. It depends on the doctrine that an action is right if it has the best consequences and wrong otherwise. It is not important, on this view, whether the agent was motivated by the consideration of consequences in any morally redeeming way. And this is due to a mere definition, which yields no moral insights.

VII

On the other hand, the utilitarian who chooses to cling to a thoroughgoing consequentialism by denying that there are any actions which only a bad man could perform is making a significant claim which leads to an important view of human character.

To see this, it is worth noting that our absolutism does not depend on any particular description of an action. Many people would not agree that it would be impossible for a good man to procure the judicial execution of an innocent man. But many of these people would hesitate to agree that there is no action whatsoever that would be within the powers of a human being but beyond those of a good man. Here of course we exclude question-begging descriptions of actions (such as 'behaving as only a bad man could').

For example, consider the actual case of a Polish doctor who was sent to a prison camp for resistance activities against the Nazis. He was offered a safe position if he would assist the Nazis in their 'medical' experiments on Jewish prisoners. The doctor agreed to this arrangement. He defended his action on the grounds that the sadistic operations required of him would do even more harm to the prisoners if performed by the medically un-trained Nazis. We may suppose that this claim was true and that various maimed and castrated prisoners survived who would otherwise have died. And many people defended the doctor on this ground. But many others regarded him as a bad man and admired the other doctors who refused to participate. And those who condemned this doctor probably felt that even if it really was not just a desire for personal safety that motivated him, the ability to perform, directly and with full awareness, acts of sadism, proves the absence of genuinely human feeling.

Furthermore, we may set aside many features of the actual case that may favourably affect our estimate of the doctor's character without making it a fantastic or unreal case. A good man may gather some strength to do terrible things if he is frequently confronted with the positive effects that are supposed to justify his behaviour. But consequentialist reasons could be found in favour of someone's going through a whole war performing nothing but acts of horrible torture and pretending to enjoy them, just because they would be done by someone else anyway, and doing them put the agent into a position to reveal enemy secrets or in some other way produce distant, but favourable consequences.

The consequentialist hero is a man whose reason is in complete control of his actions. As far as he is physically able, he will always act to bring about the best total consequences. And he is not supposed to be a mere calculating-machine reckoning consequences. He will have normal feelings for his fellow men and normal regret if he has to make any of them suffer. It is just that he keeps the total good always in view.

Our absolutism denies the possibility of such a man as this. Of course he may go through all the motions in the description. But he cannot if he is a good man. It is like suggesting that there could be a sinner who could undergo redemption every day while lapsing again each night. He may be a Jekyll and Hyde case. But one integral person cannot behave this way. It is not really redemption. And similarly, some actions are so vicious that the motives of anyone performing them cannot be those of a good man, no matter what good consequences there are to point to.

This is not meant merely as a psychological claim. A race of thorough-going consequentialists would not be human, and what could be cited as moral questions among them would be a one-dimensional mockery of the real thing. It is an essential feature of humanity that we recoil more strongly from directly inflicting pain than we do from merely knowing that an equal amount of pain is inflicted. Sometimes this trait should be overridden. Perhaps, for example, those who favour capital punishment deserve to be challenged to serve as executioners. But ultimately, the effects produced by direct bodily involvement will be more real and will have more influence on the mind of the human agent than effects less directly produced which are recognized to be equal by the intellect. And this will be reflected in a breakdown of the ability to optimize consequences in some cases.

V

JUSTICE AS FAIRNESS

JOHN RAWLS

1

It might seem at first sight that the concepts of justice and fairness are the same, and that there is no reason to distinguish them, or to say that one is more fundamental than the other. I think that this impression is mistaken. In this paper I wish to show that the fundamental idea in the concept of justice is fairness; and I wish to offer an analysis of the concept of justice from this point of view. To bring out the force of this claim, and the analysis based upon it, I shall then argue that it is this aspect of justice for which utilitarianism, in its classical form, is unable to account, but which is expressed, even if misleadingly, by the idea of the social contract.

To start with I shall develop a particular conception of justice by stating and commenting upon two principles which specify it, and by considering the circumstances and conditions under which they may be thought to arise. The principles defining this conception, and the conception itself, are, of course, familiar. It may be possible, however, by using the notion of fairness as a framework, to assemble and to look at them in a new way. Before stating this conception, however, the following preliminary matters should be kept in mind.

Throughout I consider justice only as a virtue of social institutions, or what I shall call practices.[1] The principles of justice are regarded as formulating restrictions as to how practices may define positions and offices, and assign thereto powers and liabilities, rights and duties. Justice as a virtue of particular actions or of persons I do not take up at all. It is important to

From *Philosophical Review*, 67 (1958), 164–94. Material in public domain.

[1] I use the word 'practice' throughout as a sort of technical term meaning any form of activity specified by a system of rules which defines offices, roles, moves, penalties, defences, and so on, and which gives the activity its structure. As examples one may think of games and rituals, trials and parliaments, markets and systems of property. I have attempted a partial analysis of the notion of a practice in a paper 'Two Concepts of Rules', *Philosophical Review*, 64 (1955), 3–32.

distinguish these various subjects of justice, since the meaning of the concept varies according to whether it is applied to practices, particular actions, or persons. These meanings are, indeed, connected, but they are not identical. I shall confine my discussion to the sense of justice as applied to practices, since this sense is the basic one. Once it is understood, the other senses should go quite easily.

Justice is to be understood in its customary sense as representing but *one* of the many virtues of social institutions, for these may be antiquated, inefficient, degrading, or any number of other things, without being unjust. Justice is not to be confused with an all-inclusive vision of a good society; it is only one part of any such conception. It is important, for example, to distinguish that sense of equality which is an aspect of the concept of justice from that sense of equality which belongs to a more comprehensive social ideal. There may well be inequalities which one concedes are just, or at least not unjust, but which, nevertheless, one wishes, on other grounds, to do away with. I shall focus attention, then, on the usual sense of justice in which it is essentially the elimination of arbitrary distinctions and the establishment, within the structure of a practice, of a proper balance between competing claims.

Finally, there is no need to consider the principles discussed below as *the* principles of justice. For the moment it is sufficient that they are typical of a family of principles normally associated with the concept of justice. The way in which the principles of this family resemble one another, as shown by the background against which they may be thought to arise, will be made clear by the whole of the subsequent argument.

2

The conception of justice which I want to develop may be stated in the form of two principles as follows: first, each person participating in a practice, or affected by it, has an equal right to the most extensive liberty compatible with a like liberty for all; and second, inequalities are arbitrary unless it is reasonable to expect that they will work out for everyone's advantage, and provided the positions and offices to which they attach, or from which they may be gained, are open to all. These principles express justice as a complex of three ideas: liberty, equality, and reward for services contributing to the common good.[2]

[2] These principles are, of course, well known in one form or another and appear in many analyses of justice even where the writers differ widely on other matters. Thus if the principle of equal liberty is commonly associated with Kant (see *The Philosophy of Law*, tr. W. Hastie

The term 'person' is to be construed variously depending on the circumstances. On some occasions it will mean human individuals, but in others it
may refer to nations, provinces, business firms, churches, teams, and so on.
The principles of justice apply in all these instances, although there is a
certain logical priority to the case of human individuals. As I shall use the
term 'person', it will be ambiguous in the manner indicated.

The first principle holds, of course, only if other things are equal: that is,
while there must always be a justification for departing from the initial
position of equal liberty (which is defined by the pattern of rights and
duties, powers and liabilities, established by a practice), and the burden of
proof is placed on him who would depart from it, nevertheless, there can
be, and often there is, a justification for doing so. Now, that similar particular cases, as defined by a practice, should be treated similarly as they arise,
is part of the very concept of a practice; it is involved in the notion of an
activity in accordance with rules.[3] The first principle expresses an analogous conception, but as applied to the structure of practices themselves. It
holds, for example, that there is a presumption against the distinctions and
classifications made by legal systems and other practices to the extent that
they infringe on the original and equal liberty of the persons participating in them. The second principle defines how this presumption may be
rebutted.

It might be argued at this point that justice requires only an equal
liberty. If, however, a greater liberty were possible for all without loss or
conflict, then it would be irrational to settle on a lesser liberty. There is no
reason for circumscribing rights unless their exercise would be incompatible, or would render the practice defining them less effective. Therefore
no serious distortion of the concept of justice is likely to follow from
including within it the concept of the greater equal liberty.

The second principle defines what sorts of inequalities are permissible; it
specifies how the presumption laid down by the first principle may be put
aside. Now by inequalities it is best to understand not *any* differences
between offices and positions, but differences in the benefits and burdens

(Edinburgh, 1887), 56–7), it may be claimed that it can be also be found in J. S. Mill's *On Liberty*
and elsewhere, and in many other liberal writers. Recently H. L. A. Hart has argued for
something like it in his paper 'Are there any Natural Rights?' *Philosophical Review*, 64 (1955),
175–91. The injustice of inequalities which are not won in return for a contribution to the
common advantage is, of course, widespread in political writings of all sorts. The conception of
justice here discussed is distinctive, if at all, only in selecting these two principles in this form; but
for another similar analysis, see the discussion by W. D. Lamont, *The Principles of Moral
Judgment* (Oxford: Clarendon Press, 1946), ch. v.

[3] This point was made by Sidgwick, *The Methods of Ethics* (1874; 6th edn. London, 1901), III.
v. 1. It has recently been emphasized by Sir Isaiah Berlin in a symposium, 'Equality', *Proceedings of the Aristotelian Society*, NS 56 (1955–6), 305–6.

attached to them either directly or indirectly, such as prestige and wealth, or liability to taxation and compulsory services. Players in a game do not protest against there being different positions, such as batter, pitcher, catcher, and the like, nor to there being various privileges and powers as specified by the rules; nor do the citizens of a country object to there being the different offices of government such as president, senator, governor, judge, and so on, each with their special rights and duties. It is not differences of this kind that are normally thought of as inequalities, but differences in the resulting distribution established by a practice, or made possible by it, of the things men strive to attain or avoid. Thus they may complain about the pattern of honours and rewards set up by a practice (e.g. the privileges and salaries of government officials) or they may object to the distribution of power and wealth which results from the various ways in which men avail themselves of the opportunities allowed by it (e.g. the concentration of wealth which may develop in a free price system allowing large entrepreneurial or speculative gains).

It should be noted that the second principle holds that an inequality is allowed only if there is reason to believe that the practice with the inequality, or resulting in it, will work for the advantage of *every* party engaging in it. Here it is important to stress that *every* party must gain from the inequality. Since the principle applies to practices, it implies that the representative man in every office or position defined by a practice, when he views it as a going concern, must find it reasonable to prefer his condition and prospects with the inequality to what they would be under the practice without it. The principle excludes, therefore, the justification of inequalities on the grounds that the disadvantages of those in one position are outweighed by the greater advantages of those in another position. This rather simple restriction is the main modification I wish to make in the utilitarian principle as usually understood. When coupled with the notion of a practice, it is a restriction of consequence,[4] and one which

---

[4] In 'Two Concepts of Rules', I have tried to show the importance of taking practices as the proper subject of the utilitarian principle. The criticisms of so-called 'restricted utilitarianism' by J. J. C. Smart, 'Extreme and Restricted Utilitarianism', *Philosophical Quarterly*, 6 (1956), 344–54 (Ch. II of this volume), and by H. J. McCloskey, 'An Examination of Restricted Utilitarianism', *Philosophical Review*, 66 (1957), 466–85, do not affect my argument. These papers are concerned with the very general proposition, which is attributed (with what justice I shall not consider) to S. E. Toulmin and P. H. Nowell-Smith (and in the case of the latter paper, also, apparently, to me); namely, the proposition that particular moral actions are justified by appealing to moral rules, and moral rules in turn by reference to utility. But clearly I meant to defend no such view. My discussion of the concept of rules as maxims is an explicit rejection of it. What I did argue was that, in the *logically special* case of practices (although actually quite a common case) where the rules have special features and are not moral rules at all but legal rules or rules of games and the like (except, perhaps, in the case of promises), there is a peculiar force to the distinction between justifying particular actions and justifying the system of rules themselves.

some utilitarians, e.g. Hume and Mill, have used in their discussions of justice without realizing apparently its significance, or at least without calling attention to it.[5] Why it is a significant modification of principle, changing one's conception of justice entirely, the whole of my argument will show.

Further, it is also necessary that the various offices to which special benefits or burdens attach are open to all. It may be, for example, to the common advantage, as just defined, to attach special benefits to certain offices. Perhaps by doing so the requisite talent can be attracted to them and encouraged to give its best efforts. But any offices having special benefits must be won in a fair competition in which contestants are judged on their merits. If some office were not open, those excluded would normally be justified in feeling unjustly treated, even if they benefited from the greater efforts of those who were allowed to compete for them. Now if one can assume that offices are open, it is necessary only to consider the design of practices themselves and how they jointly, as a system, work together. It will be a mistake to focus attention on the varying relative positions of particular persons, who may be known to us by their proper names, and to require that each such change, as a once for all transaction viewed in isolation, must be in itself just. It is the system of practices which is to be judged, and judged from a general point of view: unless one is prepared to criticize it from the standpoint of a representative man holding some particular office, one has no complaint against it.

3

Given these principles one might try to derive them from a priori principles of reason, or claim that they were known by intuition. These are familiar enough steps and, at least in the case of the first principle, might be

Even then I claimed only that restricting the utilitarian principle to practices as defined strengthened it. I did not argue for the position that this amendment alone is sufficient for a complete defence of utilitarianism as a general theory of morals. In this paper I take up the question as to how the utilitarian principle itself must be modified, but here, too, the subject of inquiry is not all of morality at once, but a limited topic, the concept of justice.

[5] It might seem as if J. S. Mill, in para. 36 of ch. v of *Utilitarianism* (1861), expressed the utilitarian principle in this modified form, but in the remaining two paragraphs of the chapter, and elsewhere, he would appear not to grasp the significance of the change. Hume often emphasizes that *every* man must benefit. For example, in discussing the utility of general rules, he holds that they are requisite to the 'well-being of every individual'; from a stable system of property 'every individual person must find himself a gainer in balancing the account'. 'Every member of society is sensible of this interest; everyone expresses this sense to his fellows along with the resolution he has taken of squaring his actions by it, on the conditions that others will do the same' (*A Treatise of Human Nature* (1739–40), III. ii, 2, 22).

made with some success. Usually, however, such arguments, made at this point, are unconvincing. They are not likely to lead to an understanding of the basis of the principles of justice, not at least as principles of justice. I wish, therefore, to look at the principles in a different way.

Imagine a society of persons amongst whom a certain system of practices is *already* well established. Now suppose that by and large they are mutually self-interested; their allegiance to their established practices is normally founded on the prospect of self-advantage. One need not assume that, in all senses of the term 'person', the persons in this society are mutually self-interested. If the characterization as mutually self-interested applies when the line of division is the family, it may still be true that members of families are bound by ties of sentiment and affection and willingly acknowledge duties in contradiction to self-interest. Mutual self-interestedness in the relations between families, nations, churches, and the like, is commonly associated with intense loyalty and devotion on the part of individual members. Therefore, one can form a more realistic conception of this society if one thinks of it as consisting of mutually self-interested families, or some other association. Further, it is not necessary to suppose that these persons are mutually self-interested under all circumstances, but only in the usual situations in which they participate in their common practices.

Now suppose also that these persons are rational: they know their own interests more or less accurately; they are capable of tracing out the likely consequences of adopting one practice rather than another; they are capable of adhering to a course of action once they have decided upon it; they can resist present temptations and the enticements of immediate gain; and the bare knowledge or perception of the difference between their condition and that of others is not, within certain limits and in itself, a source of great dissatisfaction. Only the last point adds anything to the usual definition of rationality. This definition should allow, I think, for the idea that a rational man would not be greatly downcast from knowing, or seeing, that others are in a better position than himself, unless he thought their being so was the result of injustice, or the consequence of letting chance work itself out for no useful common purpose, and so on. So if these persons strike us as unpleasantly egoistic, they are at least free in some degree from the fault of envy.[6]

[6] It is not possible to discuss here this addition to the usual conception of rationality. If it seems peculiar, it may be worth remarking that it is analogous to the modification of the utilitarian principle which the argument as a whole is designed to explain and justify. In the same way that the satisfaction of interests, the representative claims of which violate the principles of justice, is not a reason for having a practice (see Sect. 7), unfounded envy, within limits, need not to be taken into account.

Finally, assume that these persons have roughly similar needs and interests, or needs and interests in various ways complementary, so that fruitful co-operation amongst them is possible; and suppose that they are sufficiently equal in power and ability to guarantee that in normal circumstances none is able to dominate the others. This condition (as well as the others) may seem excessively vague; but in view of the conception of justice to which the argument leads, there seems no reason for making it more exact here.

Since these persons are conceived as engaging in their common practices, which are already established, there is no question of our supposing them to come together to deliberate as to how they will set these practices up for the first time. Yet we can imagine that from time to time they discuss with one another whether any of them has a legitimate complaint against their established institutions. Such discussions are perfectly natural in any normal society. Now suppose that they have settled on doing this in the following way. They first try to arrive at the principles by which complaints, and so practices themselves, are to be judged. Their procedure for this is to let each person propose the principles upon which he wishes his complaints to be tried with the understanding that, if acknowledged, the complaints of others will be similarly tried, and that no complaints will be heard at all until everyone is roughly of one mind as to how complaints are to be judged. They each understand further that the principles proposed and acknowledged on this occasion are binding on future occasions. Thus each will be wary of proposing a principle which would give him a peculiar advantage, in his present circumstances, supposing it to be accepted. Each person knows that he will be bound by it in future circumstances the peculiarities of which cannot be known, and which might well be such that the principle is then to his disadvantage. The idea is that everyone should be required to make *in advance* a firm commitment, which others also may reasonably be expected to make, and that no one be given the opportunity to tailor the canons of a legitimate complaint to fit his own special condition, and then to discard them when they no longer suit his purpose. Hence each person will propose principles of a general kind which will, to a large degree, gain their sense from the various applications to be made of them, the particular circumstances of which being as yet unknown. These principles will express the conditions in accordance with which each is the least unwilling to have his interests limited in the design of practices, given the competing interests of the others, on the supposition that the interests of others will be limited likewise. The restrictions which would so arise might be thought of as those a person would keep in mind if he were designing a practice in which his enemy were to assign him his place.

The two main parts of this conjectural account have a definite significance. The character and respective situations of the parties reflect the typical circumstances in which questions of justice arise. The procedure whereby principles are proposed and acknowledged represents constraints, analogous to those of having a morality, whereby rational and mutually self-interested persons are brought to act reasonably. Thus the first part reflects the fact that questions of justice arise when conflicting claims are made upon the design of a practice and where it is taken for granted that each person will insist, as far as possible, on what he considers his rights. It is typical of cases of justice to involve persons who are pressing on one another their claims, between which a fair balance or equilibrium must be found. On the other hand, as expressed by the second part, having a morality must at least imply the acknowledgement of principles as impartially applying to one's own conduct as well as to another's, and moreover principles which may constitute a constraint, or limitation, upon the pursuit of one's own interests. There are, of course, other aspects of having a morality: the acknowledgement of moral principles must show itself in accepting a reference to them as reasons for limiting one's claims, in acknowledging the burden of providing a special explanation, or excuse, when one acts contrary to them, or else in showing shame and remorse and a desire to make amends, and so on. It is sufficient to remark here that having a morality is analogous to having made a firm commitment in advance; for one must acknowledge the principles of morality even when to one's disadvantage.[7] A man whose moral judgements always coincided with his interests could be suspected of having no morality at all.

Thus the two parts of the foregoing account are intended to mirror the kinds of circumstances in which questions of justice arise and the constraints which having a morality would impose upon persons so situated. In this way one can see how the acceptance of the principles of justice might come about, for given all these conditions as described, it would be natural if the two principles of justice were to be acknowledged. Since there is no way for anyone to win special advantages for himself, each might consider it reasonable to acknowledge equality as an initial principle. There is, however, no reason why they should regard this position as final; for if there are inequalities which satisfy the second principle, the immediate

---

[7] The idea that accepting a principle as a moral principle implies that one generally acts on it, failing a special explanation, has been stressed by R. M. Hare, *The Language of Morals* (Oxford: Oxford University Press, 1952). His formulation of it needs to be modified, however, along the lines suggested by P. L. Gardiner, 'On Assenting to a Moral Principle', *Proceedings of the Aristotelian Society*, NS 55 (1955), 23–44. See also C. K. Grant, 'Akrasia and the Criteria of Assent to Practical Principles', *Mind*, 65 (1956), 400–7, where the complexity of the criteria for assent is discussed.

gain which equality would allow can be considered as intelligently invested in view of its future return. If, as is quite likely, these inequalities work as incentives to draw out better efforts, the members of this society may look upon them as concessions to human nature: they, like us, may think that people ideally should want to serve one another. But as they are mutually self-interested, their acceptance of these inequalities is merely the acceptance of the relations in which they actually stand, and a recognition of the motives which lead them to engage in their common practices. *They* have no title to complain of one another. And so provided that the conditions of the principle are met, there is no reason why they should not allow such inequalities. Indeed, it would be short-sighted of them to do so, and could result, in most cases, only from their being dejected by the bare knowledge, or perception, that others are better situated. Each person will, however, insist on an advantage to himself, and so on a common advantage, for none is willing to sacrifice anything for the others.

These remarks are not offered as a proof that persons so conceived and circumstanced would settle on the two principles, but only to show that these principles could have such a background, and so can be viewed as those principles which mutually self-interested and rational persons, when similarly situated and required to make in advance a firm commitment, could acknowledge as restrictions governing the assignment of rights and duties in their common practices, and thereby accept as limiting their rights against one another. The principles of justice may, then, be regarded as those principles which arise when the constraints of having a morality are imposed upon parties in the typical circumstances of justice.

4

These ideas are, of course, connected with a familiar way of thinking about justice which goes back at least to the Greek Sophists, and which regards the acceptance of the principles of justice as a compromise between persons of roughly equal power who would enforce their will on each other if they could, but who, in view of the equality of forces amongst them and for the sake of their own peace and security, acknowledge certain forms of conduct in so far as prudence seems to require. Justice is thought of as a pact between rational egoists the stability of which is dependent on a balance of power and a similarity of circumstances.[8] While the previous

---

[8] Perhaps the best-known statement of this conception is that given by Glaucon at the beginning of book 2 of Plato's *Republic*. Presumably it was, in various forms, a common view among the Sophists; but that Plato gives a fair representation of it is doubtful. See K. R. Popper,

account is connected with this tradition, and with its most recent variant, the theory of games,[9] it differs from it in several important respects which, to forestall misinterpretations, I will set out here.

First, I wish to use the previous conjectural account of the background of justice as a way of analysing the concept. I do not want, therefore, to be interpreted as assuming a general theory of human motivation: when I suppose that the parties are mutually self-interested, and are not willing to have their (substantial) interests sacrificed to others, I am referring to their conduct and motives as they are taken for granted in cases where questions of justice ordinarily arise. Justice is the virtue of practices where there are assumed to be competing interests and conflicting claims, and where it is supposed that persons will press their rights on each other. That persons are mutually self-interested in certain situations and for certain purposes is what gives rise to the question of justice in practices covering those circumstances. Amongst an association of saints, if such a community could really exist, the disputes about justice could hardly occur; for they would all work selflessly together for one end, the glory of God as defined by their common religion, and reference to this end would settle every question of right. The justice of practices does not come up until there are several different parties (whether we think of these as individuals, associations, or nations, and so on, is irrelevant) who do press their claims on one another, and who do regard themselves as representatives of interests which deserve to be considered. Thus the previous account involves no general theory of human motivation. Its intent is simply to incorporate into the conception of justice the relations of men to one another which set the stage for questions of justice. It makes no difference how wide or general

---

The Open Society and its Enemies, rev. edn. (Princeton: Princeton University Press, 1950), 112–18. Certainly Plato usually attributes to it a quality of manic egoism which one feels must be an exaggeration; on the other hand, see the Melian Debate in Thucydides, *The Peloponnesian War*, 5. 7, although it is impossible to say to what extent the views expressed there reveal any current philosophical opinion. Also in this tradition are the remarks of Epicurus on justice in *Principal Doctrines*, 31–8. In modern times elements of the conception appear in a more sophisticated form in Hobbes, *The Leviathan* (1651) and in Hume, *A Treatise of Human Nature* (1740), III. ii, as well as in the writings of the school of natural law such as Pufendorf's *De jure naturae et gentium* (1672). Hobbes and Hume are especially instructive. For Hobbes's argument, see Howard Warrender's *The Political Philosophy of Hobbes* (Oxford: Oxford University Press, 1957). W. J. Baumol's *Welfare Economics and the Theory of the State* (London: Harvard University Press, 1952) is valuable in showing the wide applicability of Hobbes's fundamental idea (interpreting his natural law as principles of prudence), although in this book it is traced back only to Hume's *Treatise*.

[9] See J. von Neumann and O. Morgenstern, *The Theory of Games and Economic Behavior*, 2nd edn. (Princeton: Princeton University Press, 1947). For a comprehensive and not too technical discussion of the developments since, see R. Duncan Luce and Howard Raiffa, *Games and Decisions: Introduction and Critical Survey* (New York: Wiley, 1957). Chs. VI and XIV discuss the developments most obviously related to the analysis of justice.

these relations are, as this matter does not bear on the analysis of the concept.

Again, in contrast to the various conceptions of the social contract, the several parties do not establish any particular society or practice; they do not covenant to obey a particular sovereign body or to accept a given constitution.[10] Nor do they, as in the theory of games (in certain respects a marvellously sophisticated development of this tradition), decide on individual strategies adjusted to their respective circumstances in the game. What the parties do is to *jointly* acknowledge certain *principles* of appraisal relating to their common *practices* either as already established or merely proposed. They accede to standards of judgement, not to a given practice; they do not make any specific agreement, or bargain, or adopt a particular strategy. The subject of their acknowledgement is, therefore, very general indeed; it is simply the acknowledgement of certain principles of judgement, fulfilling certain general conditions, to be used in criticizing the arrangement of their common affairs. The relations of mutual self-interest between the parties who are similarly circumstanced mirror the conditions under which questions of justice arise, and the procedure by which the principles of judgement are proposed and acknowledged reflects the constraints of having a morality. Each aspect, then, of the preceding hypothetical account serves the purpose of bringing out a feature of the notion of justice. One could, if one liked, view the principles of justice as the 'solution' of this highest-order 'game' of adopting subject to the procedure described, principles of argument for all coming particular 'games' whose peculiarities one can in no way foresee. But this comparison, while no doubt helpful, must not obscure the fact that this highest-order 'game' is of a special sort.[11] Its significance is that its various pieces represent aspects of the concept of justice.

[10] For a general survey, see J. W. Gough, *The Social Contract*, 2nd edn. (Oxford: Oxford University Press, 1957), and Otto von Gierke, *The Development of Political Theory*, tr. B. Freyd (London: W. W. Norton, 1939), pt. II, ch. II.

[11] The difficulty one gets into by a mechanical application of the theory of games to moral philosophy can be brought out by considering among several possible examples, R. B. Braithwaite's study *Theory of Games as a Tool for the Moral Philosopher* (Cambridge: Cambridge University Press, 1955). On the analysis there given, it turns out that the fair division of playing time between Matthew and Luke depends on their preferences, and these in turn are connected with the instruments they wish to play. Since Matthew has a threat advantage over Luke, arising purely from the fact that Matthew, the trumpeter, prefers both of them playing at once to neither of them playing, whereas Luke, the pianist, prefers silence to cacophony. Matthew is allotted twenty-six evenings of play to Luke's seventeen. If the situation were reversed, the threat advantage would be with Luke. See pp. 36–7. But now we have only to suppose that Matthew is a jazz enthusiast who plays the drums, and Luke a violinist who plays sonatas, in which case it will be fair, on this analysis, for Matthew to play whenever and as often as he likes, assuming, of course, as it is plausible to assume, that he does not care whether Luke plays or not. Certainly something has gone wrong. To each according to his threat advantage is

Finally, I do not, of course, conceive the several parties as necessarily coming together to establish their common practices for the first time. Some institutions may, indeed, be set up *de novo*; but I have framed the preceding account so that it will apply when the full complement of social institutions already exists and represents the result of a long period of development. Nor is the account in any way fictitious. In any society where people reflect on their institutions they will have an idea of what principles of justice would be acknowledged under the conditions described, and there will be occasions when questions of justice are actually discussed in this way. Therefore if their practices do not accord with these principles, this will affect the quality of their social relations. For in this case there will be some recognized situations wherein the parties are mutually aware that one of them is being forced to accept what the other would concede is unjust. The foregoing analysis may then be thought of as representing the actual quality of relations between persons as defined by practices accepted as just. In such practices the parties will acknowledge the principles on which it is constructed, and the general recognition of this fact shows itself in the absence of resentment and in the sense of being justly treated. Thus one common objection to the theory of the social contract, its apparently historical and fictitious character, is avoided.

5

That the principles of justice may be regarded as arising in the manner described illustrates an important fact about them. Not only does it bring out the idea that justice is a primitive moral notion in that it arises once the concept of morality is imposed on mutually self-interested agents similarly circumstanced, but it emphasizes that, fundamental to justice, is the concept of fairness which relates to right dealing between persons who are co-

hardly the principle of fairness. What is lacking is the concept of morality, and it must be brought into the conjectural account in some way or other. In the text this is done by the form of the procedure whereby principles are proposed and acknowledged (sect. 3). If one starts directly with the particular case as known, and if one accepts as given and definitive the preferences and relative positions of the parties, whatever they are, it is impossible to give an analysis of the moral concept of fairness. Braithwaite's use of the theory of games, in so far as it is intended to analyse the concept of fairness, is, I think, mistaken. This is not, of course, to criticize in any way the theory of games as a mathematical theory, to which Braithwaite's book certainly contributes, nor as an analysis of how rational (and amoral) egoists might behave (and so as an analysis of how people sometimes actually do behave). But it is to say that if the theory of games is to be used to analyse moral concepts, its formal structure must be interpreted in a special and general manner as indicated in the text. Once we do this, though, we are in touch again with a much older tradition.

operating with or competing against one another, as when one speaks of
fair games, fair competition, and fair bargains. The question of fairness
arises when free persons, who have no authority over one another, are
engaging in a joint activity and amongst themselves settling or acknowledging the rules which define it and which determine the respective shares
in its benefits and burdens. A practice will strike the parties as fair if none
feels that, by participating in it, they or any of the others are taken advantage of, or forced to give in to claims which they do not regard as legitimate. This implies that each has a conception of legitimate claims which he
thinks it reasonable for others as well as himself to acknowledge. If one
thinks of the principles of justice as arising in the manner described, then
they do define this sort of conception. A practice is just or fair, then, when
it satisfies the principles which those who participate in it could propose
to one another for mutual acceptance under the aforementioned circumstances. Persons engaged in a just, or fair, practice can face one another
openly and support their respective positions, should they appear questionable, by reference to principles which it is reasonable to expect each to
accept.

It is this notion of the possibility of mutual acknowledgement of principles by free persons who have no authority over one another which
makes the concept of fairness fundamental to justice. Only if such acknowledgement is possible can there be true community between persons
in their common practices; otherwise their relations will appear to them as
founded to some extent on force. If, in ordinary speech, fairness applies
more particularly to practices in which there is a choice whether to engage
or not (e.g. in games, business competition), and justice to practices in
which there is no choice (e.g. in slavery), the element of necessity does not
render the conception of mutual acknowledgement inapplicable, although
it may make it much more urgent to change unjust than unfair institutions.
For one activity in which one can always engage is that of proposing and
acknowledging principles to one another supposing each to be similarly
circumstanced; and to judge practices by the principles so arrived at is to
apply the standard of fairness to them.

Now if the participants in a practice accept its rules as fair, and so have
no complaint to lodge against it, there arises a prima-facie duty (and a
corresponding prima-facie right) of the parties to each other to act in
accordance with the practice when it falls upon them to comply. When any
number of persons engage in a practice, or conduct a joint undertaking
according to rules, and thus restrict their liberty, those who have submitted
to these restrictions when required have the right to a similar acquiescence
on the part of those who have benefited by their submission. These condi-

tions will obtain if a practice is correctly acknowledged to be fair, for in this case all who participate in it will benefit from it. The rights and duties so arising are special rights and duties in that they depend on previous actions voluntarily undertaken, in this case on the parties having engaged in a common practice and knowingly accepted its benefits.[12] It is not, however, an obligation which presupposes a deliberate performative act in the sense of a promise, or contract, and the like.[13] An unfortunate mistake of proponents of the idea of the social contract was to suppose that political obligation does require some such act, or at least to use language which suggests it. It is sufficient that one has knowingly participated in and accepted the benefits of a practice acknowledged to be fair. This prima-facie obligation may, of course, be overridden: it may happen, when it comes one's turn to follow a rule, that other considerations will justify not doing so. But one cannot, in general, be released from this obligation by denying the justice of the practice only when it falls on one to obey. If a person rejects a practice, he should, so far as possible, declare his intention in advance, and avoid participating in it or enjoying its benefits.

This duty I have called that of fair play, but it should be admitted that to refer to it in this way is, perhaps, to extend the ordinary notion of fairness. Usually acting unfairly is not so much the breaking of any particular rule, even if the infraction is difficult to detect (cheating), but taking advantage of loopholes or ambiguities in rules, availing oneself of unexpected or special circumstances which make it impossible to enforce them, insisting that rules be enforced to one's advantage when they should be suspended, and more generally, acting contrary to the intention of a practice. It is for this reason that one speaks of the sense of fair play: acting fairly requires more than simply being able to follow rules; what is fair must often be felt, or perceived, one wants to say. It is not, however, an unnatural extension of the duty of fair play to have it include the obligation which participants who have knowingly accepted the benefits of their common practice owe to each other to act in accordance with it when their performance falls due; for it is usually considered unfair if someone accepts the benefits of a practice but refuses to do his part in maintaining it. Thus one might say of the tax-dodger that he violates the duty of fair play: he accepts the benefits of government but will not do his part in releasing resources to it; and members of labour unions often say that fellow workers who refuse to join are being unfair: they refer to them as 'free riders', as persons who enjoy

[12] For the definition of this prima-facie duty, and the idea that it is a special duty, I am indebted to H. L. A. Hart. See his paper 'Are there any Natural Rights?', 185–6.
[13] The sense of 'performative' here is to be derived from J. L. Austin's paper in the symposium 'Other Minds', *Proceedings of the Aristotelian Society*, suppl. vol. 20 (1946), 170–4.

what are the supposed benefits of unionism, higher wages, shorter hours, job security, and the like, but who refuse to share in its burdens in the form of paying dues, and so on.

The duty of fair play stands beside other prima-facie duties such as fidelity and gratitude as a basic moral notion; yet it is not to be confused with them.[14] These duties are all clearly distinct, as would be obvious from their definitions. As with any moral duty, that of fair play implies a constraint on self-interest in particular cases; on occasion it enjoins conduct which a rational egoist strictly defined would not decide upon. So while justice does not require of anyone that he sacrifice his interests in that *general position* and procedure whereby the principles of justice are proposed and acknowledged, it may happen that in particular situations, arising in the context of engaging in a practice, the duty of fair play will often cross his interests in the sense that he will be required to forgo particular advantages which the peculiarities of his circumstances might permit him to take. There is, of course, nothing surprising in this. It is simply the consequence of the firm commitment which the parties may be supposed to have made, or which they would make, in the general position, together with the fact that they have participated in and accepted the benefits of a practice which they regard as fair.

Now the acknowledgement of this constraint in particular cases, which is manifested in acting fairly or wishing to make amends, feeling ashamed, and the like, when one has evaded it, is one of the forms of conduct by which participants in a common practice exhibit their recognition of each other as persons with similar interests and capacities. In the same way that, failing a special explanation, the criterion for the recognition of suffering is helping one who suffers, acknowledging the duty of fair play is a necessary part of the criterion for recognizing another as a person with similar interests and feelings as oneself.[15] A person who never under any circum-

---

[14] This, however, commonly happens. Hobbes, for example, when invoking the notion of a 'tacit covenant', appeals not to the natural law that promises should be kept but to his fourth law of nature, that of gratitude. On Hobbes's shift from fidelity to gratitude, see Warrender, *The Political Philosophy of Hobbes*, 51–2, 233–7. While it is not a serious criticism of Hobbes, it would have improved his argument had he appealed to the duty of fair play. On his premisses he is perfectly entitled to do so. Similarly Sidgwick thought that a principle of justice, such as every man ought to receive adequate requital for his labour, is like gratitude universalized. See *The Methods of Ethics*, III. v. 5. There is a gap in the stock of moral concepts used by philosophers into which the concept of the duty of fair play fits quite naturally.

[15] I am using the concept of criterion here in what I take to be Wittgenstein's sense. See *Philosophical Investigations* (Oxford: Basil Blackwell, 1953); and Norman Malcolm's review 'Wittgenstein's *Philosophical Investigations*', *Philosophical Review*, 63 (1954), 543–7. That the response of compassion, under appropriate circumstances, is part of the criterion for whether or not a person understands what 'pain' means, is, I think, in the *Philosophical Investigations*. The view in the text is simply an extension of this idea. I cannot, however, attempt to justify it here.

stances showed a wish to help others in pain would show, at the same time, that he did not recognize that they were in pain; nor could he have any feelings of affection or friendship for anyone; for having these feelings implies, failing special circumstances, that he comes to their aid when they are suffering. Recognition that another is a person in pain shows itself in sympathetic action; this primitive natural response of compassion is one of those responses upon which the various forms of moral conduct are built.

Similarly, the acceptance of the duty of fair play by participants in a common practice is a reflection in each person of the recognition of the aspirations and interests of the others to be realized by their joint activity. Failing a special explanation, their acceptance of it is a necessary part of the criterion for their recognizing one another as persons with similar interests and capacities, as the conception of their relations in the general position supposes them to be. Otherwise they would show no recognition of one another as persons with similar capacities and interests, and indeed, in some cases perhaps hypothetical, they would not recognize one another as persons at all, but as complicated objects involved in a complicated activity. To recognize another as a person one must respond to him and act towards him in certain ways; and these ways are intimately connected with the various prima-facie duties. Acknowledging these duties in *some* degree, and so having the elements of morality, is not a matter of choice, or of intuiting moral qualities, or a matter of the expression of feelings or attitudes (the three interpretations between which philosophical opinion frequently oscillates); it is simply the possession of one of the forms of conduct in which the recognition of others as persons is manifested.

These remarks are unhappily obscure. Their main purpose here, however, is to forestall, together with the remarks in Section 4, the misinterpretation that, on the view presented, the acceptance of justice and the acknowledgement of the duty of fair play depend in every day life solely on there being a *de facto* balance of forces between the parties. It would indeed be foolish to underestimate the importance of such a balance in securing justice; but it is not the only basis thereof. The recognition of one another as persons with similar interests and capacities engaged in a common practice must, failing a special explanation, show itself in the acceptance of the principles of justice and the acknowledgement of the duty of fair play.

The conception at which we have arrived, then, is that the principles of

Similar thoughts are to be found, I think, in Max Scheler, *The Nature of Sympathy*, tr. Peter Heath (New Haven: Yale University Press, 1954). His way of writing is often so obscure that I cannot be certain.

justice may be thought of as arising once the constraints of having a morality are imposed upon rational and mutually self-interested parties who are related and situated in a special way. A practice is just if it is in accordance with the principles which all who participate in it might reasonably be expected to propose or to acknowledge before one another when they are similarly circumstanced and required to make a firm commitment in advance without knowledge of what will be their peculiar condition, and thus when it meets standards which the parties could accept as fair should occasion arise for them to debate its merits. Regarding the participants themselves, once persons knowingly engage in a practice which they acknowledge to be fair and accept the benefits of doing so, they are bound by the duty of fair play to follow the rules when it comes their turn to do so, and this implies a limitation on their pursuit of self-interest in particular cases.

Now one consequence of this conception is that, where it applies, there is no moral value in the satisfaction of a claim incompatible with it. Such a claim violates the conditions of reciprocity and community amongst persons, and he who presses it, not being willing to acknowledge it when pressed by another, has no grounds for complaint when it is denied; whereas he against whom it is pressed can complain. As it cannot be mutually acknowledged it is a resort to coercion; granting the claim is possible only if one party can compel acceptance of what the other will not admit. But it makes no sense to concede claims the denial of which cannot be complained of in preference to claims the denial of which can be objected to. Thus in deciding on the justice of a practice it is not enough to ascertain that it answers to wants and interests in the fullest and most effective manner. For if any of these conflict with justice, they should not be counted, as their satisfaction is no reason at all for having a practice. It would be irrelevant to say, even if true, that it resulted in the greatest satisfaction of desire. In tallying up the merits of a practice one must toss out the satisfaction of interests the claims of which are incompatible with the principles of justice.

6

The discussion so far has been excessively abstract. While this is perhaps unavoidable, I should now like to bring out some of the features of the conception of justice as fairness by comparing it with the conception of justice in classical utilitarianism as represented by Bentham and Sidgwick, and its counterpart in welfare economics. This conception assimilates justice to benevolence and the latter in turn to the most efficient design of institutions to promote the general welfare. Justice is a kind of efficiency.[16]

Now it is said occasionally that this form of utilitarianism puts no restrictions on what might be a just assignment of rights and duties in that there might be circumstances which, on utilitarian grounds, would justify institutions highly offensive to our ordinary sense of justice. But the classical utilitarian conception is not totally unprepared for this objection. Beginning with the notion that the general happiness can be represented by a social utility function consisting of a sum of individual utility functions with identical weights (this being the meaning of the maxim that each counts for one and no more than one),[17] it is commonly assumed that the utility functions of individuals are similar in all essential respects. Differences between individuals are ascribed to accidents of education and upbringing, and they should not be taken into account. This assumption, coupled with that of diminishing marginal utility, results in a prima-facie case for equality, e.g. of equality in the distribution of income during any given period of time, laying aside indirect effects on the future. But even if utilitarianism is interpreted as having such restrictions built into the utility function, and even if it is supposed that these restrictions have in practice much the same result as the application of the principles of justice (and appear, perhaps, to be ways of expressing these principles in the language of mathematics and

[16] While this assimilation is implicit in Bentham's and Sidgwick's moral theory, explicit statements of it as applied to justice are relatively rare. One clear instance in *The Principles of Morals and Legislation* occurs in ch. x, sect. xl, n. 2: 'justice, in the only sense in which it has a meaning, is an imaginary personage, feigned for the convenience of discourse, whose dictates are the dictates of utility, applied to certain particular cases. Justice, then, is nothing more than an imaginary instrument, employed to forward on certain occasions, and by certain means, the purposes of benevolence. The dictates of justice are nothing more than a part of the dictates of benevolence, which, on certain occasions, are applied to certain subjects.' Likewise in *The Limits of Jurisprudence Defined*, ed. C. W. Everett (New York: Columbia University Press, 1945), 117–18. Bentham criticizes Grotius for denying that justice derives from utility; and in *The Theory of Legislation*, ed. C. K. Ogden (London: Kegan Paul, 1931), 3, he says that he uses the words 'just' and 'unjust' along with other words 'simply as collective terms including the ideas of certain pains or pleasures'. That Sidgwick's conception of justice is similar to Bentham's is admittedly not evident from his discussion of justice in book III, ch. v of *The Methods of Ethics*. But it follows, I think, from the moral theory he accepts. Hence C. D. Broad's criticisms of Sidgwick in the matter of distributive justice in *Five Types of Ethical Theory* (London: Kegan Paul, 1930), 249–53, do not rest on a misinterpretation.

[17] This maxim is attributed to Bentham by J. S. Mill in *Utilitarianism*, ch. v, para. 36. I have not found it in Bentham's writings, nor seen such a reference. Similarly James Bonar, *Philosophy and Political Economy* (London, 1893), 234 n. But it accords perfectly with Bentham's ideas. See the hitherto unpublished MS in David Baumgardt, *Bentham and the Ethics of Today* (Princeton: Princeton University Press, 1952), app. IV. For example, 'the total value of the stock of pleasure belonging to the whole community is to be obtained by multiplying the number expressing the value of it as respecting any one person, by the number expressing the multitude of such individuals' (p. 556).

psychology), the fundamental idea is very different from the conception of justice as fairness. For one thing, that the principles of justice should be accepted is interpreted as the contingent result of a higher-order administrative decision. The form of this decision is regarded as being similar to that of an entrepreneur deciding how much to produce of this or that commodity in view of its marginal revenue, or to that of someone distributing goods to needy persons according to the relative urgency of their wants. The choice between practices is thought of as being made on the basis of the allocation of benefits and burdens to individuals (these being measured by the present capitalized value of their utility over the full period of the practice's existence), which results from the distribution of rights and duties established by a practice.

Moreover, the individuals receiving these benefits are not conceived as being related in any way: they represent so many different directions in which limited resources may be allocated. The value of assigning resources to one direction rather than another depends solely on the preferences and interests of individuals as individuals. The satisfaction of desire has its value irrespective of the moral relations between persons, say as members of a joint undertaking, and of the claims which, in the name of these interests, they are prepared to make on one another;[18] and it is this value which is to be taken into account by the (ideal) legislator who is conceived as adjusting the rules of the system from the centre so as to maximize the value of the social utility function.

It is thought that the principles of justice will not be violated by a legal

---

[18] An idea essential to the classical utilitarian conception of justice. Bentham is firm in his statement of it: 'It is only upon that principle [the principle of asceticism], and not from the principle of utility, that the most abominable pleasure which the vilest of malefactors ever reaped from his crime would be reprobated, if it stood alone. The case is, that it never does stand alone; but is necessarily followed by such a quantity of pain (or, what comes to the same thing, such a chance for a certain quantity of pain) that the pleasure in comparison of it, is as nothing; and this is the true and sole, but perfectly sufficient, reason for making it a ground for punishment' (*The Principles of Morals and Legislation*, ch. ii, sect. iv. See also ch. x, sect. x, n. I). The same point is made in *The Limits of Jurisprudence Defined*, 115–16. Although much recent welfare economies, as found in such important works as I. M. D. Little, *A Critique of Welfare Economics*, 2nd edn. (Oxford: Clarendon Press, 1957) and K. J. Arrow, *Social Choice and Individual Values* (New York: Wiley, 1951), dispenses with the idea of cardinal utility, and use instead the theory of ordinal utility as stated by J. R. Hicks. *Value and Capital*, 2nd edn. (Oxford: Clarendon Press, 1946), pt. i, it assumes with utilitarianism that individual preferences have value as such, and so accepts the idea being criticized here. I hasten to add, however, that this is no objection to it as a means of analysing economic policy, and for that purpose it may, indeed, be a necessary simplifying assumption. Nevertheless it is an assumption which cannot be made in so far as one is trying to analyse moral concepts, especially the concept of justice, as economists would, I think, agree. Justice is usually regarded as a separate and distinct part of any comprehensive criterion of economic policy. See, for example, Tibor Scitovsky, *Welfare and Competition* (London: Allen & Unwin, 1952), 59–69, and Little, *A Critique of Welfare Economics*, ch. vii.

system so conceived provided these executive decisions are correctly made. In this fact the principles of justice are said to have their derivation and explanation; they simply express the most important general features of social institutions in which the administrative problem is solved in the best way. These principles have, indeed, a special urgency because, given the facts of human nature, so much depends on them; and this explains the peculiar quality of the moral feelings associated with justice.[19] This assimilation of justice to a higher-order executive decision, certainly a striking conception, is central to classical utilitarianism; and it also brings out its profound individualism, in one sense of this ambiguous word. It regards persons as so many *separate* directions in which benefits and burdens may be assigned; and the value of the satisfaction or dissatisfaction of desire is not thought to depend in any way on the moral relations in which individuals stand, or on the kinds of claims which they are willing, in the pursuit of their interests, to press on each other.

7

Many social decisions are, of course, of an administrative nature. Certainly this is so when it is a matter of social utility in what one may call its ordinary sense: that is, when it is a question of the efficient design of social institutions for the use of common means to achieve common ends. In this case either the benefits and burdens may be assumed to be impartially distributed, or the question of distribution is misplaced, as in the instance of maintaining public order and security or national defence. But as an interpretation of the basis of the principles of justice, classical utilitarianism is mistaken. It *permits* one to argue, for example, that slavery is unjust on the grounds that the advantages to the slaveholder as slaveholder do not counterbalance the disadvantages to the slave and to society at large burdened by a comparatively inefficient system of labour. Now the conception of justice as fairness, when applied to the practice of slavery with its offices of slaveholder and slave, would not allow one to consider the advantages of the slaveholder in the first place. As that office is not in accordance with principles which could be mutually acknowledged, the gains accruing to the slaveholder, assuming them to exist, cannot be counted as in *any* way mitigating the injustice of the practice. The question whether these gains outweigh the disadvantages to the slave and to society cannot arise, since in considering the justice of slavery these gains have no

---

[19] See J. S. Mill's argument in *Utilitarianism*, ch. v, paras. 16–25.

weight at all which requires that they be overridden. Where the conception of justice as fairness applies, slavery is *always* unjust.

I am not, of course, suggesting the absurdity that the classical utilitarians approved of slavery. I am only rejecting a type of argument which their view allows them to use in support of their disapproval of it. The conception of justice as derivative from efficiency implies that judging the justice of a practice is always, in principle at least, a matter of weighing up advantages and disadvantages, each having an intrinsic value or disvalue as the satisfaction of interests, irrespective of whether or not these interests necessarily involve acquiescence in principles which could not be mutually acknowledged. Utilitarianism cannot account for the fact that slavery is always unjust, nor for the fact that it would be recognized as irrelevant in defeating the accusation of injustice for one person to say to another, engaged with him in a common practice and debating its merits, that nevertheless it allowed of the greatest satisfaction of desire. The charge of injustice cannot be rebutted in this way. If justice were derivative from a higher-order executive efficiency, this would not be so.

But now, even if it is taken as established that, so far as the ordinary conception of justice goes, slavery is always unjust (that is, slavery by definition violates commonly recognized principles of justice), the classical utilitarian would surely reply that these principles, as other moral principles subordinate to that of utility, are only generally correct. It is simply for the most part true that slavery is less efficient than other institutions; and while common sense may define the concept of justice so that slavery is unjust, nevertheless, where slavery would lead to the greatest satisfaction of desire, it is not wrong. Indeed, it is then right, and for the very same reason that justice, as ordinarily understood, is usually right. If, as ordinarily understood, slavery is always unjust, to this extent the utilitarian conception of justice might be admitted to differ from that of common moral opinion. Still the utilitarian would want to hold that, as a matter of moral principle, his view is correct in giving no special weight to considerations of justice beyond that allowed for by the general presumption of effectiveness. And this, he claims, is as it should be. The every day opinion is morally in error, although, indeed, it is a useful error, since it protects rules of general high utility.

The question, then, relates not simply to the analysis of the concept of justice as common sense defines it, but the analysis of it in the wider sense as to how much weight considerations of justice, as defined, are to have when laid against other kinds of moral considerations. Here again I wish to argue that reasons of justice have a *special* weight for which only the conception of justice as fairness can account. Moreover, it belongs to the concept of justice that they do have this special weight. While Mill recognized that this was so, he thought that it could be accounted for by the special urgency of the moral feelings which naturally support principles of such high utility. But it is a mistake to resort to the urgency of feeling; as with the appeal to intuition, it manifests a failure to pursue the question far enough. The special weight of considerations of justice can be explained from the conception of justice as fairness. It is only necessary to elaborate a bit what has already been said as follows.

If one examines the circumstances in which a certain tolerance of slavery is justified, or perhaps better, excused, it turns out that these are of a rather special sort. Perhaps slavery exists as an inheritance from the past and it proves necessary to dismantle it piece by piece; at times slavery may conceivably be an advance on previous institutions. Now while there may be some excuse for slavery in special conditions, it is never an excuse for it that it is sufficiently advantageous to the slaveholder to outweigh the disadvantages to the slave and to society. A person who argues in this way is not perhaps making a wildly irrelevant remark; but he is guilty of a moral fallacy. There is disorder in his conception of the ranking of moral principles. For the slaveholder, by his own admission, has no moral title to the advantages which he receives as a slaveholder. He is no more prepared than the slave to acknowledge the principle upon which is founded the respective positions in which they both stand. Since slavery does not accord with principles which they could mutually acknowledge, they each may be supposed to agree that it is unjust: it grants claims which it ought not to grant and in doing so denies claims which it ought not to deny. Amongst persons in a general position who are debating the form of their common practices, it cannot, therefore, be offered as a reason for a practice, that, in conceding these very claims that ought to be denied, it nevertheless meets existing interests more effectively. By their very nature the satisfaction of these claims is without weight and cannot enter into any tabulation of advantages and disadvantages.

Furthermore, it follows from the concept of morality that, to the extent that the slaveholder recognizes his position *vis-à-vis* the slave to be unjust, he would not choose to press his claims. His not wanting to receive his special advantages is one of the ways in which he shows that he thinks slavery is unjust. It would be fallacious for the legislator to suppose, then, that it is a ground for having a practice that it brings advantages greater than disadvantages, if those for whom the practice is designed, and to whom the advantages flow, acknowledge that they have no moral title to them and do not wish to receive them.

For these reasons the principles of justice have a special weight; and with respect to the principle of the greatest satisfaction of desire, as cited in the general position amongst those discussing the merits of their common practices, the principles of justice have an absolute weight. In this sense they are not contingent; and this is why their force is greater than can be accounted for by the general presumption (assuming that there is one) of the effectiveness, in the utilitarian sense, of practices which in fact satisfy them.

If one wants to continue using the concepts of classical utilitarianism, one will have to say, to meet this criticism, that at least the individual or social utility functions must be so defined that no value is given to the satisfaction of interests the representative claims of which violate the principles of justice. In this way it is no doubt possible to include these principles within the form of the utilitarian conception; but to do so is, of course, to change its inspiration altogether as a moral conception. For it is to incorporate within it principles which cannot be understood on the basis of a higher order executive decision aiming at the greatest satisfaction of desire.

It is worth remarking, perhaps, that this criticism of utilitarianism does not depend on whether or not the two assumptions, that of individuals having similar utility functions and that of diminishing marginal utility, are interpreted as psychological propositions to be supported or refuted by experience, or as moral and political principles expressed in a somewhat technical language. There are, certainly, several advantages in taking them in the latter fashion.[20] For one thing, one might say that this is what Bentham and others really meant by them, as least as shown by how they were used in arguments for social reform. More importantly, one could hold that the best way to defend the classical utilitarian view is to interpret these assumptions as moral and political principles. It is doubtful whether, taken as psychological propositions, they are true of men in general as we know them under normal conditions. On the other hand, utilitarians would not have wanted to propose them merely as practical working principles of legislation, or as expedient maxims to guide reform, given the egalitarian sentiments of modern society.[21] When pressed they might well have invoked the idea of a more or less equal capacity of men

[20] See D. G. Ritchie, *Natural Rights* (London, 1894), 95 ff., 249 ff. Lionel Robbins has insisted on this point on several occasions. See *An Essay on the Nature and Significance of Economic Science*, 2nd edn. (London: Macmillan, 1935), 134–43, 'Interpersonal Comparisons of Utility: A Comment', *Economic Journal*, 48 (1938), 635–41, and more recently, 'Robertson on Utility and Scope', *Economica*, NS 20 (1953), 108–9.

[21] As Sir Henry Maine suggested Bentham may have regarded them. See *The Early History of Institutions* (London, 1875), 398 ff.

in relevant respects if given an equal chance in a just society. But if the argument above regarding slavery is correct, then granting these assumptions as moral and political principles makes no difference. To view individuals as equally fruitful lines for the allocation of benefits, even as a matter of moral principle, still leaves the mistaken notion that the satisfaction of desire has value in itself irrespective of the relations between persons as members of a common practice, and irrespective of the claims upon one another which the satisfaction of interests represents. To see the error of this idea one must give up the conception of justice as an executive decision altogether and refer to the notion of justice as fairness: that participants in a common practice be regarded as having an original and equal liberty and that their common practices be considered unjust unless they accord with principles which persons so circumstanced and related could freely acknowledge before one another, and so could accept as fair. Once the emphasis is put upon the concept of the mutual recognition of principles by participants in a common practice the rules of which are to define their several relations and give form to their claims on one another, then it is clear that the granting of a claim the principle of which could not be acknowledged by each in the general position (that is, in the position in which the parties propose and acknowledge principles before one another) is not a reason for adopting a practice. Viewed in this way, the background of the claim is seen to exclude it from consideration; that it can represent a value in itself arises from the conception of individuals as separate lines for the assignment of benefits, as isolated persons who stand as claimants on an administrative or benevolent largesse. Occasionally persons do so stand to one another; but this is not the general case, nor, more importantly, is it the case when it is a matter of the justice of practices themselves in which participants stand in various relations to be appraised in accordance with standards which they may be expected to acknowledge before one another. Thus however mistaken the notion of the social contract may be as history, and however far it may overreach itself as a general theory of social and political obligation, it does express, suitably interpreted, an essential part of the concept of justice.[22]

---

[22] Thus Kant was not far wrong when he interpreted the original contract merely as an 'Idea of Reason'; yet he still thought of it as a *general* criterion of right and as providing a general theory of political obligation. See the second part of the essay, 'On the Saying "That may be right in theory but has no value in practice" ' (1793), in *Kant's Principles of Politics*, tr. W. Hastie (Edinburgh, 1891). I have drawn on the contractarian tradition not for a general theory of political obligation but to clarify the concept of justice.

8

By way of conclusion I should like to make two remarks: first, the original modification of the utilitarian principle (that it require of practices that the offices and positions defined by them be equal unless it is reasonable to suppose that the representative man in *every* office would find the inequality to his advantage), slight as it may appear at first sight, actually has a different conception of justice standing behind it. I have tried to show how this is so by developing the concept of justice as fairness and by indicating how this notion involves the mutual acceptance, from a general position, of the principles on which a practice is founded, and how this in turn requires the exclusion from consideration of claims violating the principles of justice. Thus the slight alteration of principle reveals another family of notions, another way of looking at the concept of justice.

Second, I should like to remark also that I have been dealing with the *concept* of justice. I have tried to set out the kinds of principles upon which judgements concerning the justice of practices may be said to stand. The analysis will be successful to the degree that it expresses the principles involved in these judgements when made by competent persons upon deliberation and reflection.[23] Now every people may be supposed to have the concept of justice, since in the life of every society there must be at least some relations in which the parties consider themselves to be circumstanced and related as the concept of justice as fairness requires. Societies will differ from one another not in having or in failing to have this notion but in the range of cases to which they apply it and in the emphasis which they give to it as compared with other moral concepts.

A firm grasp of the concept of justice itself is necessary if these variations, and the reasons for them, are to be understood. No study of the development of moral ideas and of the differences between them is more sound than the analysis of the fundamental moral concepts upon which it must depend. I have tried, therefore, to give an analysis of the concept of

---

[23] For a further discussion of the idea expressed here, see my paper 'Outline of a Decision Procedure for Ethics', *Philosophical Review*, 60 (1951), 177–97. For an analysis, similar in many respects but using the notion of the ideal observer instead of that of the considered judgement of a competent person, see Roderick Firth, 'Ethical Absolutism and the Ideal Observer', *Philosophy and Phenomenological Research*, 12 (1952), 317–45. While the similarities between these two discussions are more important than the differences, an analysis based on the notion of a considered judgement of a competent person, as it is based on a kind of judgement, may prove more helpful in understanding the features of moral judgement than an analysis based on the notion of an ideal observer, although this remains to be shown. A man who rejects the conditions imposed on a considered judgement of a competent person could no longer profess to *judge* at all. This seems more fundamental than his rejecting the conditions of observation, for these do not seem to apply, in an ordinary sense, to making a moral judgement.

justice which should apply generally, however large a part the concept may have in a given morality, and which can be used in explaining the course of men's thoughts about justice and its relations to other moral concepts. How it is to be used for this purpose is a large topic which I cannot, of course, take up here. I mention it only to emphasize that I have been dealing with the concept of justice itself and to indicate what use I consider such an analysis to have.

VI

CONTRACTUALISM AND UTILITARIANISM

T. M. SCANLON

Utilitarianism occupies a central place in the moral philosophy of our time. It is not the view which most people hold; certainly there are very few who would claim to be act-utilitarians. But for a much wider range of people it is the view towards which they find themselves pressed when they try to give a theoretical account of their moral beliefs. Within moral philosophy it represents a position one must struggle against if one wishes to avoid it. This is so in spite of the fact that the implications of act-utilitarianism are wildly at variance with firmly held moral convictions, while rule-utilitarianism, the most common alternative formulation, strikes most people as an unstable compromise.

The wide appeal of utilitarianism is due, I think, to philosophical considerations of a more or less sophisticated kind which pull us in a quite different direction than our first-order moral beliefs. In particular, utilitarianism derives much of its appeal from alleged difficulties about the foundations of rival views. What a successful alternative to utilitarianism must do, first and foremost, is to sap this source of strength by providing a clear account of the foundations of non-utilitarian moral reasoning. In what follows I will first describe the problem in more detail by setting out the questions which a philosophical account of the foundations of morality must answer. I will then put forward a version of contractualism which, I will argue, offers a better set of responses to these questions than that supplied by straightforward versions of utilitarianism. Finally I will explain why contractualism, as I understand it, does not lead back to some utilitarian formula as its normative outcome.

From Amartya Sen and Bernard Williams (eds.), *Utilitarianism and Beyond* (Cambridge: Cambridge University Press, 1982), 103–28. Reprinted by permission of Cambridge University Press and the author.

I am greatly indebted to Derek Parfit for patient criticism and enormously helpful discussion of many earlier versions of this paper. Thanks are due also to the many audiences who have heard parts of those versions delivered as lectures and kindly responded with helpful comments. In particular, I am indebted to Marshall Cohen, Ronald Dworkin, Owen Fiss, and Thomas Nagel for valuable criticism.

Contractualism has been proposed as the alternative to utilitarianism before, notably by John Rawls in *A Theory of Justice*.[1] Despite the wide discussion which this book has received, however, I think that the appeal of contractualism as a foundational view has been underrated. In particular, it has not been sufficiently appreciated that contractualism offers a particularly plausible account of moral motivation. The version of contractualism that I shall present differs from Rawls's in a number of respects. In particular, it makes no use, or only a different and more limited kind of use, of his notion of choice from behind a veil of ignorance. One result of this difference is to make the contrast between contractualism and utilitarianism stand out more clearly.

I

There is such a subject as moral philosophy for much the same reason that there is such a subject as the philosophy of mathematics. In moral judgements, as in mathematical ones, we have a set of putatively objective beliefs in which we are inclined to invest a certain degree of confidence and importance. Yet on reflection it is not at all obvious what, if anything, these judgements can be about, in virtue of which some can be said to be correct or defensible and others not. This question of subject-matter, or the grounds of truth, is the first philosophical question about both morality and mathematics. Second, in both morality and mathematics it seems to be possible to discover the truth simply by thinking or reasoning about it. Experience and observation may be helpful, but observation in the normal sense is not the standard means of discovery in either subject. So, given any positive answer to the first question—any specification of the subject-matter or ground of truth in mathematics or morality—we need some compatible epistemology explaining how it is possible to discover the facts about this subject-matter through something like the means we seem to use.

Given this similarity in the questions giving rise to moral philosophy and to the philosophy of mathematics, it is not surprising that the answers commonly given fall into similar general types. If we were to interview students in a freshman mathematics course many of them would, I think, declare themselves for some kind of conventionalism. They would hold that mathematics proceeds from definitions and principles that are either arbitrary or instrumentally justified, and that mathematical reasoning consists in perceiving what follows from these definitions and principles. A

[1] (Cambridge, Mass.: Harvard University Press, 1971.)

few others, perhaps, would be realists or platonists according to whom mathematical truths are a special kind of non-empirical fact that we can perceive through some form of intuition. Others might be naturalists who hold that mathematics, properly understood, is just the most abstract empirial science. Finally there are, though perhaps not in an average freshman course, those who hold that there are no mathematical facts in the world 'outside of us', but that the truths of mathematics are objective truths about the mental constructions of which we are capable. Kant held that pure mathematics was a realm of objective mind-dependent truths, and Brouwer's mathematical intuitionism is another theory of this type (with the important difference that it offers grounds for the warranted assertability of mathematical judgements rather than for their truth in the classical sense). All of these positions have natural correlates in moral philosophy. Intuitionism of the sort espoused by W. D. Ross is perhaps the closest analogue to mathematical platonism, and Kant's theory is the most familiar version of the thesis that morality is a sphere of objective, mind-dependent truths.

All of the views I have mentioned (with some qualification in the case of conventionalism) give positive (i.e. non-sceptical) answers to the first philosophical question about mathematics. Each identifies some objective, or at least intersubjective, ground of truth for mathematical judgements. Outright scepticism and subjective versions of mind-dependence (ana-logues of emotivism or prescriptivism) are less appealing as philosophies of mathematics than as moral philosophies. This is so in part simply because of the greater degree of intersubjective agreement in mathematical judge-ment. But it is also due to the difference in the further questions that philosophical accounts of the two fields must answer.

Neither mathematics nor morality can be taken to describe a realm of facts existing in isolation from the rest of reality. Each is supposed to be connected with other things. Mathematical judgements give rise to predic-tions about those realms to which mathematics is applied. This connection is something that a philosophical account of mathematical truth must explain, but the fact that we can observe and learn from the correctness of such predictions also gives support to our belief in objective mathematical truth. In the case of morality the main connection is, or is generally supposed to be, with the will. Given any candidate for the role of subject-matter of morality we must explain why anyone should care about it, and the need to answer this question of motivation has given strong support to subjectivist views.

But what must an adequate philosophical theory of morality say about moral motivation? It need not, I think, show that the moral truth gives anyone who knows it a reason to act which appeals to that person's present desires or to the advancement of his or her interests. I find it entirely intelligible that moral requirement might correctly apply to a person even though that person had no reason of either of these kinds for complying with it. Whether moral requirements give those to whom they apply reasons for compliance of some third kind is a disputed question which I shall set aside. But what an adequate moral philosophy must do, I think, is to make clearer to us the nature of the reasons that morality does provide, at least to those who are concerned with it. A philosophical theory of morality must offer an account of these reasons that is, one the one hand, compatible with its account of moral truth and moral reasoning and, on the other, supported by a plausible analysis of moral experience. A satisfactory moral philosophy will not leave concern with morality as a simple special preference, like a fetish or a special taste, which some people just happen to have. It must make it understandable why moral reasons are ones that people can take seriously, and why they strike those who are moved by them as reasons of a special stringency and inescapability.

There is also a further question whether susceptibility to such reasons is compatible with a person's good or whether it is, as Nietzsche argued, a psychological disaster for the person who has it. If one is to defend morality one must show that it is not disastrous in this way, but I will not pursue this second motivational question here. I mention it only to distinguish it from the first question, which is my present concern.

The task of giving a philosophical explanation of the subject-matter of morality differs both from the task of analysing the meaning of moral terms and from that of finding the most coherent formulation of our first-order moral beliefs. A maximally coherent ordering of our first-order moral beliefs could provide us with a valuable kind of explanation: it would make clear how various, apparently disparate moral notions, precepts, and judgements are related to one another, thus indicating to what degree conflicts between them are fundamental and to what degree, on the other hand, they can be resolved or explained away. But philosophical inquiry into the subject-matter of morality takes a more external view. It seeks to explain what kind of truths moral truths are by describing them in relation to other things in the world and in relation to our particular concerns. An explanation of how we can come to know the truth about morality must be based on such an external explanation of the kind of things moral truths are rather than on a list of particular moral truths, even a maximally coherent list. This seems to be true as well about explanations of how moral beliefs can give one a reason to act.[2]

---

[2] Though here the ties between the nature of morality and its content are more important. It is not clear that an account of the nature of morality which left its content *entirely* open could be the basis for a plausible account of moral motivation.

Coherence among our first-order moral beliefs—what Rawls has called narrow reflective equilibrium[3]—seems unsatisfying[4] as an account of moral truth or as an account of the basis of justification in ethics just because, taken by itself, a maximally coherent account of our moral beliefs need not provide us with what I have called a philosophical explanation of the subject-matter of morality. However internally coherent our moral beliefs may be rendered, the nagging doubt may remain that there is nothing to them at all. They may be merely a set of socially inculcated reactions, mutually consistent perhaps but not judgements of a kind which can properly be said to be correct or incorrect. A philosophical theory of the nature of morality can contribute to our confidence in our first-order moral beliefs chiefly by allaying these natural doubts about the subject. In so far as it includes an account of moral epistemology, such a theory may guide us towards new forms of moral argument, but it need not do this. Moral argument of more or less the kind we have been familiar with may remain as the only form of justification in ethics. But whether or not it leads to revision in our modes of justification, what a good philosophical theory should do is to give us a clearer understanding of what the best forms of moral argument amount to and what kind of truth it is that they can be a way of arriving at. (Much the same can be said, I believe, about the contribution which philosophy of mathematics makes to our confidence in particular mathematical judgements and particular forms of mathematical reasoning.)

Like any thesis about morality, a philosophical account of the subject-matter of morality must have some connection with the meaning of moral terms: it must be plausible to claim that the subject-matter described is in fact what these terms refer to at least in much of their normal use. But the current meaning of moral terms is the product of many different moral beliefs held by past and present speakers of the language, and this meaning is surely compatible with a variety of moral views and with a variety of views about the nature of morality. After all, moral terms are used to express many different views of these kinds, and people who express these views are not using moral terms incorrectly, even though what some of

---

[3] See John Rawls, 'The Independence of Moral Theory', *Proceedings and Addresses of the American Philosophical Association*, 47 (1974–5), 8, and Norman Daniels, 'Wide Reflective Equilibrium and Theory Acceptance in Ethics', *Journal of Philosophy*, 76 (1979), 257–8. How closely the process of what I am calling philosophical explanation will coincide with the search for 'wide reflective equilibrium' as this is understood by Rawls and by Daniels is a further question which I cannot take up here.

[4] For expression of this dissatisfaction, see Peter Singer, 'Sidgwick and Reflective Equilibrium', *Monist*, 58 (1974), 490–517, and R. B. Brandt, *A Theory of the Good and the Right* (Oxford: Oxford University Press, 1979), 16–21.

them say must be mistaken. Like a first-order moral judgement, a philosophical characterization of the subject-matter of morality is a substantive claim about morality, albeit a claim of a different kind.

While a philosophical characterization of morality makes a kind of claim that differs from a first-order moral judgement, this does not mean that a philosophical theory of morality will be neutral between competing normative doctrines. The adoption of a philosophical thesis about the nature of morality will almost always have some effect on the plausibility of particular moral claims, but philosophical theories of morality vary widely in the extent and directness of their normative implications. At one extreme is intuitionism, understood as the philosophical thesis that morality is concerned with certain non-natural properties. Rightness, for example, is held by Ross[5] to be the property of 'fittingness' or 'moral suitability'. Intuitionism holds that we can identify occurrences of these properties, and that we can recognize as self-evident certain general truths about them, but that they cannot be further analysed or explained in terms of other notions. So understood, intuitionism is in principle compatible with a wide variety of normative positions. One could, for example, be an intuitionistic utilitarian or an intuitionistic believer in moral rights, depending on the general truths about the property of moral rightness which one took to be self-evident.

The other extreme is represented by philosophical utilitarianism. The term 'utilitarianism' is generally used to refer to a family of specific normative doctrines—doctrines which might be held on the basis of a number of different philosophical theses about the nature of morality. In this sense of the term one might, for example, be a utilitarian on intuitionist or on contractualist grounds. But what I will call 'philosophical utilitarianism' is a particular philosophical thesis about the subject-matter of morality, namely the thesis that the only fundamental moral facts are facts about individual well-being.[6] I believe that this thesis has a great deal of plausibility for many people, and that, while some people are utilitarians for other reasons, it is the attractiveness of philosophical utilitarianism which accounts for the widespread influence of utilitarian principles.

It seems evident to people that there is such a thing as individuals' being made better or worse off. Such facts have an obvious motivational force; it is quite understandable that people should be moved by them in much the way that they are supposed to be moved by moral considerations. Further,

[5] W. D. Ross, *Foundations of Ethics* (Oxford: Oxford University Press, 1939), 52–4, 315.
[6] For purposes of this discussion I leave open the important questions of which individuals are to count and how 'well-being' is to be understood. Philosophical utilitarianism will retain the appeal I am concerned with under many different answers to these questions.

these facts are clearly relevant to morality as we now understand it. Claims about individual well-being are one class of valid starting-points for moral argument. But many people find it much harder to see how there could be any other, independent starting-points. Substantive moral requirements independent of individual well-being strike people as intuitionist in an objectionable sense. They would represent 'moral facts' of a kind it would be difficult to explain. There is no problem about recognizing it as a fact that a certain act is, say, an instance of lying or of promise-breaking. And a utilitarian can acknowledge that such facts as these often have (derivative) moral significance: they are morally significant because of their consequences for individual well-being. The problems, and the charge of 'intuitionism', arise when it is claimed that such acts are wrong in a sense that is not reducible to the fact that they decrease individual well-being. How could this independent property of moral wrongness be understood in a way that would give it the kind of importance and motivational force which moral considerations have been taken to have? If one accepts the idea that there are no moral properties having this kind of intrinsic significance, then philosophical utilitarianism may seem to be the only tenable account of morality. And once philosophical utilitarianism is accepted, some form of normative utilitarianism seems to be forced on us as the correct first-order moral theory. Utilitarianism thus has, for many people, something like the status which Hilbert's formalism and Brouwer's intuitionism have for their believers. It is a view which seems to be forced on us by the need to give a philosophically defensible account of the subject. But it leaves us with a hard choice: we can either abandon many of our previous first-order beliefs or try to salvage them by showing that they can be obtained as derived truths or explained away as useful and harmless fictions.

It may seem that the appeal of philosophical utilitarianism as I have described it is spurious, since this theory must amount either to a form of intuitionism (differing from others only in that it involves just one appeal to intuition) or else to definitional naturalism of a kind refuted by Moore and others long ago. But I do not think that the doctrine can be disposed of so easily. Philosophical utilitarianism is a philosophical thesis about the nature of morality. As such, it is on a par with intuitionism or with the form of contractualism which I will defend later in this paper. None of these theses need claim to be true as a matter of definition; if one of them is true it does not follow that a person who denies it is misusing the words 'right', 'wrong', and 'ought'. Nor are all these theses forms of intuitionism, if intuitionism is understood as the view that moral facts concern special non-natural properties, which we can apprehend by intuitive insight but which do not need or admit of any further analysis. Both contractualism and philosophical utilitarianism are specifically incompatible with this claim. Like other philosophical theses about the nature of morality (including, I would say, intuitionism itself), contractualism and philosophical utilitarianism are to be appraised on the basis of their success in giving an account of moral belief, moral argument, and moral motivation that is compatible with our general beliefs about the world: our beliefs about what kinds of things there are in the world, what kinds of observation and reasoning we are capable of, and what kinds of reasons we have for action. A judgement as to which account of the nature of morality (or of mathematics) is most plausible in this general sense is just that: a judgement of overall plausibility. It is not usefully described as an insight into concepts or as a special intuitive insight of some other kind.

If philosophical utilitarianism is accepted then some form of utilitarianism appears to be forced upon us as a normative doctrine, but further argument is required to determine which form we should accept. If all that counts morally is the well-being of individuals, no one of whom is singled out as counting for more than the others, and if all that matters in the case of each individual is the degree to which his or her well-being is affected, then it would seem to follow that the basis of moral appraisal is the goal of maximizing the sum^7 of individual well-being. Whether this standard is to be applied to the criticism of individual actions, or to the selection of rules or policies, or to the inculcation of habits and dispositions to act is a further question, as is the question of how 'well-being' itself is to be understood. Thus the hypothesis that much of the appeal of utilitarianism as a normative doctrine derives from the attractiveness of philosophical utilitarianism explains how people can be convinced that some form of utilitarianism must be correct while yet being quite uncertain as to which form it is, whether it is 'direct' or 'act-' utilitarianism or some form of indirect 'rule-' or 'motive-' utilitarianism. What these views have in common, despite their differing normative consequences, is the identification of the same class of fundamental moral facts.

II

If what I have said about the appeal of utilitarianism is correct, then what a rival theory must do is to provide an alternative to philosophical utilitarianism as a conception of the subject-matter of morality. This is what the

---

[7] 'Average utilitarianism' is most plausibly arrived at through quite a different form of argument, one more akin to contractualism. I discuss one such argument is sect. IV below.

theory which I shall call contractualism seeks to do. Even if it succeeds in this, however, and is judged superior to philosophical utilitarianism as an account of the nature of morality, normative utilitarianism will not have been refuted. The possibility will remain that normative utilitarianism can be established on other grounds, for example as the normative outcome of contractualism itself. But one direct and, I think, influential argument for normative utilitarianism will have been set aside.

To give an example of what I mean by contractualism, a contractualist account of the nature of moral wrongness might be stated as follows. 'An act is wrong if its performance under the circumstances would be disallowed by any system of rules for the general regulation of behaviour which no one could reasonably reject as a basis for informed, unforced general agreement.' This is intended as a characterization of the kind of property which moral wrongness is. Like philosophical utilitarianism, it will have normative consequences, but it is not my present purpose to explore these in detail. As a contractualist account of one moral notion, what I have set out here is only an approximation, which may need to be modified considerably. Here I can offer a few remarks by way of clarification.

The idea of 'informed agreement' is meant to exclude agreement based on superstition or false belief about the consequences of actions, even if these beliefs are ones which it would be reasonable for the person in question to have. The intended force of the qualification 'reasonably', on the other hand, is to exclude rejections that would be unreasonable *given* the aim of finding principles which could be the basis of informed, unforced general agreement. Given this aim, it would be unreasonable, for example, to reject a principle because it imposed a burden on you when every alternative principle would impose much greater burdens on others. I will have more to say about grounds for rejection later in the paper.

The requirement that the hypothetical agreement which is the subject of moral argument be unforced is meant not only to rule out coercion, but also to exclude being forced to accept an agreement by being in a weak bargaining position, for example because others are able to hold out longer and hence to insist on better terms. Moral argument abstracts from such considerations. The only relevant pressure for agreement comes from the desire to find and agree on principles which no one who had this desire could reasonably reject. According to contractualism, moral argument concerns the possibility of agreement among persons who are all moved by this desire, and moved by it to the same degree. But this counterfactual assumption characterizes only the agreement with which morality is concerned, not the world to which moral principles are to apply. Those who are concerned with morality look for principles for application to their imperfect world which they could not reasonably reject, and which others in this world, who are not now moved by the desire for agreement, could not reasonably reject should they come to be so moved.[8]

The contractualist account of moral wrongness refers to principles 'which no one could reasonably reject' rather than to principles 'which everyone could reasonably accept' for the following reason.[9] Consider a principle under which some people will suffer severe hardships, and suppose that these hardships are avoidable. That is, there are alternative principles under which no one would have to bear comparable burdens. It might happen, however, that the people on whom these hardships fall are particularly self-sacrificing, and are willing to accept these burdens for the sake of what they see as the greater good of all. We would not say, I think, that it would be unreasonable of them to do this. On the other hand, it might not be unreasonable for them to refuse these burdens, and, hence, not unreasonable for someone to reject a principle requiring him to bear them. If this rejection would be reasonable, then the principle imposing these burdens is put in doubt, despite the fact that some particularly self-sacrificing people could (reasonably) accept it. Thus it is the reasonableness of rejecting a principle, rather than the reasonableness of accepting it, on which moral argument turns.

It seems likely that many non-equivalent sets of principles will pass the test of non-rejectability. This is suggested, for example, by the fact that there are many different ways of defining important duties, no one of which is more or less 'rejectable' than the others. There are, for example, many different systems of agreement-making and many different ways of assigning responsibility to care for others. It does not follow, however, that any action allowed by at least one of these sets of principles cannot be morally wrong according to contractualism. If it is important for us to have *some* duty of a given kind (some duty of fidelity to agreements, or some duty of mutual aid) of which there are many morally acceptable forms, then one of these forms needs to be established by convention. In a setting in which one of these forms *is* conventionally established, acts disallowed by it will be wrong in the sense of the definition given. For, given the need for such conventions, one thing that could not be generally agreed to would be a set of principles allowing one to disregard conventionally established (and morally acceptable) definitions of important duties. This dependence on convention introduces a degree of cultural relativity into contractualist morality. In addition, what a person can reasonably reject

[8] Here I am indebted to Gilbert Harman for comments which have helped me to clarify my statement of contractualism.
[9] A point I owe to Derek Parfit.

will depend on the aims and conditions that are important in his life, and these will also depend on the society in which he lives. The definition given above allows for variation of both of these kinds by making the wrongness of an action depend on the circumstances in which it is performed.

The partial statement of contractualism which I have given has the abstract character appropriate in an account of the subject-matter of morality. On its face, it involves no specific claim as to which principles could be agreed to or even whether there is a unique set of principles which could be the basis of agreement. One way, though not the only way, for a contractualist to arrive at substantive moral claims would be to give a technical definition of the relevant notion of agreement, e.g. by specifying the conditions under which agreement is to be reached, the parties to this agreement and the criteria of reasonableness to be employed. Different contractualists have done this in different ways. What must be claimed for such a definition is that (under the circumstances in which it is to apply) what it describes is indeed the kind of unforced, reasonable agreement at which moral argument aims. But contractualism can also be understood as an informal description of the subject-matter of morality on the basis of which ordinary forms of moral reasoning can be understood and appraised without proceeding via a technical notion of agreement.

Who is to be included in the general agreement to which contractualism refers? The scope of morality is a difficult question of substantive morality, but a philosophical theory of the nature of morality should provide some basis for answering it. What an adequate theory should do is to provide a framework within which what seem to be relevant arguments for and against particular interpretations of the moral boundary can be carried out. It is often thought that contractualism can provide no plausible basis for an answer to this question. Critics charge either that contractualism provides no answer at all, because it must begin with some set of contracting parties taken as given, or that contractualism suggests an answer which is obviously too restrictive, since a contract requires parties who are able to make and keep agreements and who are each able to offer the others some benefit in return for their co-operation. Neither of these objections applies to the version of contractualism that I defending. The general specification of the scope of morality which it implies seems to me to be this: morality applies to a being if the notion of justification to a being of that kind makes sense. What is required in order for this to be the case? Here I can only suggest some necessary conditions. The first is that the being have a good, that is, that there be a clear sense in which things can be said to go better or worse for that being. This gives partial sense to the idea of what it would be reasonable for a trustee to accept on the being's behalf. It would be reasonable for a trustee to accept at least those things that are good, or not bad, for the being in question. Using this idea of trusteeship we can extend the notion of acceptance to apply to beings that are incapable of literally agreeing to anything. But this minimal notion of trusteeship is too weak to provide a basis for morality, according to contractualism. Contractualist morality relies on notions of what it would be reasonable to accept, or reasonable to reject, which are essentially comparative. Whether it would be unreasonable for me to reject a certain principle, given the aim of finding principles which no one with this aim could reasonably reject, depends not only on how much actions allowed by that principle might hurt me in absolute terms but also on how that potential loss compares with other potential losses to others under this principle and alternatives to it. Thus, in order for a being to stand in moral relations with us it is not enough that it have a good, it is also necessary that its good be sufficiently similar to our own to provide a basis for some system of comparability. Only on the basis of such a system can we give the proper kind of sense to the notion of what a trustee could reasonably reject on a being's behalf.

But the range of possible trusteeship is broader than that of morality. One could act as a trustee for a tomato plant, a forest, or an ant colony, and such entities are not included in morality. Perhaps this can be explained by appeal to the requirement of comparability: while these entities have a good, it is not comparable to our own in a way that provides a basis for moral argument. Beyond this, however, there is in these cases insufficient foothold for the notion of justification *to* a being. One further minimum requirement for this notion is that the being constitute a point of view; that is, that there be such a thing as what it is like to be that being, such a thing as what the world seems like to it. Without this, we do not stand in a relation to the being that makes even hypothetical justification *to it* appropriate.

On the basis of what I have said so far contractualism can explain why the capacity to feel pain should have seemed to many to count in favour of moral status: a being which has this capacity seems also to satisfy the three conditions I have just mentioned as necessary for the idea of justification to it to make sense. If a being can feel pain, then it constitutes a centre of consciousness to which justification can be addressed. Feeling pain is a clear way in which the being can be worse off; having its pain alleviated a way in which it can be benefited; and these are forms of weal and woe which seem directly comparable to our own.

It is not clear that the three conditions I have listed as necessary are also sufficient for the idea of justification to a being to make sense. Whether they are, and, if they are not, what more may be required, are difficult and disputed questions. Some would restrict the moral sphere to those to whom justifications could in principle be communicated, or to those who can actually agree to something, or to those who have the capacity to understand moral argument. Contractualism as I have stated it does not settle these issues at once. All I claim is that it provides a basis for argument about them which is at least as plausible as that offered by rival accounts of the nature of morality. These proposed restrictions on the scope of morality are naturally understood as debatable claims about the conditions under which the relevant notion of justification makes sense, and the arguments commonly offered for and against them can also be plausibly understood on this basis.

Some other possible restrictions on the scope of morality are more evidently rejectable. Morality might be restricted to those who have the capacity to observe its constraints, or to those who are able to confer some reciprocal benefit on other participants. But it is extremely implausible to suppose that the beings excluded by these requirements fall entirely outside the protection of morality. Contractualism as I have formulated it[10] can explain why this is so: the absence of these capacities alone does nothing to undermine the possibility of justification to a being. What it may do in some cases, however, is to alter the justifications which are relevant. I suggest that whatever importance the capacities for deliberative control and reciprocal benefit may have is as factors altering the duties which beings have and the duties others have towards them, not as conditions whose absence suspends the moral framework altogether.

III

I have so far said little about the normative content of contractualism. For all I have said, the act-utilitarian formula might turn out to be a theorem of contractualism. I do not think that this is the case, but my main thesis is that whatever the normative implications of contractualism may be it still

[10] On this view (as contrasted with some others in which the notion of a contract is employed) what is fundamental to morality is the desire for reasonable agreement, not the pursuit of mutual advantage. See Sect. v below. It should be clear that this version of contractualism can account for the moral standing of future persons who will be better or worse off as a result of what we do now. It is less clear how it can deal with the problem presented by future people who would not have been born but for actions of ours which also made the conditions in which they live worse. Do such people have reason to reject principles allowing these actions to be performed? This difficult problem, which I cannot explore here, is raised by Derek Parfit in 'On Doing the Best for our Children', in M. Bayles (ed.), *Ethics and Population* (Cambridge, Mass.: Schenkman), 100–15.

has distinctive content as a philosophical thesis about the nature of morality. This content—the difference, for example, between being a utilitarian because the utilitarian formula is the basis of general agreement and being a utilitarian on other grounds—is shown most clearly in the answer that a contractualist gives to the first motivational question.

Philosophical utilitarianism is a plausible view partly because the facts which it identifies as fundamental to morality—facts about individual well-being—have obvious motivational force. Moral facts can motivate us, on this view, because of our sympathetic identification with the good of others. But as we move from philosophical utilitarianism to a specific utilitarian formula as the standard of right action, the form of motivation that utilitarianism appeals to becomes more abstract. If classical utilitarianism is the correct normative doctrine then the natural source of moral motivation will be a tendency to be moved by changes in aggregate well-being, however these may be composed. We must be moved in the same way by an aggregate gain of the same magnitude whether it is obtained by relieving the acute suffering of a few people or by bringing tiny benefits to a vast number, perhaps at the expense of moderate discomfort for a few. This is very different from sympathy of the familiar kind toward particular individuals, but a utilitarian may argue that this more abstract desire is what natural sympathy becomes when it is corrected by rational reflection. This desire has the same content as sympathy—it is a concern for the good of others—but it is not partial or selective in its choice of objects.

Leaving aside the psychological plausibility of this even-handed sympathy, how good a candidate is it for the role of moral motivation? Certainly sympathy of the usual kind is one of the many motives that can sometimes impel one to do the right thing. It may be the dominant motive, for example, when I run to the aid of a suffering child. But when I feel convinced by Peter Singer's article[11] on famine, and find myself crushed by the recognition of what seems a clear moral requirement, there is something else at work. In addition to the thought of how much good I could do for people in drought-stricken lands, I am overwhelmed by the further, seemingly distinct thought that it would be wrong for me to fail to aid them when I could do so at so little cost to myself. A utilitarian may respond that his account of moral motivation cannot be faulted for not capturing this aspect of moral experience, since it is just a reflection of our non-utilitarian moral upbringing. Moreover, it must be groundless. For what kind of fact could this supposed further fact of moral wrongness be, and how

[11] Peter Singer, 'Famine, Affluence, and Morality', *Philosophy and Public Affairs*, 1 (1972), 229–43.

could it give us a further, special reason for acting? The question for contractualism, then, is whether it can provide a satisfactory answer to this challenge.

According to contractualism, the source of motivation that is directly triggered by the belief that an action is wrong is the desire to be able to justify one's actions to others on grounds they could not reasonably[12] reject. I find this an extremely plausible account of moral motivation—a better account of at least my moral experience than the natural utilitarian alternative—and it seems to me to constitute a strong point for the contractualist view. We all might like to be in actual agreement with the people around us, but the desire which contractualism identifies as basic to morality does not lead us simply to conform to the standards accepted by others whatever these may be. The desire to be able to justify one's actions to others on grounds they could not reasonably reject will be satisfied when we know that there is adequate justification for our action even though others in fact refuse to accept it (perhaps because they have no interest in finding principles which we and others could not reasonably reject). Similarly, a person moved by this desire will not be satisfied by the fact that others accept a justification for his action if he regards this justification as spurious.

One rough test of whether you regard a justification as sufficient is whether you would accept that justification if you were in another person's position. This connection between the idea of 'changing places' and the motivation which underlies morality explains the frequent occurrence of 'Golden Rule' arguments within different systems of morality and in the teachings of various religions. But the thought experiment of changing places is only a rough guide; the fundamental question is what would it be unreasonable to reject as a basis for informed, unforced, general agreement. As Kant observed,[13] our different individual points of view, taken as they are, may in general be simply irreconcilable. 'Judgemental harmony' requires the construction of a genuinely interpersonal form of justification which is none the less something that each individual could agree to. From this interpersonal standpoint, a certain amount of how things look from another person's point of view, like a certain amount of how they look from my own, will be counted as bias.

I am not claiming that the desire to be able to justify one's actions to others on grounds they could not reasonably reject is universal or 'natural'.

---

[12] Reasonably, that is, given the desire to find principles which others similarly motivated could not reasonably reject.

[13] *Grundlegung zur Metaphysik der Sitten*, tr. H. J. Paton as *The Moral Law* (London: Hutchinson, 1948), sect. 2, n. 14.

'Moral education' seems to me plausibly understood as a process of cultivating this desire and shaping it, largely by learning what justifications others are in fact willing to accept, by finding which ones you yourself find acceptable as you confront them from a variety of perspectives, and by appraising your own and others' acceptance or rejection of these justifications in the light of greater experience.

In fact it seems to me that the desire to be able to justify one's actions (and institutions) on grounds one takes to be acceptable is quite strong in most people. People are willing to go to considerable lengths, involving quite heavy sacrifices, in order to avoid admitting the unjustifiability of their actions and institutions. The notorious insufficiency of moral motivation as a way of getting people to do the right thing is not due to simple weakness of the underlying motive, but rather to the fact that it is easily deflected by self-interest and self-deception.

It could reasonably be objected here that the source of motivation I have described is not tied exclusively to the contractualist notion of moral truth. The account of moral motivation which I have offered refers to the idea of a justification which it would be unreasonable to reject, and this idea is potentially broader than the contractualist notion of agreement. For let M be some non-contractualist account of moral truth. According to M, we may suppose, the wrongness of an action is simply a moral characteristic of that action in virtue of which it ought not to be done. An act which has this characteristic, according to M, has it quite independently of any tendency of informed persons to come to agreement about it. However, since informed persons are presumably in a position to recognize the wrongness of a type of action, it would seem to follow that if an action is wrong then such persons would agree that it is not to be performed. Similarly, if an act is not morally wrong, and there is adequate moral justification to perform it, then there will presumably be a moral justification for it which an informed person would be unreasonable to reject. Thus, even if M, and not contractualism, is the correct account of moral truth, the desire to be able to justify my actions to others on grounds they could not reasonably reject could still serve as a basis for moral motivation.

What this shows is that the appeal of contractualism, like that of utilitarianism, rests in part on a qualified scepticism. A non-contractualist theory of morality can make use of the source of motivation to which contractualism appeals. But a moral argument will trigger this source of motivation only in virtue of being a good justification for acting in a certain way, a justification which others would be unreasonable not to accept. So a non-contractualist theory must claim that there are moral properties which have justificatory force quite independent of their recognition in any ideal agreement. These would represent what John Mackie has called instances of intrinsic 'to-be-doneness' and 'not-to-be-doneness'.[14] Part of contractualism's appeal rests on the view that, as Mackie puts it, it is puzzling how there could be such properties 'in the world'. By contrast, contractualism seeks to explain the justificatory status of moral properties, as well as their motivational force, in terms of the notion of reasonable agreement. In some cases the moral properties are themselves to be understood in terms of this notion. This is so, for example, in the case of the property of moral wrongness, considered above. But there are also right- and wrong-making properties which are themselves independent of the contractualist notion of agreement. I take the property of being an act of killing for the pleasure of doing so to be a wrong-making property of this kind. Such properties are wrong-making because it would be reasonable to reject any set of principles which permitted the acts they characterize. Thus, while there are morally relevant properties 'in the world' which are independent of the contractualist notion of agreement, these do not constitute instances of intrinsic 'to-be-doneness' and 'not-to-be-doneness': their moral relevance—their force in justifications as well as their link with motivation—is to be explained on contractualist grounds.

In particular, contractualism can account for the apparent moral significance of facts about individual well-being, which utilitarianism takes to be fundamental. Individual well-being will be morally significant, according to contractualism, not because it is intrinsically valuable or because promoting it is self-evidently a right-making characteristic, but simply because an individual could reasonably reject a form of argument that gave his well-being no weight. This claim of moral significance is, however, only approximate, since it is a further difficult question exactly how 'well-being' is to be understood and in what ways we are required to take account of the well-being of others in deciding what to do. It does not follow from this claim, for example, that a given desire will always and everywhere have the same weight in determining the rightness of an action that would promote its satisfaction, a weight proportional to its strength or 'intensity'. The right-making force of a person's desires is specified by what might be called a conception of morally legitimate interests. Such a conception is a product of moral argument; it is not given, as the notion of individual well-being may be, simply by the idea of what it is rational for an individual to desire. Not everything for which I have a rational desire will be something in which others need concede me to have a legitimate interest which they undertake to weigh in deciding what to do. The range of things which may

<hr />

[14] J. L. Mackie, *Ethics: Inventing Right and Wrong* (Harmondsworth: Pelican, 1977), 42.

be objects of my rational desires is very wide indeed, and the range of claims which others could not reasonably refuse to recognize will almost certainly be narrower than this. There will be a tendency for interests to conform to rational desire—for those conditions making it rational to desire something also to establish a legitimate interest in it—but the two will not always coincide.

One effect of contractualism, then, is to break down the sharp distinction, which arguments for utilitarianism appeal to, between the status of individual well-being and that of other moral notions. A framework of moral argument is required to define our legitimate interests and to account for their moral force. This same contractualist framework can also account for the force of other moral notions such as rights, individual responsibility, and procedural fairness.

IV

It seems unlikely that act-utilitarianism will be a theorem of the version of contractualism which I have described. The positive moral significance of individual interests is a direct reflection of the contractualist requirement that actions be defensible to each person on grounds he could not reasonably reject. But it is a long step from here to the conclusion that each individual must agree to deliberate always from the point of view of maximum aggregate benefit and to accept justifications appealing to this consideration alone. It is quite possible that, according to contractualism, *some* moral questions may be properly settled by appeal to maximum aggregate well-being, even though this is not the sole or ultimate standard of justification.

What seems less improbable is that contractualism should turn out to coincide with some form of 'two-level' utilitarianism. I cannot fully assess this possibility here. Contractualism does share with these theories the important features that the defence of individual actions must proceed via a defence of principles that would allow those acts. But contractualism differs from *some* forms of two-level utilitarianism in an important way. The role of principles in contractualism is fundamental; they do not enter merely as devices for the promotion of acts that are right according to some other standard. Since it does not establish two potentially conflicting forms of moral reasoning, contractualism avoids the instability which often plagues rule-utilitarianism.

The fundamental question here, however, is whether the principles to which contractualism leads must be ones whose general adoption (either ideally or under some more realistic conditions) would promote maximum aggregate well-being. It has seemed to many that this must be the case. To indicate why I do not agree I will consider one of the best known arguments for this conclusion and explain why I do not think it is successful. This will also provide an opportunity to examine the relation between the version of contractualism I have advocated here and the version set forth by Rawls.

The argument I will consider, which is familiar from the writings of Harsanyi[15] and others, proceeds via an interpretation of the contractualist notion of acceptance and leads to the principle of maximum average utility. To think of a principle as a candidate for unanimous agreement I must think of it not merely as acceptable to *me* (perhaps in virtue of my particular position, my tastes, etc.) but as acceptable[16] to others as well. To be relevant, my judgement that the principle is acceptable must be impartial. What does this mean? To judge impartially that a principle is acceptable is, one might say, to judge that it is one which you would have reason to accept no matter who you were. That is, and here is the interpretation, to judge that it is a principle which it would be rational to accept if you did not know which person's position you occupied and believed that you had an equal chance of being in any of these positions. ('Being in a person's position' is here understood to mean being in his objective circumstances and evaluating these from the perspective of his tastes and preferences.) But, it is claimed, the principle which it would be rational to prefer under these circumstances—the one which would offer the chooser greatest expected utility—would be that principle under which the average utility of the affected parties would be highest.

This argument might be questioned at a number of points, but what concerns me at present is the interpretation of impartiality. The argument can be broken down into three stages. The first of these is the idea that moral principles must be impartially acceptable. The second is the idea of choosing principles in ignorance of one's position (including one's tastes, preferences, etc.). The third is the idea of rational choice under the assumption that one has an equal chance of occupying anyone's position. Let me leave aside for the moment the move from stage two to stage three, and

[15] See John C. Harsanyi, 'Cardinal Welfare, Individualistic Ethics, and Interpersonal Comparisons of Utility', *Journal of Political Economy*, 63 (1955), sect. IV. He is there discussing an argument which he presented earlier in Harsanyi, 'Cardinal Utility in Welfare Economics and in the Theory of Risk-Taking', *Journal of Political Economy*, 61 (1953), 434–5.

[16] In discussing Harsanyi and Rawls I will generally follow them in speaking of the acceptability of principles rather than their unrejectability. The difference between these, pointed out above, is important only within the version of contractualism I am presenting; accordingly, I will speak of rejectability only when I am contrasting my own version with theirs.

concentrate on the first step, from stage one to stage two. There is a way of making something like this step which is, I think, quite valid, but it does not yield the conclusion needed by the argument. If I believe that a certain principle, P, could not reasonably be rejected as a basis for informed, unforced general agreement, then I must believe not only that it is something which it would be reasonable for me to accept but something which it would be reasonable for others to accept as well, in so far as we are all seeking a ground for general agreement. Accordingly, I must believe that I would have reason to accept P no matter which social position I were to occupy (though, for reasons mentioned above, I may not believe that I *would* agree to P if I were in some of these positions). Now it may be thought that no sense can be attached to the notion of choosing or agreeing to a principle in ignorance of one's social position, especially when this includes ignorance of one's tastes, preferences, etc. But there is at least a minimal sense that might be attached to this notion. If it would be reasonable for everyone to choose or agree to P, then my knowledge that I have reason to do so need not depend on my knowledge of my particular position, tastes, preferences, etc. So, in so far as it makes any sense at all to speak of choosing or agreeing to something in the absence of this knowledge, it could be said that I have reason to choose or agree to those things which everyone has reason to choose or agree to (assuming, again, the aim of finding principles on which all could agree). And indeed, this same reasoning can carry us through to a version of stage three. For if I judge P to be a principle which everyone has reason to agree to, then it could be said that I would have reason to agree to it if I thought that I had an equal chance of being anybody, or indeed, if I assign any other set of probabilities to being one or another of the people in question.

But it is clear that this is not the conclusion at which the original argument aimed. That conclusion concerned what it would be rational for a self-interested person to choose or agree to under the assumption of ignorance or equal probability of being anyone. The conclusion we have reached appeals to a different notion: the idea of what it would be unreasonable for people to reject given that they are seeking a basis for general agreement. The direction of explanation in the two arguments is quite different. The original argument sought to explain the notion of impartial acceptability of an ethical principle by appealing to the notion of rational self-interested choice under special conditions, a notion which appears to be a clearer one. My revised argument explains how *a* sense might be attached to the idea of choice or agreement in ignorance of one's position given some idea of what it would be unreasonable for someone to reject as a basis for general agreement. This indicates a problem for my

version of contractualism: it may be charged with failure to explain the
central notion on which it relies. Here I would reply that my version of
contractualism does not seek to explain this notion. It only tries to describe
it clearly and to show how other features of morality can be understood in
terms of it. In particular, it does not try to explain this notion by reducing
it to the idea of what would maximize a person's self-interested expectations if he were choosing from a position of ignorance or under the assumption of equal probability of being anyone.

The initial plausibility of the move from stage one to stage two of the
original argument rests on a subtle transition from one of these notions to
the other. To believe that a principle is morally correct one must believe
that it is one which all could reasonably agree to and none could reasonably reject. But my belief that this is the case may often be distorted by a
tendency to take its advantage to me more seriously than its possible costs
to others. For this reason, the idea of 'putting myself in another's place' is
a useful corrective device. The same can be said for the thought experiment of asking what I could agree to in ignorance of my true position. But
both of these thought experiments are devices for considering more accurately the question of what *everyone* could reasonably agree to or what no
one could reasonably reject. That is, they involve the pattern of reasoning
exhibited in my revised form of the three-stage argument, not that of the
argument as originally given. The question, what would maximize the
expectations of a single self-interested person choosing in ignorance of his
true position, is a quite different question. This can be seen by considering
the possibility that the distribution with the highest average utility, call
it A, might involve extremely low utility levels for some people, levels
much lower than the minimum anyone would enjoy under a more equal
distribution.

Suppose that A is a principle which it would be rational for a self-
interested chooser with an equal chance of being in anyone's position to
select. Does it follow that no one could reasonably reject A? It seems
evident that this does not follow.[17] Suppose that the situation of those who
would fare worst under A, call them the Losers, is extremely bad, and that
there is an alternative to A, call it E, under which no one's situation would
be nearly as bad as this. Prima facie, the Losers would seem to have a
reasonable ground for complaint against A. Their objection may be rebutted, by appeal to the sacrifices that would be imposed on some other

---

[17] The discussion which follows has much in common with the contrast between majority
principles and unanimity principles drawn by Thomas Nagel in 'Equality', ch. 8 of *Mortal
Questions* (Cambridge: Cambridge University Press, 1979). I am indebted to Nagel's discussion
of this idea.

individual by the selection of E rather than A. But the mere fact that A yields higher average utility, which might be due to the fact that many people do very slightly better under A than under E while a very few do much worse, does not settle the matter.

Under contractualism, when we consider a principle our attention is naturally directed first to those who would do worst under it. This is because if anyone has reasonable grounds for objecting to the principle it is *likely* to be them. It does not follow, however, that contractualism always requires us to select the principle under which the expectations of the worse off are highest. The reasonableness of the Losers' objection to A is not established simply by the fact that they are worse off under A and no-one would be this badly off under E. The force of their complaint depends also on the fact that their position under A is, in absolute terms, very bad, and would be significantly better under E. This complaint must be weighed against those of individuals who would do worse under E. The question to be asked is, is it unreasonable for someone to refuse to put up with the Losers' situation under A in order that someone else should be able to enjoy the benefits which he would have to give up under E? As the supposed situation of the Loser under A becomes better, or his gain under E smaller in relation to the sacrifices required to produce it, his case is weakened.

One noteworthy feature of contractualist argument as I have presented it so far is that it is non-aggregative: what are compared are individual gains, losses, and levels of welfare. How aggregative considerations can enter into contractualist argument is a further question too large to be entered into here.

I have been criticizing an argument for average utilitarianism that is generally associated with Harsanyi, and my objections to this argument (leaving aside the last remarks about maximin) have an obvious similarity to objections raised by Rawls.[18] But the objections I have raised apply as well against some features of Rawls's own argument. Rawls accepts the first step of the argument I have described. That is, he believes that the correct principles of justice are those which 'rational persons concerned to advance their interests' would accept under the conditions defined by his original position, where they would be ignorant of their own particular talents, their conception of the good, and the social position (or generation) into which they were born. It is the second step of the argument which Rawls rejects, i.e. the claim that it would be rational for persons so

---

[18] For example, the intuitive argument against utilitarianism on p. 14 of Rawls, *A Theory of Justice*, and his repeated remark that we cannot expect some people to accept lower standards of life for the sake of the higher expectations of others.

situated to choose those principles which would offer them greatest expected utility under the assumption that they have an equal chance of being anyone in the society in question. I believe, however, that a mistake has already been made once the first step is taken.

This can be brought out by considering an ambiguity in the idea of acceptance by persons 'concerned to advance their interests'. On one reading, this is an essential ingredient in contractual argument; on another it is avoidable and, I think, mistaken. On the first reading, the interests in question are simply those of the members of society to whom the principles of justice are to apply (and by whom those principles must ultimately be accepted). The fact that they have interests which may conflict, and which they are concerned to advance, is what gives substance to questions of justice. On the second reading, the concern 'to advance their interests' that is in question is a concern of the parties to Rawls's original position, and it is this concern which determines, in the first instance,[19] what principles of justice they will adopt. Unanimous agreement among these parties, each motivated to do as well for himself as he can, is to be achieved by depriving them of any information that could give them reason to choose differently from one another. From behind the veil of ignorance, what offers the best prospects for one will offer the best prospects for all, since no one can tell what would benefit him in particular. Thus the choice of principles can be made, Rawls says, from the point of view of a single rational individual behind the veil of ignorance.

Whatever rules of rational choice this single individual, concerned to advance his own interests as best he can, is said to employ, this reduction of the problem to the case of a single person's self-interested choice should arouse our suspicion. As I indicated in criticizing Harsanyi, it is important to ask whether this single individual is held to accept a principle because he judges that it is one he could not reasonably reject whatever position he turns out to occupy, or whether, on the contrary, it is supposed to be acceptable to a person in any social position because it would be the rational choice for a single self-interested person behind the veil of ignorance. I have argued above that the argument for average utilitarianism involves a covert transition from the first pattern of reasoning to the second. Rawls's argument also appears to be of this second form; his defence of his two principles of justice relies, at least initially, on claims about what it would be rational for a person, concerned to advance his own

---

[19] Though they must then check to see that the principles they have chosen will be stable, not produce intolerable strains of commitment, and so on. As I argue below, these further considerations can be interpreted in a way that brings Rawls's theory closer to the version of contractualism presented here.

interests, to choose behind a veil of ignorance. I would claim, however, that the plausibility of Rawls's arguments favouring his two principles over the principle of average utility is preserved, and in some cases enhanced, when they are interpreted as instances of the first form of contractualist argument.

Some of these arguments are of an informal moral character. I have already mentioned his remark about the unacceptability of imposing lower expectations on some for the sake of the higher expectations of others. More specifically, he says of the parties to the original position that they are concerned 'to choose principles the consequences of which they are prepared to live with whatever generation they turn out to belong to'[20] or, presumably, whatever their social position turns out to be. This is a clear statement of the first form of contractualist argument. Somewhat later he remarks, in favour of the two principles, that they 'are those a person would choose for the design of a society in which his enemy is to assign him a place'.[21] Rawls goes on to dismiss this remark, saying that the parties 'should not reason from false premises',[22] but it is worth asking why it seemed a plausible thing to say in the first place. The reason, I take it, is this. In a contractualist argument of the first form, the object of which is to find principles acceptable to each person, assignment by a malevolent opponent is a thought experiment which has a heuristic role like that of a veil of ignorance: it is a way of testing whether one really does judge a principle to be acceptable from all points of view or whether, on the contrary, one is failing to take seriously its effect on people in social positions other than one's own.

But these are all informal remarks, and it is fair to suppose that Rawls's argument, like the argument for average utility, is intended to move from the informal contractualist idea of principles 'acceptable to all' to the idea of rational choice behind a veil of ignorance, an idea which is, he hopes, more precise and more capable of yielding definite results. Let me turn then to his more formal arguments for the choice of the difference principle by the parties to the original position. Rawls cites three features of the decision faced by parties to the original position which, he claims, make it rational for them to use the maximin rule and, therefore, to select his difference principle as a principle of justice. These are (1) the absence of any objective basis for estimating probabilities, (2) the fact that some principles could have consequences for them which 'they could hardly accept', while (3) it is possible for them (by following maximin) to ensure themselves of a minimum prospect, advances above which, in comparison,

---

[20] Rawls, *A Theory of Justice*, 137.   [21] Ibid. 152.   [22] Ibid. 153.

matter very little.[23] The first of these features is slightly puzzling, and I leave it aside. It seems clear, however, that the other considerations mentioned have at least as much force in an informal contractualist argument about what all could reasonably agree to as they do in determining the rational choice of a single person concerned to advance his interests. They express the strength of the objection that the 'losers' might have to a scheme that maximized average utility at their expense, as compared with the counter-objections that others might have to a more egalitarian arrangement.

In addition to this argument about rational choice, Rawls invokes among 'the main grounds for the two principles' other considerations which, as he says, use the concept of contract to a greater extent.[24] The parties to the original position, Rawls says, can agree to principles of justice only if they think that this agreement is one that they will actually be able to live up to. It is, he claims, more plausible to believe this of his two principles than of the principle of average utility, under which the sacrifices demanded ('the strains of commitment') could be much higher. A second, related claim is that the two principles of justice have greater psychological stability than the principle of average utility. It is more plausible to believe, Rawls claims, that in a society in which they were fulfilled people would continue to accept them and to be motivated to act in accordance with them. Continuing acceptance of the principle of average utility, on the other hand, would require an exceptional degree of identification with the good of the whole on the part of those from who sacrifices were demanded.

These remarks can be understood as claims about the 'stability' (in a quite practical sense) of a society founded on Rawls's two principles of justice. But they can also be seen as an attempt to show that a principle arrived at via the second form of contractualist reasoning will also satisfy the requirements of the first form, i.e. that it is something no one could reasonably reject. The question 'Is the acceptance of this principle an agreement you could actually live up to?' is, like the idea of assignment by one's worst enemy, a thought experiment through which we can use our own reactions to test our judgement that certain principles are ones that no one could reasonably reject. General principles of human psychology can also be invoked to this same end.

Rawls's final argument is that the adoption of his two principles gives public support to the self-respect of individual members of society, and 'give a stronger and more characteristic interpretation of Kant's idea'[25]

[23] Rawls, Ibid. 154.   [24] Ibid., sect. 29, pp. 175 ff.   [25] Ibid. 183.

that people must be treated as ends, not merely as means to the greater collective good. But, whatever difference there may be here between Rawls's two principles of justice and the principle of average utility, there is at least as sharp a contrast between the two patterns of contractualist reasoning distinguished above. The connection with self-respect, and with the Kantian formula, is preserved by the requirement that principles of justice be ones which no member of the society could reasonably reject. This connection is weakened when we shift to the idea of a choice which advances the interests of a single rational individual for whom the various individual lives in a society are just so many different possibilities. This is so whatever decision rule this rational chooser is said to employ. The argument from maximin seems to preserve this connection because it reproduces as a claim about rational choice what is, in slightly different terms, an appealing moral argument.

The 'choice situation' that is fundamental to contractualism as I have described it is obtained by beginning with 'mutually disinterested' individuals with full knowledge of their situations and adding to this (not, as is sometimes suggested, benevolence but) a desire on each of their parts to find principles which none could reasonably reject in so far as they too have this desire. Rawls several times considers such an idea in passing.[26] He rejects it in favour of his own idea of mutually disinterested choice from behind a veil of ignorance on the ground that only the latter enables us to reach definite results: 'if in choosing principles we required unanimity even where there is full information, only a few rather obvious cases could be decided'.[27] I believe that this supposed advantage is questionable. Perhaps this is because my expectations for moral argument are more modest than Rawls's. However, as I have argued, almost all of Rawls's own arguments have at least as much force when they are interpreted as arguments within the form of contractualism which I have been proposing. One possible exception is the argument from maximin. If the difference principle were taken to be generally applicable to decisions of public policy, then the second form of contractualist reasoning through which it is derived would have more far reaching implications than the looser form of argument by comparison of losses, which I have employed. But these wider applications of the principle are not always plausible, and I do not think that Rawls intends it to be applied so widely. His intention is that the difference principle should be applied only to major inequalities generated by the basic institutions of a society, and this limitation is a reflection of the

---

[26] e.g. ibid. 141, 148, although these passages may not clearly distinguish between this alternative and an assumption of benevolence.

[27] Ibid. 141.

special conditions under which he holds maximin to be the appropriate basis for rational choice: some choices have outcomes one could hardly accept, while gains above the minimum one can assure oneself matter very little, and so on. It follows, then, that in applying the difference principle—in identifying the limits of its applicability—we must fall back on the informal comparison of losses which is central to the form of contractualism I have described.

V

I have described this version of contractualism only in outline. Much more needs to be said to clarify its central notions and to work out its normative implications. I hope that I have said enough to indicate its appeal as a philosophical theory of morality and as an account of moral motivation. I have put forward contractualism as an alternative to utilitarianism, but the characteristic feature of the doctrine can be brought out by contrasting it with a somewhat different view.

It is sometimes said[28] that morality is a device for our mutual protection. According to contractualism, this view is partly true but in an important way incomplete. Our concern to protect our central interests will have an important effect on what we could reasonably agree to. It will thus have an important effect on the content of morality if contractualism is correct. To the degree that this morality is observed, these interests will gain from it. If we had no desire to be able to justify our actions to others on grounds they could reasonably accept, the hope of gaining this protection would give us reason to try to instil this desire in others, perhaps through mass hypnosis or conditioning, even if this also meant acquiring it ourselves. But given that we have this desire already, our concern with morality is less instrumental.

The contrast might be put as follows. On one view, concern with protection is fundamental, and general agreement becomes relevant as a means or a necessary condition for securing this protection. On the other, contractualist view, the desire for protection is an important factor determining the content of morality because it determines what can reasonably be agreed to. But the idea of general agreement does not arise as a means of securing protection. It is, in a more fundamental sense, what morality is about.

---

[28] In different ways by G. J. Warnock in *The Object of Morality* (London: Methuen, 1971), and by J. L. Mackie in *Ethics: Inventing Right and Wrong*. See also Richard Brandt's remarks on justification in ch. x of Brandt, *A Theory of the Good and the Right*.

VII

CAN THERE BE A RIGHT-BASED
MORAL THEORY?

J. L. MACKIE

In the course of a discussion of Rawls's theory of justice, Ronald Dworkin suggests a 'tentative initial classification' of political theories into goal-based, right-based, and duty-based theories.[1] Though he describes this, too modestly, as superficial and trivial ideological sociology, it in fact raises interesting questions. In particular, does some such classification hold for moral as well as for political theories? We are familiar with goal-based or consequentialist moral views and with duty-based or deontological ones; but it is not easy to find right-based examples, and in discussions of consequentialism and deontology this third possibility is commonly ignored. Dworkin's own example of a right-based theory is Tom Paine's theory of revolution; another, recent, example might be Robert Nozick's theory of the minimal state.[2] But each of these is a political theory; the scope of each is restricted to the criticism of some political structures and policies and the support of others; neither is a fully developed general moral theory. If Rawls's view is, as Dworkin argues, fundamentally right-based, it may be the only member of this class. Moreover, it is only for Rawls's 'deep theory' that Dworkin can propose this identification: as explicitly formulated, Rawls's moral philosophy is not right-based. The lack of any convincing and decisive example leaves us free to ask the abstract question 'Could there be a right-based general moral theory, and, if there were one, what would it be like?'

It is obvious that most ordinary moral theories include theses about

Reprinted by permission of the University of Minnesota Press and Mrs J. Mackie, from Peter A. French, Theodore E. Uehling, Jr., and Howard K. Wettstein (eds.), *Studies in Ethical Theory*, Midwest Studies in Philosophy, 3 (Minneapolis: University of Minnesota Press, 1978), copyright © 1978 by the University of Minnesota.

[1] R. Dworkin, *Taking Rights Seriously* (London: Duckworth, 1977), ch. 6, 'Justice and Rights', esp. pp. 171–2. This chapter appeared first as an article, 'The Original Position', *University of Chicago Law Review*, 40 (1973), 500–33; repr. as ch. 2 in N. Daniels (ed.), *Reading Rawls* (Oxford: Oxford University Press, 1975).

[2] R. Nozick, *Anarchy, State, and Utopia* (New York: Basic Books, 1974).

items of all three kinds, goals, duties, and rights, or, equivalently, about what is good as an end, about what is obligatory, or about what ought or ought not to be done or must or must not be done, and about what people are entitled to have or receive or do. But it is also obvious that moral theories commonly try to derive items of some of these sorts from items of another of them. It is easy to see how a consequentialist, say a utilitarian, may derive duties and rights from his basic goal. There are certain things that people must or must not do if the general happiness is to be maximized. Equally, the securing for people of certain entitlements and protections, and therefore of areas of freedom in which they can act as they choose, is, as Mill says, something which concerns the essentials of human well-being more nearly, and is therefore of more absolute obligation, than any other rules for the guidance of life.[3]

Again, it is possible to derive both goals and rights from duties. Trivially, there could just be a duty to pursue a certain end or to respect and defend a certain right. More interestingly, though more obscurely, it is conceivable that sets of goals and rights should follow from a single fundamental duty. Kant, for example, attempts to derive the principle of treating humanity as an end from the categorical imperative 'Act only on that maxim through which you can at the same time will that it should become a universal law.'[4] Taken as literally as it can be taken, the principle of treating humanity— that is, persons, or more generally rational beings—as an end would seem to set up a goal. But it could well be interpreted as assigning rights to persons. Alternatively it could be argued that some general assignment of rights would follow directly from the choice of maxims which one could will to be universal. In either of these ways rights might be derived from duties.

But is it possible similarly to derive goals and duties from rights? And, if we are seeking a systematic moral theory, is it possible to derive a multiplicity of rights from a single fundamental one or from some small number of basic rights?

A right, in the most important sense, is the conjunction of a freedom and a claim-right. That is, if someone, A, has the moral right to do X, not only is he entitled to do X if he chooses—he is not morally required not to do X—but he is also protected in his doing of X—others are morally required not to interfere or prevent him. This way of putting it suggests that duties are at least logically prior to rights: this sort of right is built up out of two facts about duties, that A does not have a duty not to do X and that others

---

[3] J. S. Mill, *Utilitarianism* (1861), ch. 5.
[4] I. Kant, *Groundwork of the Metaphysic of Morals* (1785), sect. 2.

have a duty not to interfere with A's doing of X. But we could look at it the other way round: what is primary is A's having this right in a sense indicated by the prescription 'Let A be able to do X if he chooses', and the duty of others not to interfere follows from this (as does the absence of a duty for A not to do X). Here we have one way, at least, in which duties (and negations of duties) may be derived from rights.

I cannot see any way in which the mere fact of someone's having a certain right would in itself entail that anyone should take something as a goal. Nor does someone's having a right in itself require the achievement or realization of any goal. But the achievement of certain things as goals, or of things that may be taken as goals, may well be a necessary condition for the exercise of a right. Things must be thus and so if A is really to be able to do X, his merely having the right is not in itself sufficient. In this way a goal may be derived from a right, as a necessary condition of its exercise.

Rights can be derived from other rights in fairly obvious logical ways. For example, if I have a right to walk from my home to my place of work by the most direct route, and the most direct route is across Farmer Jones's potato field, then I have a right to walk across Farmer Jones's potato field. Again, there may be a right to create rights—in Hohfeld's terminology, a power. If someone has a certain power, and exercises it appropriately, then it follows that there will be the rights he has thus created. But what may be of more interest is a causal derivation of rights from rights. Suppose that A has a right to do X, but it is causally impossible for him to do X unless he does Y. It does not follow from this alone that he has a right to do Y. But at least a prima-facie case for his having the right to do Y could be based on the fact that doing Y is causally necessary for doing X, which he already has the right to do.

It seems, then, to be at least formally possible to have a system of moral ideas in which some rights are fundamental and other rights, and also goals and duties, are derived from these. But is it substantially possible? Are rights really the sort of thing that could be fundamental?

It is true that rights are not plausible candidates for objective existence. But neither are goods or intrinsic goals, conceived as things whose nature in itself requires that they should be pursued, or duties taken as intrinsic requirements, as constituting something like commands for which there need be, and is, no commander, which issue from no source. A belief in objective prescriptivity has flourished within the tradition of moral thinking, but it cannot in the end be defended.[5] So we are not looking for

---

[5] This is argued at length in ch. 1 of my *Ethics: Inventing Right and Wrong* (Harmondsworth: Penguin, 1977).

objective truth or reality in a moral system. Moral entities—values or standards or whatever they may be—belong within human thinking and practice: they are either explicitly or implicitly posited, adopted, or laid down. And the positing of rights is no more obscure or questionable than the positing of goals or obligations.

We might, then, go on to consider what rights to posit as fundamental. But it will be better, before we do this, to consider the comparative merits of right-based, goal-based, and duty-based theories. When we know what advantages a right-based theory might secure, we shall be better able to specify the rights that would secure them.

Rights have obvious advantages over duties as the basis and ground of morality. Rights are something that we may well want to have; duties are irksome. We may be glad that duties are imposed on others, but only (unless we are thoroughly bloody-minded) for the sake of the freedom, protection, or other advantages that other people's duties secure for us and our friends. The point of there being duties must lie elsewhere. Duty for duty's sake is absurd, but rights for their own sake are not. Duty is, as Wordsworth says, the stern daughter of the voice of God, and if we deny that there is a god, her parentage becomes highly dubious. Even if we accepted a god, we should expect his commands to have some further point, though possibly one not known to us; pointless commands, even from a god, would be gratuitous tyranny. Morality so far as we understand it might conceivably be thus based on divine commands, and therefore have, for us, a duty-based form, but if we reject this mythology and see morality as a human product we cannot intelligibly take duties as its starting-point. Despite Kant, giving laws to oneself is not in itself a rational procedure. For a group to give laws to its members may be, but not for the sake of the restrictions they impose, or even for the sake of the similarity of those restrictions, but only for the sake of the correlative rights they create or the products of the co-operation they maintain.

However, such points as these can be and commonly are made against duty-based theories on behalf of goal-based ones. When duties have been eliminated from the contest, is there anything to be said for rights as against goals?

A central embarrassment for the best-known goal-based theories, the various forms of utilitarianism, is that they not merely allow but positively require, in certain circumstances, that the well-being of one individual should be sacrificed, without limits, for the well-being of others. It is not that these theories are collectivist in principle; it is not that the claims of individual welfare are overridden by those of some unitary communal welfare. They can and usually do take utility to be purely a resultant of individual satisfactions and frustrations. It is, quite literally, to other individuals that they allow one individual to be sacrificed. If some procedure produces a greater sum of happiness made up of the enjoyments experienced separately by *B* and *C* and *D* and so on than the happiness that this procedure takes away from *A*—or a sum greater than that needed to balance the misery that this procedure imposes on *A*—then, at least on a simple utilitarian view, that procedure is to be followed. And of course this holds whether the quantity to be maximized is total or average utility.

I have called this an embarrassment for utilitarianism, and it is no more than this. There are at least three well-known possible reactions to it. The tough-minded act-utilitarian simply accepts this consequence of his principles, and is prepared to dismiss any contrary 'intuitions'. Indirect utilitarianism, of which rule-utilitarianism is only one variety, distinguishes two levels of moral thinking.[6] At the level of ordinary practical day-to-day thinking, actions and choices are to be guided by rules, principles, dispositions (virtues), and so on, which will indeed protect the welfare of each individual against the claims of the greater happiness of others: rights, in fact, will be recognized at this level. But at a higher level of critical or philosophical thinking these various provisions are to be called in question, tested, explained, justified, amended, or rejected by considering how well practical thinking that is guided by them is likely to promote the general happiness. Such intermediate devices, interposed between practical choices and the utilitarian goal, may for various reasons do more for that goal than the direct application of utility calculations to everyday choices. But in this goal itself, the general happiness which constitutes the ultimate moral aim and the final test in critical moral thought, the well-being of all individuals is simply aggregated, and the happiness of some can indeed compensate for the misery (even the undeserved misery) of others. This, then, is the second possible reaction. The third says that the difficulty or embarrassment results, not because utilitarianism is a goal-based theory, but because it is a purely aggregative one, and that what is required is the addition to it of a distributive principle that prescribes fairness in the distribution of happiness. It is not fair to sacrifice one individual to others.

Of these three reactions, the first would be attractive only if there were some strong prima-facie case for adopting a simple utilitarian morality; but there is not.[7] The indirect view also has to assume that there are good

---

[6] For example, R. M. Hare, 'Ethical Theory and Utilitarianism', in H. D. Lewis (ed.), *Contemporary British Philosophy: Personal Statements*, 4th ser. (London: Allen & Unwin, 1976).
[7] I have tried to show this in ch. 6 of *Ethics: Inventing Right and Wrong*, appealing to radical weaknesses in anything like Mill's proof of utility.

general grounds for taking a sheer aggregate of happiness as the ultimate moral aim. But its great difficulty lies in maintaining the two levels of thinking while keeping them insulated from one another. There is, I admit, no difficulty in distinguishing them. The problem is rather the practical difficulty, for someone who is for part of the time a critical moral philosopher in this utilitarian style, to keep this from infecting his everyday moral thought and conduct. It cannot be easy for him to retain practical dispositions of honesty, justice, and loyalty if in his heart of hearts he feels that these don't really matter, and sees them merely as devices to compensate for the inability of everyone, himself included, to calculate reliably and without bias in terms of aggregate utility. And a thinker who does achieve this is still exposed to the converse danger that his practical morality may weaken his critical thinking. He will be tempted to believe that the virtues built into his own character, the principles to which he automatically appeals in practice, are the very ones that will best promote the general happiness, not because he has reached this conclusion by cogent reasoning, but just because his belief reconciles his theory with his practice. He may come to cultivate a quite artificial distrust of his own ability to work out the consequences of actions for the general happiness. And what happens if the two levels cannot be kept apart? If the critical thinkers let their higher-level thinking modify their own day-to-day conduct, the division will cease to be between two levels of thinking for at least some people, and become a division between two classes of people, those who follow a practical morality devised for them by others, and those who devise this but themselves follow a different, more directly utilitarian, morality. If, alternatively, the critical thinkers let their practical morality dominate their criticism, there can indeed be the same moral system for everyone, but it will have ceased to be a goal-based one. The derivation of the working principles from utility will have become a mere rationalization. Altogether, then, indirect utilitarianism is a rather unhappy compromise. And it is inadequately motivated. Why should it not be a *fundamental* moral principle that the well-being of one person cannot be simply replaced by that of another? There is no cogent proof of purely aggregative consequentialism at any level.[8]

Is the remedy, then, to add a distributive principle? This is still not quite what we need. If one individual is sacrificed for advantages accruing to others, what is deplorable is the ill-treatment of this individual, the invasion of his rights, rather than the relational matter of the unfairness of his treatment in comparison with others. Again, how are we to understand

---

[8] The discussion referred to in n. 7 applies here also.

fairness itself? Within a purely goal-based theory it would have to be taken as an end or good, presumably a collective good, a feature of multi-person distributions which it is good to have in a group, or perhaps good for the group, though not good for any one member. And this would be rather mysterious. Further, within a goal-based theory it would be natural to take fairness, if it were recognized, as one additional constituent of utility, and then, unless it were given an infinite utility value, it in turn could be outweighed by a sufficient aggregate of individual satisfactions. There could still be a moral case for sacrificing not only A's welfare but also fairness along with it to the greater utility summed up in the welfare of B and C and so on.

Fairness as a distributive principle, added to an otherwise aggregative theory, would prescribe some distribution of utility. But what distribution? Presumably an equal one would be the ideal, to which distribution in practice would be expected to approximate as closely as was reasonably possible. But though extreme inequalities of satisfaction are deplorable, it is not clear that simple equality of satisfaction is the ideal. We surely want to leave it open to people to make what they can of their lives. But then it is inevitable that some will do better for themselves than others. This same point can be made about groups rather than individuals. Consider a society containing two groups, A and B, where the members of each group are in contact mainly with co-members of their own group. Suppose that the members of A are more co-operative, less quarrelsome, and so more successful in co-ordinating various activities than the members of B. Then the members of A are likely to do better, achieve more satisfaction, than the members of B. And why shouldn't they? Would there be any good reason for requiring an equal distribution of welfare in such circumstances? There is, of course, no need to adopt the extravagances and the myths of sturdy individualism, above all no ground for supposing that all actual inequalities of satisfaction result from some kind of merit and are therefore justified. All I am suggesting is that inequalities may be justified, and in particular that we should think of protecting each individual in an opportunity to do things rather than of distributing satisfactions.

Perhaps when fairness is added to an otherwise goal-based theory it should be thought of as a duty-based element. But then the arguments against duty-based systems apply to this element. What merit has even the duty to be fair for its own sake? It would be easier to endorse something like fairness as a right-based element, giving us a partly goal-based and partly right-based system.

But even this is not enough. A plausible goal, or good for man, would have to be something like Aristotle's *eudaimonia*: it would be in the category of activity. It could not be just an end, a possession, a termination of pursuit. The absurdity of taking satisfaction in the sense in which it is such a termination as the moral goal is brought out by the science-fictional pleasure machine described by Smart.[9] But Aristotle went wrong in thinking that moral philosophy could determine that a particular sort of activity constitutes the good for man in general, and is objectively and intrinsically the best way of life. People differ radically about the kinds of life that they choose to pursue. Even this way of putting it is misleading: in general people do not and cannot make an overall choice of a total plan of life. They choose successively to pursue various activities from time to time, not once and for all. And while there is room for other sorts of evaluation of human activities, morality as a source of constraints on conduct cannot be based on such comparative evaluations.[10] I suggest that if we set out to formulate a goal-based moral theory, but in identifying the goal try to take adequate account of these three factors, namely that the 'goal' must belong to the category of activity, that there is not one goal but indefinitely many diverse goals, and that there are the objects of progressive (not once-for-all or conclusive) choices, then our theory will change insensibly into a right-based one. We shall have to take as central the right of persons progressively to choose how they shall live.

This suggestion is dramatically illustrated by some of the writings of the best known of utilitarian moralists, John Stuart Mill. When he reiterates, in *On Liberty*, that he regards utility 'as the ultimate appeal on all ethical questions', he hastens to add that 'it must be utility in the largest sense, grounded on the permanent interests of a man as a progressive being'. Not, as it is sometimes misquoted, 'of man as a progressive being': that would imply a collectivist view, but here the stress is on the claims of each individual. 'These interests, I contend, authorize the subjection of individual spontaneity to external control, only in respect to those actions of each, which concern the interest of other people.' And the next few lines make it clear that he is thinking not of any interests of other people, but particularly of their rights and the defence of their rights. It is at least as plausible to say that the deep theory of *On Liberty* is right-based as that this holds of Rawls's *A Theory of Justice*.[11] The same point emerges from a close examination of the last chapter of *Utilitarianism*, 'On the Connection between Justice and Utility'. There Mill argues that what is morally

[9] J. J. C. Smart and Bernard Williams, *Utilitarianism, For and Against* (Cambridge: Cambridge University Press, 1973), 18–21.

[10] I am speaking here of what I call morality in the narrow sense in *Ethics: Inventing Right and Wrong*, ch. 5.

[11] Dworkin makes this point, at least implicitly, in ch. 11, 'Liberty and Liberalism', of *Taking Rights Seriously*.

required or obligatory is included in but not coextensive with what is expedient or worthy, and that what is just (or rather, what is required for justice) is similarly a proper subclass of what is obligatory. By 'justice' he makes it clear that he means the body of rules which protect rights which 'reside in persons'. They are 'The moral rules which forbid mankind to hurt one another (in which we must never forget to include wrongful interference with each other's freedom)' and 'are more vital to human well-being than any maxims, however important, which only point out the best way of managing some department of human affairs'. And though he still says that general utility is the reason why society ought to defend me in the possession of these rights, he explains that it is an 'extraordinarily important and impressive kind of utility which is concerned'. 'Our notion, therefore, of the claim we have on our fellow-creatures to join in making safe for us the very groundwork of our existence, gathers feelings around it so much more intense than those concerned in any of the more common cases of utility, that the difference in degree . . . becomes a real difference in kind.' In such passages as these we can see Mill, while still working within the framework of a goal-based theory, moving towards a right-based treatment of at least the central part of morality.

When we think it out, therefore, we see that not only can there be a right-based moral theory, there cannot be an acceptable moral theory that is not right-based. Also, in learning why this approach is superior to those based either on duties or on goals, we have at least roughly identified what we may take as the fundamental right. If we assume that, from the point of view of the morality we are constructing, what matters in human life is activity, but diverse activities determined by successive choices, we shall, as I have said, take as central the right of persons progressively to choose how they shall live. But this is only a rough specification, and at once raises problems. Who is to have this right? Let us make what is admittedly a further decision and say that all persons are to have it, and all equally. It is true that this leaves in a twilight zone sentient and even human beings that are not and never will be persons; let us simply admit that there are problems here, but postpone them to another occasion.[12] Other problems are more pressing. The rights we have assigned to all persons will in practice come into conflict with one another. One person's choice of how to live will constantly be interfering with the choices of others. We have come close to Jefferson's formulation of fundamental rights to life, liberty and the pursuit of happiness. But one person's pursuit of happiness will obstruct another's, and diverse liberties, and even the similar liberties of

[12] I have touched on it in ch. 8, sect. 8, of *Ethics: Inventing Right and Wrong*.

different people, are notoriously incompatible. Liberty is an all-purpose slogan: in all wars and all revolutions both sides have been fighting for freedom. This means that the rights we have called fundamental can be no more than prima-facie rights: the rights that in the end people have, their final rights, must result from compromises between their initially conflicting rights. These compromises will have to be worked out in practice, but will be morally defensible only in so far as they reflect the equality of the prima-facie rights. This will not allow the vital interests of any to be sacrificed for the advantage of others, to be outweighed by an aggregate of less vital interests. Rather we might think in terms of a model in which each person is represented by a point-centre of force, and the forces (representing prima-facie rights) obey an inverse square law, so that a right decreases in weight with the remoteness of the matter on which it bears from the person whose right it is. There will be some matters so close to each person that, with respect to them, his rights will nearly always outweigh any aggregate of other rights, though admittedly it will sometimes happen that issues arise in which the equally vital interests of two or more people clash.

In discussing what rights we have, Dworkin has argued against any general right to liberty and in favour of a fundamental right to equal concern and respect.[13] The latter has, indeed, the advantage that it could be a final, not merely a prima-facie right: one person's possession or enjoyment of it does not conflict with another's. But it will not serve as the foundation of a right-based moral theory. Dworkin is, indeed, putting it forward as a fundamental *political* right: it is governments that must treat those whom they govern with equal concern and respect, or, more generally, social and economic arrangements that must represent these in a concrete form. But this cannot be what is morally fundamental. The right to be treated in a certain way rests on a prior, even if somewhat indeterminate, right to certain opportunities of living. Dworkin's main reason for rejecting a general right to liberty is that it cannot explain or justify the discriminations we want between legitimate and illegitimate restrictions of freedom, or the special stress liberals place on freedom of speech and political activity. But we can discriminate in terms of how closely a certain freedom is bound up with a person's vital central interests—but, of course, it may tell against a freedom which is fairly vital in this sense to someone if his exercise of it tends to affect adversely at least equally central interests of some others. The specifically political liberties may not be thus vital to many people, but they are important, far more widely, in an indirect way,

---

[13] *Taking Rights Seriously*, ch. 12, 'What Rights do we Have?'.

as providing means for the defence of more central freedoms. That their importance is, morally speaking, thus derivative, and therefore contingent and relative to circumstances, is a conclusion which we should accept.

Dworkin is unwilling to recognize a general right to liberty also because this supposed right is commonly used to support a right to the free use of property. However, on the view I am putting forward such a right would be qualified and restricted by the consideration of how the ways in which this or that kind of property was acquired and used affect the central interests not only of the owner but of other people as well. I believe that a right to some sorts of property and some uses of it would be supported by such considerations; but by no means all the kinds and uses of property that are current in 'bourgeois' society.

Any right-based moral or political theory has to face the issue whether the rights it endorses are 'natural' or 'human' rights, universally valid and determinable a priori by some kind of reason, or are historically determined in and by the concrete institutions of a particular society, to be found out by analysis of its actual laws and practices. However, the view I am suggesting straddles this division. The fundamental right is put forward as universal. On the other hand I am not claiming that it is objectively valid, or that its validity can be found out by reason: I am merely adopting it and recommending it for general adoption as a moral principle. Also, I have argued that this fundamental right has to be formulated only as a prima-facie right. Derived specific rights (which can be final, not merely prima facie) will be historically determined and contingent upon concrete circumstances and upon the interplay of the actual interests and preferences that people have. But the fact that something is an institutional right, recognized and defended by the laws and practices of a particular society, does not necessarily establish it as a moral right. It can be criticized from the moral point of view by considering how far the social interactions which have generated and maintain this institutional right express the fundamental right of persons progressively to choose how they shall live, interpreted along the lines of our model of centres of force, and to what extent they violate it. Our theory could have conservative implications in some contexts, but equally it could have reforming or revolutionary implications in others.

It may be asked whether this theory is individualist, perhaps too individualist. It is indeed individualist in that individual persons are the primary bearers of rights, and the sole bearers of fundamental rights, and one of its chief merits is that, unlike aggregate goal-based theories, it offers a persistent defence of some interests of each individual. It is, however, in no way committed to seeing individuals as spontaneous originators of their thoughts and desires. It can recognize that the inheritance of cultural traditions and being caught up in movements help to make each individual what he is, and that even the most independent individuals constitute their distinctive characters not by isolating themselves or making 'existential' choices but by working with and through inherited traditions. Nor need it be opposed to co-operation or collective action. I believe that Rousseau's description of a community with a general will, general 'both in its object and in its essence', that is, bearing in its expression upon all members alike and located in every member of the community, provides a model of a conceivable form of association, and there is nothing in our theory that would be hostile to such genuine co-operation. But I do not believe that there could actually be a community with a genuine, not fictitious, general will of this sort of the size of an independent political unit, a sovereign state. The fundamental individual rights could, however, be expressed in joint activity or communal life on a smaller scale, and organizations of all sorts can have derived, though not fundamental, moral rights. Our theory, therefore, is not anti-collectivist; but it will discriminate among collectivities, between those which express and realize the rights of their members and those which sacrifice some of even most of their members to a supposed collective interest, or to the real interest of some members, or even to some maximized aggregate of interests.

I hope I have not given the impression that I think it an easy matter to resolve conflicts of rights and to determine, in concrete cases, what the implications of our theory will be. What I have offered is not an algorithm or decision procedure, but only, as I said, a model, an indication of a framework of ideas within which the discussion of actual specific issues might go on. And in general this paper is no more than a tentative initial sketch of a right-based moral theory. I hope that others will think it worth further investigation.

POSTSCRIPT

This paper has been read at a number of universities in the United States and Canada, and has met with some acute and forceful criticisms. I do not know how to cope with all of them, but at least some further clarifications are needed.

It has been asked whether this right-based theory is extensionally equivalent to some form of utilitarianism, yielding exactly the same output of practical prescriptions, and whether it is even just a notational variant of some form of utilitarianism. This question has, as yet, no determinate answer, because the right-based theory has not yet been made sufficiently precise. I hope that it will not turn out to be an extensional equivalent, let alone a mere notational variant, of any form of utilitarianism. But even if it does, there may be some merit in the formulation in terms of rights. It may be easier to keep this distinct from other forms of utilitarianism. And there would be no reason for preferring to formulate it in a utilitarian style unless there were some general presumption that *some* version of utilitarianism must be correct, that moral thinking ought somehow to be cast in a utilitarian mould; and I would argue that there is no ground for such a presumption.

It may also be asked just what is it to *base* a moral theory on goals or duties or rights. One possible view is that an *X*-based theory is one which takes *X* as its only undefined term, and defines other moral terms in relation to *X*. In this sense G. E. Moore's moral system is good-based. Since I have allowed that statements about rights can be analysed into conjunctions of affirmative and negative statements about duties, my account seems not to be right-based in this sense, but rather duty-based. However, this is not what I find most important. Another interpretation is that a moral theory is *X*-based if it forms a system in which some statements about *X*s are taken as basic and the other statements in the theory are derived from them, perhaps with the help of the non-moral, purely factual, premisses. But what would make a theory *X*-based in the most important sense is that it should be such a system not merely formally but in its purpose, that the basic statements about *X*s should be seen as capturing what gives point to the whole moral theory. The possibility into which I am inquiring is that of a theory which is right-based in this most important sense.

The greatest difficulties concern the suggestions about how to deal with conflicts of prima-facie rights. One question is whether each agent can say, authoritatively, how vital some matter is to him. If we were working out a detailed theory, we would want to give considerable weight to sincere claims of this sort, but not complete authority: we may have to tell a busybody that something is not as vital to him, from the point of view of this moral theory, as he thinks it is. Another problem is that a model of point-centres of force seems to offer no solution at all to conflicts of equally vital interests. This difficulty is partly met by the reflection that the proposed theory calls for compromises worked out in practice, for the historical development of institutional rights as derivatives from and realizations of the prima-facie rights, rather than for direct solution of conflicts as they arise at any moment by reference to the general theory alone. Institutional rights may resolve what would be insoluble conflicts of claims.

The suggested theory is only right-*based*; it does not make rights, let alone fundamental prima-facie rights, the only moral elements; it provides for the derivation of goals and duties from those fundamental rights. But this reply leads to a further difficulty: will not an indirect right-based theory be open to objections similar to those pressed against indirect utilitarianism? I think it will be less open to such objections, because the protection of rights can be seen throughout as what gives force to the derived moral judgements: there is less need to detach them from this source than there is to detach the working principles of an indirect utilitarianism from a purely aggregative basic theory. Whatever problems there are about adjusting conflicts of rights, this theory is not saddled with the embarrassing presumption that one person's well-being can be simply replaced by that of another.

Finally, it does not seem to me to be a reasonable requirement for a moral theory that it should, even when fully developed, be able to resolve all conflicts. But my main thesis is that this right-based approach is worth some further study, similar to that which has been lavished on various forms of utilitarianism.

VIII

LATER SELVES AND MORAL PRINCIPLES

DEREK PARFIT

I shall first sketch different views about the nature of personal identity, then suggest that the views support different moral claims.

I

Most of us seem to have certain beliefs about our own identity. We seem for instance to believe that, whatever happens, any future person must be either us, or someone else.

These beliefs are like those that some of us have about a simpler fact. Most of us now think that to be a person, as opposed to a mere animal, is just to have certain more specific properties, such as rationality. These are matters of degree. So we might say that the fact of personhood is just the fact of having certain other properties, which are had to different degrees.

There is a different view. Some of us believe that personhood is a further, deep, fact, and cannot hold to different degrees.

This second view may be confused with some trivial claims. Personhood is, in a sense, a further fact. And there is a sense in which all persons are equally persons.

Let us first show how these claims may be trivial. We can use a different example. There is a sense in which all our relatives are equally our relatives. We can use the phrase 'related to' so that what it means has no degrees; on this use, parents and remote cousins are as much relatives. It is obvious, though, that kinship has degrees. This is shown in the phrase 'closely related to': remote cousins are, as relatives, less close. I shall summarize such remarks in the following way. On the above use, the fact

From A. Montefiore (ed.), *Philosophy and Personal Relations* (London: Routledge & Kegan Paul, 1973), 137–69. Reprinted by permission of Routledge Publishers.

I have been helped in writing this by T. Nagel; also by S. Blackburn, E. Borowitz, S. Clark, L. Francis, H. Frankfurt, J. Griffin, R. M. Hare, S. Lukes, J. L. Mackie, A. Orenstein, C. Peacocke, A. Rorty, A. Ryan, S. Shoemaker, D. Thomas, R. Walker, and others.

of being someone's relative has in its *logic* no degrees. But in its *nature*—in what it involves—it does have degrees. So the fact's logic hides its nature. Hence the triviality of the claim that all our relatives are equally our relatives. (The last few sentences may be wrongly worded,[1] but I hope that the example suggests what I mean.)

To return to the claims about personhood. These were: that it is a further fact, and that all persons are equally persons. As claims about the fact's logic, these are trivial. Certain people think the claims profound. They believe them to be true of the fact's nature.

The difference here can be shown in many ways. Take the question 'When precisely does an embryo become a person?' If we merely make the claims about the fact's logic, we shall not believe that this question must have a precise answer.[2] Certain people do believe this. They believe that any embryo must either be, or not be, a complete person. Their view goes beyond the 'logical claims'. It concerns the nature of personhood.

We can now return to the main argument. About the facts of both personhood and personal identity, there are two views. According to the first, these facts have a special nature. They are further facts, independent of certain more specific facts; and in every case they must either hold completely, or completely fail to hold. According to the second view, these facts are not of this nature. They consist in the holding of the more specific facts; and they are matters of degree.

Let us name such opposing views. I shall call the first kind 'Simple' and the second 'Complex'.

Such views may affect our moral principles, in the following way. If we change from a Simple to a Complex View, we acquire two beliefs: we decide that a certain fact is in its nature less deep, and that it sometimes holds to reduced degrees. These beliefs may have two effects: the first belief may weaken certain principles, and the second give the principles a new scope.

Take the views about personhood. An ancient principle gives to the welfare of people absolute precedence over that of mere animals. If the difference between people and mere animals is in its nature less deep, this principle can be more plausibly denied. And if embryos are not people, and become them only by degrees, the principle forbidding murder can be more plausibly given less scope.[3]

---

[1] But compare *de dicto* versus *de re*.

[2] We might say, 'The concept of a person is too vague to yield such an answer'.

[3] Here is another example. Some of those who dislike all Jews seem to take Jewishness to be a special, deep property, equally possessed by all Jews. If they lose this belief, their attitude may be both weakened and reduced in scope. They may dislike 'typical Jews' less, and untypical Jews not at all.

I have not defended these claims. They are meant to parallel what I shall defend in the case of the two views about personal identity.

II

We must first sketch these views. It will help to revive a comparison. What is involved in the survival of a nation are just certain continuities, such as those of a people and a political system. When there is a weakening of these continuities, as there was, say, in the Norman Conquest, it may be unclear whether a nation survives. But there is here no problem. And the reason is that the survival of a nation just involves these continuities. Once we know how the continuities were weakened, we need not ask, as a question about an independent fact, 'Did a nation cease to exist?' There is nothing left to know.

We can add the following remarks. Though identity has no degrees,[4] these continuities are matters of degree. So the identity of nations over time is only in its logic 'all-or-nothing'; in its nature it has degrees.

The identity of people over time is, according to the Complex View, comparable.[5] It consists in bodily and psychological continuity. These, too, are matters of degree. So we can add the comparable remark. The identity of people over time is only in its logic 'all-or-nothing'; in its nature it has degrees.

How do the continuities of bodies and minds have degrees? We can first dismiss bodies, since they are morally trivial.[6] Let us next call 'direct' the psychological relations which hold between: the memory of an experience and this experience, the intention to perform some later action and this action, and different expressions of some lasting character trait. We can now name two general features of a person's life. One, 'connectedness', is the holding, over time, of particular 'direct' relations. The other, 'continuity', is the holding of a chain of such relations. If, say, I cannot now remember some earlier day, there are no 'connections of memory' between me now and myself on that day. But there may be 'continuity of memory'. This there is if, on every day between, I remembered the previous day.

---

[4] The thing of which X is true can only be, or not be, the thing of which Y is true.

[5] Cf. Hume: 'I cannot compare the soul more properly to anything than to a republic or commonwealth' (Hume, *A Treatise of Human Nature* (London, 1740), I. iv. 6, p. 261).

[6] They cannot be so dismissed in a full account. The Complex View is not identical to Hume's view. It is even compatible with physicalism. See, for example, A. M. Quinton, 'The Soul', *Journal of Philosophy*, 59 (1962), 393–409, and *On the Nature of Things* (London: Routledge & Kegan Paul, 1972), 88–102.

Of these two general relations, I define 'continuous with' so that, in its logic, it has no degrees. It is like 'related to' in the use on which all our relatives are equally our relatives. But 'connectedness' has degrees. Between different parts of a person's life, the connections of memory, character, and intention are—in strength and number—more or less. ('Connected to' is like 'closely related to'; different relatives can be more or less close.)

We can now restate the Complex View. What is important in personal identity are the two relations we have just sketched. One of these, continuity, is in its logic all-or-nothing. But it just involves connectedness, which clearly has degrees. In its nature, therefore, continuity holds to different degrees. So the fact of personal identity also, in its nature, has degrees.

To turn to the Simple View. Here the fact is believed to be, in its nature, all-or-nothing. This it can only be if it does not just consist in (bodily and) psychological continuity—if it is, in its nature, a further fact. To suggest why: These continuities hold, over time, to different degrees. This is true in actual cases, but is most clearly true in some imaginary cases. We can imagine cases where the continuities between each of us and a future person hold to every possible degree.[7] Suppose we think, in imagining these cases, 'Such a future person must be either, and quite simply, *me*, or *someone else*'. (Suppose we think, 'Whatever happens, any future experience must be either *wholly* mine, or *not* mine *at all*'.) If the continuities can hold to every degree, but the fact of our identity must hold completely or not at all, then this fact cannot consist in these continuities. It must be a further, independent, fact.

It is worth repeating that the Simple View is about the nature of personal identity, not its logic. This is shown by the reactions most of us have to various so-called 'problem cases'.[8] These reactions also show that even

---

[7] Here are two (crude) ranges of cases. In the first, different proportions of the cells in our brains and bodies will be replaced by exact duplicates. At the start of this range, where there is no replacement, there is full bodily continuity; at the end, where there is complete (simultaneous) 'replacement', there is no bodily continuity. In the second range, the duplication is progressively less accurate. At the start of this range, where there are perfect duplicates, there is full psychological continuity; at the end, where there are no duplicates, there is none. In the first case of the first range there is clearly personal identity. In the last case of the second range there is clearly no identity. But the two ranges can be superimposed to form a smooth spectrum. It is unbelievable that, at a precise point on the spectrum, identity would suddenly disappear. If we grant its psychophysical assumptions, the spectrum seems to show that our identity over time could *imaginably* hold to any degree. This prepares the ground for the claim that it *actually* holds to reduced degrees.

[8] The main such reaction is the belief that these cases pose problems. (Cf. our reaction to the question, 'When, precisely, does an embryo become a person?') Among the 'problem' cases would be those described in n. 7, or in B. A. O. Williams, 'The Self and the Future', *Philosophical Review*, 79 (1970), 161–80.

if, on the surface, we reject the Simple View, at a deeper level we assume it to be true.[9]

We can add this—rough—test of our assumptions. Nations are in many ways unlike people; for example, they are not organisms. But if we take the Complex View, we shall accept this particular comparison: the survival of a person, like that of a nation, is a matter of degree. If instead we reject this comparison, we take the Simple View.

One last preliminary. We can use 'I', and the other pronouns, so that they cover only the part of our lives to which, when speaking, we have the strongest psychological connections. We assign the rest of our lives to what we call our 'other selves'. When, for instance, we have undergone any marked change in character, or conviction, or style of life, we might say, 'It was not *I* who did that, but an earlier self'.

Such talk can become natural. To quote three passages:

> Our dread of a future in which we must forgo the sight of faces, the sound of voices, that we love, friends from whom we derive today our keenest joys, this dread, far from being dissipated, is intensified, if to the grief of such a privation we reflect that there will be added what seems to us now in anticipation an even more cruel grief: not to feel it as a grief at all—to remain indifferent; for if that should occur, our self would then have changed. It would be in a real sense the death of ourself, a death followed, it is true, by a resurrection, but in a different self, the life, the love of which are beyond the reach of those elements of the existing self that are doomed to die. . . .[10]

> It is not because other people are dead that our affection for them grows faint, it is because we ourself are dying. Albertine had no cause to rebuke her friend. The man who was usurping his name had merely inherited it. . . . My new self, while it grew up in the shadow of the old, had often heard the other speak of Albertine; through that other self . . . it thought that it knew her, it found her attractive . . . but this was merely an affection at second hand.[11]

> Nadya had written in her letter; 'When you return. . . .' But that was the whole horror: that there would be no *return*. . . . A new, unfamiliar person would walk in bearing the name of her husband, and she would see that the man, her beloved, for whom she had shut herself up to wait for fourteen years, no longer existed. . . .[12]

Whether we are inclined to use such talk will depend upon our view about the nature of personal identity. If we take the Simple View, we shall

[9] That we are inclined to this view is shown ibid. That the view is false I began to argue in 'Personal Identity', *Philosophical Review*, 80 (1971), 3–27.
[10] Marcel Proust, *Within a Budding Grove*, i, tr. C. K. Scott Moncrieff (London: Chatto & Windus, 1967), 349. (I have slightly altered the translation.)
[11] Marcel Proust, *The Sweet Cheat Gone*, tr. C. K. Scott Moncrieff (London: Chatto & Windus, 1949), 249.
[12] A. Solzhenitsyn, *The First Circle* (New York: Bantam, 1969), 232. (Curiously, Solzhenitsyn, like Keats (*Letters*, ed. R. Gittings (London: Oxford University Press, 1970), 322), seems to attach weight not just to psychological but to *cellular* change. Cf. Hume, *A Treatise of Human Nature*.)

not be so inclined, for we shall think it deeply true that all the parts of a person's life are as much parts of his life. If we take the Complex View, we shall be less impressed by this truth. It will seem like the truth that all the parts of a nation's history are as much parts of its history. Because this latter truth is superficial, we at times subdivide such a history into that of a series of successive nations, such as Anglo-Saxon, medieval, or post-imperial England.[13] The connections between these, though similar in kind, differ in degree. If we take the Complex View, we may also redescribe a person's life as the history of a series of successive selves. And the connections between these we shall also claim to be similar in kind, different in degree.[14]

III

We can now turn to our question. Do the different views tend to support different moral claims?

I have space to consider only three subjects: desert, commitment, and distributive justice. And I am forced to over-simplify, and to distort. So it may help to start with some general remarks.

My suggestions are of this form: 'The Complex View supports certain claims'. By 'supports' I mean both 'makes more plausible' and 'helps to explain'. My suggestions thus mean: 'If the true view is the Complex, not the Simple, View, certain claims are more plausible.[15] We may therefore[16] be, on the Complex View, more inclined to make these claims.'

I shall be discussing two kinds of case: those in which the psychological connections are as strong as they ever are, and those in which they are markedly weak. I choose these kinds of case for the following reason. If we change from the Simple to the Complex View, we believe (I shall claim) that our identity is in its nature less deep, and that it sometimes holds to reduced degrees. The first of these beliefs covers every case, even those where there are the strongest connections. But the second of the two

---

[13] Someone might say, 'These are not successive nations. They are just stages of a single nation.' What about Prussia, Germany, and West Germany? We *decide* what counts as the same nation.

[14] Talk about successive selves can be easily misunderstood. It is intended *only* to imply the weakening of psychological connections. It does *not* report the discovery of a new type of thing. We should take the question, 'When did that self end?' as like the question, 'What marked the end of medieval England?' Cf. n. 24. (There is of course another use of 'earlier self' which, because it equates 'self' and 'person', does not distinguish successive selves.)

[15] I do not mean 'more plausible than their denials'; I mean 'than they would be if the Simple View were true'.

[16] The implied factual assumption surely holds for *some* of us.

beliefs only covers cases where there are weak connections. So the two kinds of case provide separate testing-grounds for the two beliefs.

Let us start with the cases of weak connection. And our first principle can be that we deserve to be punished for certain crimes.

We can suppose that, between some convict now and himself when he committed some crime, there are only weak psychological connections. (This will usually be when conviction takes place after many years.) We can imply the weakness of these connections by calling the convict, not the criminal, but his later self.[17]

Two grounds for detaining him would be unaffected. Whether a convict should be either reformed, or preventively detained, turns upon his present state, not his relation to the criminal. A third ground, deterrence, turns upon a different question. Do potential criminals care about their later selves? Do they care, for instance, if they do not expect to be caught for many years? If they do, then detaining their later selves could perhaps deter.

Would it be deserved? Locke thought that if we forget our crimes we deserve on punishment.[18] Geach considers this view 'morally repugnant'.[19] Mere loss of memory does seem to be insufficient. Changes of character would appear to be more relevant. The subject is, though, extremely difficult. Claims about desert can be plausibly supported with a great variety of arguments. According to some of these loss of memory would be important. And according to most the nature and cause of any change in character would need to be known.

I have no space to consider these details, but I shall make one suggestion. This appeals to the following assumption. When some morally important fact holds to a lesser degree, it can be more plausibly claimed to have less importance—even, in extreme cases, none.

I shall not here defend this assumption. I shall only say that most of us apply the assumption to many kinds of principle. Take, for example, the two principles that we have special duties to help our relatives, or friends.

---

[17] Talk about successive selves can be used, like this, merely to imply the weakness of psychological connections. It can also be used to assign moral or emotional significance to such a weakness. This 'evaluative' use I have sketched elsewhere, in 'On "The Importance of Self-Identity"', *Journal of Philosophy*, 68 (1971), 683–9. It is the 'descriptive' use which I need here. On this use, if a convict says, 'It was only my past self', all that he implies is the weakening in connections. On the 'evaluative' use, his claim suggests that, because of this weakening, he does not now deserve to be punished for his crime. Since the questions I am asking here all concern whether such a weakening *does* have such significance, it is the 'descriptive' use which I here employ. The 'evaluative' use begs these questions.

[18] John Locke, *An Essay Concerning Human Understanding* (1690), II. xxvii. 26. (Cf. also the 'Defence of Mr. Locke's Opinion' in certain editions of Locke's *Works* (e.g. 11th edn., vol. iii).)

[19] P. T. Geach, *God and the Soul* (London: Routledge & Kegan Paul, 1969), 4.

On the assumption, we might claim that we have less of a special duty to help our less close relatives, or friends, and, to those who are very distant, none at all.

My suggestion is this. If the assumption is acceptable, and the Complex View correct, it becomes more plausible to make the following claim: when the connections between convicts and their past criminal selves are less, they deserve less punishment; if they are very weak, they perhaps deserve none. This claim extends the idea of 'diminished responsibility'. It does not appeal to mental illness, but instead treats a later self like a sane accomplice. Just as a man's deserts correspond to the degree of his complicity with some criminal, so his deserts, now, for some past crime correspond to the degree of connectedness between himself now and himself when committing that crime.[20]

If we add the further assumption that psychological connections are, in general, weaker over longer periods,[21] the claim provides a ground for statutes of limitations. (They of course have other grounds.)

IV

We can next consider promises. There are here two identities involved. The first is that of the person who, once, made a promise. Let us suppose that between this person now and himself then there are only weak connections. Would this wipe away his commitment? Does a later self start with a clean slate?

On the assumption that I gave, the Complex View supports the answer, 'yes'. Certain people think that only short-term promises carry moral weight. This belief becomes more plausible on the Complex View.

The second relevant identity is that of the person who received the promise. There is here an asymmetry. The possible effect of the Complex View could be deliberately blocked. We could ask for promises of this form: 'I shall help you, and all your later selves'. If the promises that I *receive* take this form, they cannot be plausibly held to be later under-

---

[20] If we are tempted to protest, 'But it was just as much *his* crime', we seems to be taking the Simple View. The comparable claim, 'Every accomplice is just as much an accomplice' is, in the sense in which it is true, clearly trivial. (See my 'On "The Importance of Self-Identity" '.) (It is perhaps worth repeating that the Complex View deals with our relations at certain times, to ourselves at other times. The convict and criminal are, timelessly, the same person. But the convict's present self and his past self are not the same, any more than Roman and Victorian Britain are the same.)

[21] This is only generally true. Old men, for instance, can be closer to themselves in childhood than to themselves in youth.

mined by any change in *my* character, or by any other weakening, over the rest of *my* life, in connectedness.

The asymmetry is this: similar forms cannot so obviously stay binding on the *maker* of a promise. I might say, 'I, and all my later selves, shall help you'. But it is plausible to reply that I can only bind my present self. This is plausible because it is like the claim that I can only bind myself. No one, though, denies that I can promise you that I shall help someone else. So I can clearly promise you that I shall help your later selves.

Such a promise may indeed seem especially binding. Suppose that you change faster than I do. I may then regard myself as committed, not to you, but to your earlier self. I may therefore think that you cannot waive my commitment. (It would be like a commitment, to someone now dead, to help his children. We cannot be released from such commitments.)

Such a case would be rare. But an example may help the argument. Let us take a nineteenth-century Russian who, in several years, should inherit vast estates. Because he has socialist ideals, he intends, now, to give the land to the peasants. But he knows that in time his ideals may fade. To guard against this possibility, he does two things. He first signs a legal document, which will automatically give away the land, and which can only be revoked with his wife's consent. He then says to his wife, 'If I ever change my mind, and ask you to revoke the document, promise me that you will not consent'. He might add, 'I regard my ideals as essential to me. If I lose these ideals, I want you to think that *I* cease to exist. I want you to regard your husband, then, not as me, the man who asks you for this promise, but only as his later self. Promise me that you would not do what he asks.'

This plea seems understandable.[22] And if his wife made this promise, and he later asked her to revoke the document, she might well regard herself as in no way released from her commitment. It might seem to her as if she has obligations to two different people. She might think that to do what her husband now asks would be to betray the young man whom she loved and married. And she might regard what her husband now says as unable to acquit her of disloyalty to this young man—of disloyalty to her husband's earlier self.

Such an example may seem not to require the distinction between successive selves. Suppose that I ask you to promise me never to give me cigarettes, even if I beg you for them. You might think that I cannot, in begging you, simply release you from this commitment. And to think this you need not deny that it is I to whom you are committed.

---

[22] It involves the new use of pronouns, and of the word 'man', to refer to one out of a series of selves.

This seems correct. But the reason is that addiction clouds judgement. Similar examples might involve extreme stress or pain, or (as with Odysseus, tied to the mast) extraordinary temptation. When, though, nothing clouds a person's judgement, most of us believe that the person to whom we are committed can always release us. He can always, if in sound mind, waive our commitment. We believe this whatever the commitment may be. So (on this view) the content of a commitment cannot stop its being waived.

To return to the Russian couple. The man's ideals fade, and he asks his wife to revoke the document. Though she promised him to refuse, he declares that he now releases her from this commitment. We have sketched two ways in which she might think that she is not released. She might, first, take her husband's change of mind as proof that he cannot now make considered judgements. But we can suppose that she has no such thought. We can also suppose that she shares our view about commitment. If so, she will only believe that her husband is unable to release her if she thinks that it is, in some sense, not *he* to whom she is committed. We have sketched such a sense. She may regard the young man's loss of his ideals as involving his replacement by a later self.

The example is of a quite general possibility. We may regard some events within a person's life as, in certain ways, like birth or death. Not in all ways, for beyond these events the person has earlier or later selves. But it may be only one out of the series of selves which is the object of some of our emotions, and to which we apply some of our principles.[23]

The young Russian socialist regards his ideals as essential to his present self. He asks his wife to promise to this present self not to act against these ideals. And, on this way of thinking, she can never be released from her commitment. For the self to whom she is committed would, in trying to release her, cease to exist.

The way of thinking may seem to be within our range of choice. We can indeed choose when to *speak* of a new self, just as we can choose when to speak of the end of medieval England. But the way of speaking would express beliefs. And the wife in our example cannot choose her beliefs. That the young man whom she loved and married has, in a sense, ceased to exist, that her middle-aged and cynical husband is at most the later self of this young man—these claims may seem to her to express more of the truth

---

[23] I have here moved from the use of talk about successive selves which is merely 'descriptive', which merely implies the weakening of connections, to the use which is also 'evaluative', which assigns to such a weakening certain kinds of significance. It may seem confusing to allow these different uses, but they cannot be sharply distinguished. The 'merely descriptive' use lies at the end-point of a spectrum.

than the simple claim, 'but they are the same person'. Just as we can give a more accurate description if we divide the history of Russia into that of the empire and of the Soviet Union, so it may be more accurate to divide her husband's life into that of two successive selves.[24]

V

I have suggested that the Complex View supports certain claims. It is worth repeating that these claims are at most more plausible on the Complex View (more, that is, than on the Simple View). They are not entailed by the Complex View.

We can sometimes show this in the following way. Some claims make sense when applied to successive generations. Such claims can obviously be applied to successive selves. For example, it perhaps makes sense to believe that we inherit the commitments of our parents. If so, we can obviously believe that commitments are inherited by later selves.

Other claims may be senseless when applied to generations. Perhaps we cannot intelligibly think that we deserve to be punished for all our parents' crimes. But even if this is so, it should still make sense to have the comparable thought about successive selves. No similarity in the form of two

---

[24] If we take the Complex View, we might add: 'It would be even more accurate to abandon talk about "selves", and to describe actions, thoughts, and experiences in a quite "impersonal" way. (Cf. P. F. Strawson, *Individuals* (London: Methuen, 1959), 81–4.) If these are not ascribed to any "subject", their various interconnections can then be directly specified. But the concept of a "subject of experience", like that of a nation, is an abbreviatory device of enormous convenience. If we remember that it is just this, and nothing more, it can be safely used.' (Cf. Mill, *An Examination of Sir William Hamilton's Philosophy* (London: Longmans, 1872), 252. Those who disagree, see n. 57.) These remarks may *not* apply to the concept of a persisting object. This may be essential to the spatio-temporal framework. But observed objects do not require observers. They require observations.

Here is another way in which the move from 'person' to 'successive self' may help to express the truth. Suppose that, in middle age, the Russian wife asks herself, 'Do I love my husband?' If it is asked in this form, she may find the question baffling. She may then realize that there is someone she loves—her husband's earlier self. (The object of love can be in the past. We can love the dead.) Cf. Solzhenitsyn, *The First Circle*, 393: 'Innokenty felt sorry for her and agreed to come. . . . He felt sorry, not for the wife he lived with and yet did not live with these days, the wife he was going to leave again soon, but for the blond girl with the curls hanging down to her shoulders, the girl he had known in the tenth grade.' Cf. also Nabokov, *Glory* (London: Weidenfeld & Nicolson, 1971), 64: 'They said the only thing this Englishman loved in the world was Russia. Many people could not understand why he had not remained there. Moon's reply to questions of that kind would invariably be: "Ask Robertson" (the orientalist) "why he did not stay in Babylon." The perfectly reasonable objection would be raised that Babylon no longer existed. Moon would nod with a sly, silent smile. He saw in the Bolshevist insurrection a certain clear-cut finality. While he willingly allowed that, by-and-by, after the primitive phases, some civilization might develop in the "Soviet Union", he nevertheless maintained that Russia was concluded and unrepeatable.'

relations could force us to admit that they are morally equivalent, for we can always appeal to the difference in their content.

There are, then, no entailments. But there seldom are in moral reasoning. So the Complex View may still support certain claims. Most of us think that our children are neither bound by our commitments, nor responsible for all we do. If we take the Complex View, we may be more inclined to think the same about our later selves. And the correctness of the view might make such beliefs more defensible.

VI

What, next, of our present selves? What of the other kind of case, where there are the strongest psychological connections? Here it makes no difference to believe that our identity has, in its nature, degrees, for there is here the strongest degree. But in the change to the Complex View we acquire a second new belief. We decide that our identity is in its nature less deep, or involves less. This belief applies to every case, even those where there are the strongest connections.

It is worth suggesting why there must be this second difference between the two views. On the Complex View, our identity over time just involves bodily and psychological continuity. On the Simple View, it does not just involve these continuities; it is in its nature a further fact. If we stop believing that it is a further fact, then (by arithmetic) we believe that it involves less. There is still the bare possibility that we thought the further fact superficial.[25] But it seems to most of us peculiarly deep.[26] This is why, if we change to the Complex View, we believe that our identity is in its nature less deep.

Would this belief affect our principles? If it has effects, they would not be confined to the special cases where there are only weak psychological connections. They would hold in every case. The effects would not be that

[25] As, for example, Leibniz may have done. See the remark that Shoemaker quotes in N. Care and R. H. Grimm, *Perception and Personal Identity* (Cleveland, Ohio: Press of Case-Western Reserve University, 1967), 127. Locke sometimes held a similar view. (I refer to his claim that 'whether it be the same identical substance, which always thinks in the same person . . . matters not at all'; *An Essay Concerning Human Understanding*.)

[26] As Williams suggests ('The Self and the Future'). Cf. Bayle's reply to Leibniz quoted by Chisholm in Care and Grimm, *Perception and Personal Identity*, 139; and, for other statements, Geach, *God and the Soul*, 1–29, T. Penelhum, *Survival and Disembodied Existence* (London: Routledge & Kegan Paul, 1970), closing chapters (both implicit), Joseph Butler, 'Of Personal Identity', app. to *The Analogy of Natural Religion*, i, ed. W. E. Gladstone (Oxford: Frowde, 1897), 385 ff., Joseph Reid, *Essays on the Intellectual Powers of Man* (1785), essay iii, chs. 4 and 6, and R. Chisholm, 'Problems of Identity', in M. K. Munitz, *Identity and Individuation* (New York: New York University Press, 1971) (more explicit).

we give certain principles a different scope. They would be that we give the principles a different weight.

Such effects could be defended on the following assumption. When some morally important fact is seen to be less deep, it can be plausibly claimed to be less important. As the limiting case, it becomes more plausible to claim that it has no importance. (This assumption is a variant of the one I used earlier.) The implications are obvious. The principles of desert and commitment presuppose that personal identity is morally important. On the assumption I have just sketched, the Complex View supports the claim that it is—because less deep—less important. So it may tend to weaken these principles.

I shall not here discuss these possible effects. I shall only say that the principle of commitment seems to be the less threatened by this weakening effect. The reason may be that, unlike the principle of desert, it is a conventional or 'artificial' principle. This may shield it from a change of view about the facts.[27]

I shall now turn to my last subject, distributive justice. Here the consequences of a change to the Complex View seem harder to assess. The reason is this: in the case of the principles of desert and commitment, both the possible effects, the weakening and the change in scope, are in theory pro-utilitarian. (Since these principles compete with the principle of utility, it is obviously in theory pro-utilitarian if they are weakened.[28] And their new scope would be a reduced scope. This should also be pro-utilitarian.[29]) Since both the possible effects would be in the same direction, we can make this general claim: if the change of view has effects upon these principles, these effects would be pro-utilitarian. In the case of distributive justice, things are different. Here, as I shall argue, the two possible effects seem to be in opposite directions. So there is a new question: which is the more plausible combined effect? My reply will again be: pro-utilitarian.

---

[27] We should perhaps add the obvious remark that the principle of desert seems itself to be more threatened by a change of view, not about personal identity, but about psychological causation.

[28] That it may in practice be anti-utilitarian is, for instance, emphasized in Henry Sidgwick, *The Methods of Ethics* (1874; 6th edn. London: Macmillan, 1901), book IV, ch. v. (In *The Ethics of Green, Spencer, and Martineau* (London: Macmillan, 1902), 114, he writes, 'It may be—I think it is—true that Utilitarianism is only adapted for practical use by human beings at an advanced stage of intellectual development.')

[29] There are some exceptions. If, for instance, we hold the principle of desert in its 'negative' form (cf. H. L. A. Hart, *Punishment and Responsibility* (Oxford: Clarendon Press, 1968), its receiving less scope may in theory seem anti-utilitarian. Useful punishments might be ruled out on the ground that they are no longer deserved. But this would in practice be a minor point. (And there seems to be no corresponding point about commitment.)

VII

Before defending this claim, I shall mention two related claims. These can be introduced in the following way.

Utilitarians reject distributive principles. They aim for the greatest net sum of benefits minus burdens, whatever its distribution. Let us say they 'maximize'.

There is, here, a well-known parallel. When we can affect only one person, we accept maximization. We do not believe that we ought to give a person fewer happy days so as to be more fair in the way we spread them out over the parts of his life. There are, of course, arguments for spreading out enjoyments. We remain fresh, and have more to look forward to. But these arguments do not count against maximization; they remind us how to achieve it.

When we can affect several people, utilitarians make similar claims. They admit new arguments for spreading out enjoyments, such as that which appeals to relative deprivation. But they treat equality as a mere means, not a separate aim.

Since their attitude to sets of lives is like ours to single lives, utilitarians disregard the boundaries between lives. We may ask, 'Why?'

Here are three suggestions.—Their approach to morality leads them to overlook these boundaries.—They believe that the boundaries are unimportant, because they think that sets of lives are like single lives.—They take the Complex View.

The first suggestion has been made by Rawls. It can be summarized like this. Utilitarians tend to approach moral questions as if they were impartial observers. When they ask themselves, as observers, what is right, or what they prefer, they tend to *identify* with *all* the affected people. This leads them to ignore the fact that *different* people are affected, and so to reject the claims of justice.[30]

In the case of some utilitarians, Rawls's explanation seems sufficient.[31] Let us call these the 'identifying observers'. But there are others who in contrast always seem '*detached* observers'. These utilitarians do not seem to overlook the distinction between people.[32] And, as Rawls remarks, there

---

[30] Rawls, *A Theory of Justice* (Cambridge, Mass.: Harvard University Press, 1971), 27 and 185–9.

[31] Rawls mentions G. I. Lewis (ibid. 188); but the explanation cannot hold for him, for he insists upon the claims of justice (Lewis, *An Analysis of Knowledge and Valuation* (La Salle, Ill.: Open Court, 1962), 553–4). The explanation may seem to apply to Hare; see his *Freedom and Reason* (Oxford: Clarendon Press, 1963), 123; but p. 121 suggests that it does not. In J. Mackaye, *The Economy of Happiness* (Boston: Little, Brown, 1906), 129–30 and p. 189 seem to fit; but again, pp. 146–50 point the other way.

[32] Among the many utilitarians who clearly remain detached is Sidgwick. To quote a typical

is no obvious reason why observers who remain *detached* cannot adopt the principles of justice. If we approach morality in a quite detached way—if we do not think of ourselves as potentially involved[33]—we may, I think, be somewhat more inclined to reject these principles.[34] But this particular approach to moral questions does not itself seem a sufficient explanation for utilitarian beliefs.

The Complex View may provide a different explanation. These two are quite compatible. Utilitarians may both approach morality as observers, and take the Complex View. (The explanations may indeed be mutually supporting.)

To turn to the remaining explanation. Utilitarians treat sets of lives in the way that we treat single lives. It has been suggested, not that they ignore the difference between people, but that they actually believe that a group of people is like a super-person. This suggestion is, in a sense, the reverse of mine. It imputes a different view about the facts. And it can seem the more plausible.

Let us start with an example. Suppose that we must choose whether to let some child undergo some hardship. If he does, this will either be for his own greater benefit in adult life, or for the similar benefit of someone else. Does it matter which?

Most of us would answer: 'Yes. If it is for the child's own benefit, there can at least be no unfairness'. We might draw the general conclusion that failure to relieve useful burdens is more likely to be justified if they are for a person's *own* good.

Utilitarians, confusingly, could accept this conclusion. They would explain it in a different way. They might, for instance, point out that such burdens are in general easier to bear.

To block this reply, we can suppose that the child in our example cannot

---

sentence: 'I as a disengaged spectator should like him to sacrifice himself to the general good: but I do not expect him to do it, any more than I should do it myself in his place' (Sidgwick, *Methods of Ethics*, pp. xvii–xviii). Sidgwick ended the first edition of his book with the word 'failure' mostly because he assigned such weight to the distinction between people. (See, for example, ibid. 404 or *The Ethics of Green, Spencer, and Martineau*, 67, or the remark in 'Some Fundamental Ethical Controversies', *Mind*, 14 (1889), 483–4, 'The distinction between any one individual and another is real, and fundamental.' (Sidgwick's own view about personal identity is hard to judge. In *The Methods of Ethics*, 418–19, he appears to disclaim one form of the Complex View. In 'Criticism of the Critical Philosophy', *Mind*, 8 (1883), 326, he admits a Kantian claim about the necessity of the 'permanent, identical self'. Perhaps (like Kant himself?) he was torn between the two views.))

[33] As we do if we are either contracting agents (Rawls), or universal prescribers (Hare).

[34] As the contrast between the two halves of the first quotation in n. 32 may suggest. For a different suggestion, see R. M. Hare, 'Rules of War and Moral Reasoning', *Philosophy and Public Affairs*, I (1972), 166–81, and review of Rawls, *Philosophical Quarterly*, 23 (1973), 144–55, 241–52.

be cheered up in this way. Let us next ignore other such arguments.[35] This simplifies the disagreement. Utilitarians would say: 'Whether it is right to let the child bear the burden only depends upon how great the benefit will be. It does not depend upon who benefits. It would make no moral difference if the benefit comes, not to the child himself, but to someone else.' Non-utilitarians might reply: 'On the contrary, if it comes to the child himself this helps to justify the burden. If it comes to someone else, that is unfair.'

We can now ask: do the two views about the nature of personal identity tend to support different sides in this debate?

Part of the answer seems clear. Non-utilitarians think it a morally important fact that it be the child himself who, as an adult, benefits. This fact, if it seems more important on one of the views, ought to do so on the Simple View, for it is on this view that the identity between the child and the adult is in its nature deeper. On the Complex View, it is less deep, and holds, over adolescence, to reduced degrees. If we take the Complex View, we may compare the lack of connections between the child and his adult self to the lack of connections between different people. That it will be *he* who receives the benefit may thus seem less important. We might say, 'It will not be *he*. It will only be his adult self.'

The Simple View seems, then, to support the non-utilitarian reply. Does it follow that the Complex View tends to support utilitarian beliefs? Not directly. For we might say, 'Just as it would be unfair if it is someone else who benefits, so if it won't be he, but only his adult self, that would also be unfair'.

The point is a general one. If we take the Complex View, we may regard the (rough) subdivisions within lives as, in certain ways, like the divisions between lives. We may therefore come to treat alike two kinds of distribution: within lives, and between lives. But there are two ways of treating these alike. We can apply distributive principles to both, or to neither.

Which of these might we do? I claim that we may abandon these principles. Someone might object: 'If we do add, to the divisions between lives, subdivisions within lives, the effects could only be these. The principles that we now apply to the divisions we come to apply to the subdivisions. (If, to use your own example, we believe that our sons do not inherit our commitments, we may come to think the same about our later selves.)

---

[35] Such as those which appeal to the undermining of the general sense of security, or to pessimism about the 'acceptance-utility' of utilitarian beliefs.

'The comparable effect would now be this. We demand fairness to later selves. We *extend* distributive principles. You instead claim that we may abandon these principles. Since this is *not* the comparable effect, your claim must be wrong.'

The objection might be pressed. We might add: 'If we did abandon these principles, we should be moving in reverse. We should not be treating parts of one life as we now treat different lives, but be treating different lives as we now treat one life. This, the reverse effect, could only come from the reverse comparison. Rather than thinking that a person's life is like the history of a nation, we must be thinking that a nation—or indeed any group—is like a person.'

To review the argument so far. Treating alike single people and groups may come from accepting some comparison between them. But there are two ways of treating them alike. We can demand fairness even within single lives, or reject this demand in the case of groups. And there are two ways of taking this comparison. We can accept the Complex View and compare a person's life to the history of a group, or accept the reverse view and compare groups of single people.

Of these four positions, I had matched the Complex View with the abandonment of fairness. The objection was that it seemed to be better matched with the demand for fairness even within lives. And the rejection of this demand, in the case of groups, seemed to require what I shall call 'the Reverse View'.

My reply will be this. Disregard for the principles of fairness could perhaps be supported by the Reverse View. But it does not have to be. And in seeing why we shall see how it may be supported by the Complex View.

Many thinkers have believed that a society, or nation, is like a person. This belief seems to weaken the demand for fairness. When we are thought to be mere parts of a social organism, it can seem to matter less how we are each treated.[36]

If the rejection of fairness has to be supported in this way, utilitarians can be justly ignored. This belief is at best superficially true when held about societies. And to support utilitarian views it would have to be held about the whole of mankind, where it is absurd.

Does the rejection of fairness need such support? Certain writers think that it does. Gauthier, for instance, suggests that to suppose that we should

---

[36] Cf. the claim of Espinas, that society 'is a living being like an individual' (R. Perry, *General Theory of Value* (Cambridge, Mass.: Harvard University Press, 1950), 402). Good Hegelians do not argue in this way.

maximize for mankind 'is to suppose that mankind is a super-person'.[37] This suggestion seems to rest on the following argument. 'We are free to maximize within one life only because it is *one* life.[38] So we could only be free to maximize over different lives if they are like parts of a single life.'

Given this argument, utilitarians would, I think, deny the premiss. They would deny that it is the unity of a life which, within this life, justifies maximization. They can then think this justified over different lives without assuming mankind to be a super-person.

The connection with the Complex View is, I think, this. It is on this view, rather than the Simple View, that the premiss is more plausibly denied. That is how the Complex View may support utilitarian beliefs.

To expand these remarks. There are two kinds of distribution: within lives, and between lives. And there are two ways of treating these alike. We can apply distributive principles to both, or to neither.

Utilitarians apply them to neither. I suggest that this may be (in part) because they take the Complex View. An incompatible suggestion is that they take the Reverse View.

My suggestion may seem clearly wrong if we overlook the following fact. There are two routes to the abandonment of distributive principles. We may give them no scope, or instead give them no weight.

Suppose we assume that the only route is the change in scope.[29] Then it may indeed seem that utilitarians must either be assuming that any group of people is like a single person (Gauthier's suggestion), or at least be forgetting that it is not (Rawls's suggestion).

I shall sketch the other route. Utilitarians may not be denying that distributive principles have scope. They may be denying that they have weight. This, the second of the kinds of effect that I earlier distinguished, *may* be supported by the Complex View.

The situation, more precisely, may be this. If the Complex View supports a change in the scope of distributive principles, it perhaps supports giving them more scope. It perhaps supports their extension even within single lives. But the other possible effect, the weakening of these prin-

---

[37] D. Gauthier, *Practical Reasoning* (Oxford: Clarendon Press, 1963), 126.

[38] Someone might say: 'No. We are free, here, because it is not a moral matter what we do with our own lives'. This cannot be right, for we are allowed to maximize within the life of *someone else*. (Medicine provides examples. Doctors are allowed to maximize on behalf of their unconscious patients.)

[39] As Rawls seems to do. Cf. his remark: 'the utilitarian extends to society the principle of choice for one man' (*A Theory of Justice*, 28, and elsewhere, e.g. p. 141). The assumption here is that the route to utilitarianism is a change in the scope, not of distributive principles, but of their correlative: our freedom to ignore these principles.

ciples, may be the more strongly supported. That is how the net effect may be pro-utilitarian.

This suggestion differs from the other two in the following way. Rawls remarks that the utilitarian attitude seems to involve 'conflating all persons into one'.[40] This remark also covers Gauthier's suggestion. But the attitude may derive, not from the conflation of persons, but from their (partial) disintegration. It may rest upon the view that a person's life is less deeply integrated than we mostly think. Utilitarians may be treating benefits and burdens, not as if they all came within the same life, but as if it made no moral difference where they came. This belief may be supported by the view that the unity of each life, and hence the difference between lives, is in its nature less deep.[41]

VIII

I shall next sketch a brief defence of this suggestion. And I shall start with a new distributive principle. Utilitarians believe that benefits and burdens can be freely weighed against each other, even if they come to different people. This is frequently denied.

We must first distinguish two kinds of weighing. The claim that a certain burden 'factually outweighs' another is the claim that it is greater. The claim that it 'morally outweighs' the other is the claim that we should relieve it even at the cost of failing to relieve the other. Similar remarks apply to the weighing of benefits against burdens, and against each other.

Certain people claim that burdens cannot even *factually* outweigh each other if they come to different people. (They claim that the sense of 'greater than' can only be provided by a single person's preferences.) I am here concerned with a different claim.[42] At its boldest this is that the burdens and benefits of different people cannot be *morally* weighed. I shall consider one part of this claim. This goes: 'Someone's burden cannot be morally outweighed by mere benefits to someone else'. I say 'mere' benefits, because the claim is not intended to deny that it *can* be right to let a person bear a burden so as to benefit another. Such acts may, for instance, be required by justice. What the claim denies is that such acts can be

---

[40] Ibid. 27; cf. p. 191; cf. also Nagel, *The Possibility of Altruism* (Oxford: Clarendon Press, 1970), 134.

[41] The utilitarian attitude is *impersonal*. Rawls suggests that it 'mistakes impersonality for impartiality' (ibid. 190). I suggest that it may in part derive from a view about the nature of persons. This suggestion, unlike his, may be no criticism. For as he writes 'the correct regulative principle for anything depends upon the nature of that thing' (p. 29).

[42] The possibility of 'factual weighing' over different lives can, I think, be shown with an argument which appeals to the Complex View. But the argument would have to be long.

justified solely upon utilitarian grounds. It denies that a person's burden can be morally outweighed by *mere* benefits to someone else.

This claim often takes qualified forms. It can be restricted to great burdens, or be made to require that the net benefit be proportionately great.[43] I shall here discuss the simplest form, for my remarks could be adapted to the other forms. Rawls puts the claim as follows: 'The reasoning which balances the gains and losses of different persons . . . is excluded.'[44] So I shall call this the 'objection to balancing'.

This objection rests in part on a different claim. This goes: 'Someone's burden cannot be *compensated* by benefits to someone else'. This second claim is, with qualifications,[45] clearly true. We cannot say, 'On the contrary, our burdens can be compensated by benefits to anyone else, even a total stranger'.

Not only is this second claim clearly true; its denial is in no way supported by the Complex View. So if the change to this view has effects upon this claim, they would be these. We might, first, extend the claim even within single lives. We might say, in the example that I gave, 'The child's burden cannot be compensated by benefits to his adult self'. This claim would be like the claims that we are sometimes not responsible for, nor bound by, our earlier selves. It would apply to certain parts of one life what we now believe about different lives. It would therefore seem to be, as a change in scope, in the right direction.[46]

---

[43] Cf. Perry, *General Theory of Value*, 674: 'We do not . . . balance one man's loss against a million's gain. We acknowledge that there are amounts or degrees of value associated with each party, between which it is impossible to discriminate.' This claim seems to be slightly qualified. (It is not wholly clear whether Perry is objecting *only* to *moral* weighing.)

[44] *A Theory of Justice*, 28. I omit the words 'as if they were one person', for I am asking whether this reasoning must involve this assumption.

[45] The main such qualification is to exclude cases where the first person wants the second to receive the benefit.

[46] It seems worth mentioning here an idea of Nagel's. Like Rawls, Nagel claims that if we imagine that we are going to *be* all of the affected parties, we may then ignore the claims of justice. He then suggests that this is only so if our future lives are to be had *seriatim*. 'We can [instead] imagine a person splitting into several persons. . . . This provides a sense in which an individual might expect to become *each* of a number of different persons—not in series, but simultaneously' (Nagel, *The Possibility of Altruism*, 141–2; cf. Rawls, *A Theory of Justice*, 190–1). *This* model, he believes, 'renders plausible the extremely strict position that there can be no interpersonal compensation for sacrifice'. Why? How can it make a difference whether the person's future lives are to be lived in series, or concurrently? The relation between the person now and the future lives is, in either case, the same. (It is 'as good as survival'; see Parfit, 'Personal Identity', 4–10.) Nagel suggests an answer: '*Each* of [the] lives would in a sense be his unique life, without deriving any compensatory or supplementary experiences, good or bad, by seepage from the other unique lives he is leading at the time.' This, of course, is the *utilitarian* answer. It treats *pure* compensation as of no value. It suggests that compensation only matters when it actually has good effects (when it produces 'compensatory . . . supplementary experiences'). The disagreement seems to disappear!

We might, next, give the claim less weight. Our ground would be the one that I earlier gave. Compensation presupposes personal identity. On the Complex View, we may think that our identity is, because less deep, less morally important. We may therefore think that the fact of compensation is itself less morally important. Though it cannot be denied, the claim about compensation may thus be given less weight.[47]

If we now return to the objection to balancing, things are different. The concept of 'greater moral weight' does not presuppose personal identity.[48] So this objection can be denied; and the Complex View seems to support this denial.

The denial might be put like this: 'Our burdens cannot indeed be *compensated* by mere benefits to someone else. But they may be *morally outweighed* by such benefits. It may still be right to give the benefits rather than relieve the burdens. Burdens are morally outweighed by benefits if they are factually outweighed by these benefits. All that is needed is that the benefits be greater than the burdens. It is unimportant, in itself, to whom both come.'

This is the utilitarian reply.[49] I shall next suggest why the Complex View seems, more than the Simple View, to support this reply.

The objection to balancing rests in part on the claim about compensation. On the Complex View, this claim can more plausibly be thought less important. If we take this view, we may (we saw) think both that there is less scope for compensation and that it has less moral weight. If the possibilities of compensation are, in these two ways, less morally important, there would then be less support for the objection to balancing. It would be more plausible to make the utilitarian reply.

The point can be made in a different way. Even those who object to balancing think it justified to let us bear burdens for our own good. So their claim must be that a person's burden, while it can be morally outweighed by benefits to him, cannot ever be outweighed by mere benefits to others. This is held to be so even if the benefits are far greater than the burden. The claim thus gives to the boundaries between lives—or to the fact of

---

[47] This distinction bears on the 'is–ought' debate. That it is unjust to punish the innocent cannot be denied; but the claim can be given no weight. We might say, 'It is just as *bad* to punish the guilty'.

[48] It might do so, indirectly, if we cannot even *factually* weigh over different lives, and adopt utility as our only principle. No one (that I know) holds this position.

[49] It would be their reply to the many arguments in which the objection to balancing and the claim about compensation are intertwined. Cf. Rawls's phrase 'cannot be justified by, or compensated for, by . . .' (*A Theory of Justice*, 61), and similar remarks on pp. 14–15, 287, and elsewhere. Perry writes: 'The happiness of a million somehow fails utterly to compensate or even to mitigate the torture of one.' This undeniable remark he seems to equate with the objection to balancing (Perry, *General Theory of Value*, 671).

non-identity—overwhelming significance. It allows within the same life what, for different lives, it totally forbids.

This claim seems to be more plausible on the Simple View. Since identity is, here, thought to involve more, non-identity could plausibly seem more important. On the Simple View, we are impressed by the truth that all of a person's life is as much his life. If we are impressed by this truth—by the unity of each life—the boundaries between lives will seem to be deeper. This supports the claim that, in the moral calculus, these boundaries cannot be crossed. On the Complex View, we are less impressed by this truth. We regard the unity of each life as in its nature less deep, and as a matter of degree. We may therefore think the boundaries between lives to be less like those between, say, the squares on a chess-board,[50] and to be more like those between different countries. They may then seem less morally decisive.[51]

IX

We can now turn to different principles, for example that of equal distribution. Most of us give such principles only *some* weight. We think, for instance, that unequal distribution can be justified if it brings an overall gain in social welfare. But we may insist that the gain be proportionately great.[52]

We do not, in making such claims, forbid utilitarian policies. We allow that every gain in welfare has moral value. But we do restrain these policies. We insist that it also matters *who* gains. Certain distributions are, we claim, morally preferable. We thus claim that we ought to favour the worst off, and to incline towards equality.

[50] Cf. 'The difference between self and another is as plain as the difference between black and white' (L. T. Hobhouse, *The Metaphysical Theory of the State* (London: Allen & Unwin, 1918), 51).

[51] Someone might object: 'On the Complex View, we may claim that the parts of each life are less deeply unified; but we do not claim that there is more unity between lives. So the boundaries between lives are, on this view, just as deep.' We could answer: 'Not so. Take for comparison the fact of personhood. We may decide that to be a person, as opposed to a mere animal, is not in its nature a further fact, beyond the fact of having certain more specific properties, but that it just consists in this fact. This belief is not itself the belief that we are more like mere animals than we thought. But it still removes a believed difference. So it makes the boundaries between us and mere animals less deep. Similar remarks apply to the two views about personal identity.'

[52] These are examples of what both Sidgwick and Rawls would call 'the intuitionism of Common Sense'. I cannot here discuss Rawls's principles, or his 'contractual' argument. (I should point out that a contractual argument for the principles of justice seems to be in no way weakened by the Complex View. But alongside the contractual argument, Rawls suggests another: that these principles are required by the *plurality* of persons (cf. *A Theory of Justice*, 29). This is the argument which, however strong, seems to me less strong on the Complex View.)

Utilitarians would reply: 'These claims are of course plausible. But the policies they recommend are the very policies which tend to increase total welfare. This coincidence suggests[53] that we ought to change our view about the status of these claims. We should regard them, not as checks upon, but as guides to, utilitarian policy. We should indeed value equal distribution. But the value lies in its typical effects.'

This reply might be developed in the following way. Most of us believe that a mere difference in *when* something happens, if it does not affect the nature of what happens, cannot be morally significant. Certain answers to the question 'When?' are of course important. We cannot ignore the timing of events. And it is even plausible to claim that if, say, we are planning when to give or to receive benefits, we should aim for an equal distribution over time. But we aim for this only because of its effects. We do not believe that the equality of benefit at different times is, as such, morally important.

Utilitarians might say: 'If it does not, as such, matter *when* something happens, why does it matter *to whom* it happens? Both of these are mere differences in position. What is important is the nature of what happens. When we choose between social policies, we need only be concerned with how *great* the benefits will be. *Where* they come, whether in space, or in time, or as between people, has in itself no importance.'

Part of the disagreement is, then, this. Non-utilitarians take the question 'Who?' to be quite unlike the question 'When?' If they are asked for the simplest possible description of the morally relevant facts, they will sometimes give them in a form which is tenseless; but it will always be personal. They will say, 'Someone gains, the same person loses, someone else gains ...'. Utilitarians would instead say, 'A gain, a loss, another gain ...'.

There are many different arguments for and against these two positions. We are only asking: would a change to the Complex View tend to support either one?

It would seem so. On the Simple View, it is more plausible to insist upon the question 'Who?' On the Complex View, it is more plausible to compare this to the question 'When?', and to present the moral data in the second, or 'impersonal', form.[54]

---

[53] See, for instance, Sidgwick, *The Methods of Ethics*, 425 (or indeed pp. 199–457).

[54] I am here claiming that the Complex View tends to weaken distributive principles. What of the other possible effect, the change in scope? Might we demand fair shares for successive selves? *Perhaps*. (Cf. J. Findlay, *Values and Intentions* (London: Allen & Unwin, 1961), 239.) But the demand would, I think (and for various reasons), be rare. And the argument in the text only requires the following claim: the weakening of distributive principles would be more supported than the widening in their scope. The effects of the former would outweigh the effects

It may help to return to our comparison. Most of us believe that the existence of a nation does not involve anything more than the existence of associated people. We do not deny the reality of nations. But we do deny that they are separately, or independently, real. They are entirely composed of associated people.[55]

This belief seems to support certain moral claims. If there is nothing to a nation but its citizens, it is less plausible to regard the nation as itself a (primary) object of duties, or possessor of rights. It is more plausible to focus upon the citizens, and to regard them less as citizens, more as people. We may therefore, on this view, think a person's nationality less morally important.[56]

On the Complex View, we hold similar beliefs. We regard the existence of a person as, in turn, involving nothing more than the occurrence of interrelated mental and physical events. We do not, of course, deny the reality of people (our own reality!). And we agree that we are not, strictly. series of events—that we are not thoughts, but thinkers, not actions, but agents. But we consider this a fact of grammar. And we do deny that we are not just conceptually distinct from our bodies, actions, and experiences, but also separately real. We deny that the identity of a person, of the so-called 'subject' of mental and physical events, is a further, deep, fact, independent of the facts about the interrelations between these events.[57]

This belief may support similar claims. We may, when thinking morally, focus less upon the person, the subject of experience, and instead focus more upon the experiences themselves. Just as we often ignore whether people come from the same or different nations, so we may more often ignore whether experiences come within the same or different lives.

Take, for example, the relief of suffering. Suppose that we can only help one of two people. We shall achieve more if we help the first; but it is the second who, in the past, suffered more.

of the latter. As the limiting case, if we give distributive principles no weight, nothing follows from a change in their scope.

[55] This is ontological reductionism. It may not require the truth of analytical reductionism (or 'methodological individualism'). See, for instance, Strawson, *Individuals*, 201, Dummett, 'The Reality of the Past', *Proceedings of the Aristotelian Society*, 69 (1968–9), 242, and S. Kripke, 'Naming and Necessity', in D. Davidson and G. Harman (eds.), *Semantics of Natural Language* (Dordrecht: Reidel, 1972), 271. I have no space to pursue this point here.

[56] We could, of course, still claim that the fact of being associated-in-a-nation has supreme importance. But this claim, though possible, may still be less supported by this view. This it will be if the independent reality, which this view denies would have helped to support the claim.

[57] Someone might object: 'The comparison fails. The interrelations between citizens could in theory be described without mentioning nations. The interrelations between mental and physical events could *not* in theory be described without mentioning the "subject of experience".' This seems to me false. The difference is only one of practical convenience. (See Parfit, 'Personal Identity',) sect. III, for a very brief statement.) But even if the comparison *does* fail in this respect, it would still hold in the respects which are morally important.

Those who believe in fair shares may decide to help the second person. This will be less effective; so the amount of suffering in the two people's lives will, in sum, be greater; but the amounts in each life will be made more equal.

If we take the Complex View, we may reject this line of thought. We may decide to do the most we can to relieve suffering. To suggest why, we can vary the example. Suppose that we can only help one of two nations. Here again, the one that we can help most is the one whose history was, in earlier centuries, the more fortunate. Most of us would not believe that it could be right to allow mankind to suffer more, so that its suffering could be more equally divided between the histories of different nations.

On the Complex View, we compare the lives of people to the histories of nations. We may therefore think the same about them too. We may again decide to aim for the least possible suffering, whatever its distribution.[58]

X

We can next explain what, earlier, may have seemed puzzling. Besides the Complex View, which compares people to nations, I mentioned a reverse view, which compares nations to people. How can these be different?

It will help to introduce two more terms. With respect to many types of thing, we may take one of two views. We may believe that the existence of this type of thing does not involve anything more than the existence of certain other (interrelated) things. Such a view can be called 'atomistic'. We may instead believe that the things in question have a quite separate existence, over and above that of these other things. Such a view can be called 'holistic'.

One example of an atomistic view is the one we mostly take about nations. Most of us do not (here and now) believe that there is more to nations than associated people. On the other hand, we mostly do seem to assume that there is more to us than a series of mental and physical events. We incline to what I call the Simple View. Most of us are therefore atomists about nations, holists about people.

It is the difference between these common views which explains the two comparisons. The claim that X is like Y typically assumes the common

---

[58] Someone might object: 'This reasoning only applies to the demand for equal distribution as between entire lives. But we might make the demand in a form which ignores both the past and the future. We might value equal distribution as between people (or "successive selves") at any given time.' True. But this new demand seems, on reflection, implausible. Why the restriction to the *same* (given) time? How can simultaneity have intrinsic moral weight? (The new demand may, of course, have good effects. This is here irrelevant.)

view of *Y*. We shall therefore say 'People are like nations' if we are atomists about both. We shall instead say 'Nations are like people' if we are holists about both. Either way, we assume one of the common views and deny the other.[59]

We can end by considering a remark in Rawls. There is, he writes, 'a curious anomaly':[60] 'It is customary to think of utilitarianism as individualistic, and certainly there are good reasons for this. The utilitarians ... held that the good of society is constituted by the advantages enjoyed by individuals. Yet utilitarianism is not individualistic ... in that ... it applies to society the principle of choice for one man.'

Our account suggests an explanation. Individualists claim that the welfare of society only consists in the welfare of its members, and that the members have rights to fair shares.

Suppose that we are holists about society. We believe that the existence of society transcends that of its members. This belief threatens the first of the individualist claims. It supports the view that the welfare of society also transcends that of its members. This in turn threatens the second claim, for in the pursuit of a transcendent social goal, fair shares may seem less important. Social holists may thus reject both of the individualist claims.

Utilitarians reject the second claim, but accept the first. This would indeed be anomalous if their attitude to these claims rested upon social holism. If this were their ground, we should expect them to reject *both* claims.

We have sketched a different ground. Rather than being holists about society, utilitarians may be atomists about people. This dissolves the anomaly. For they are also atomists about society, and this double atomism seems to support the two positions Rawls describes. If we are atomists about society, we can then more plausibly accept the first of the individualist claims, viz. that the welfare of society only consists in that of its members.[61] If we are also atomists about people, we can then more plausibly reject the second claim, the demand for fair shares. We may tend to

[59] I am here forced (by lack of space) into gross over-simplification. There are many intermediate views. To give one example: if we are atomists about organisms, we shall find it easier to compare nations to organisms. For some of the complexities see Perry, *General Theory of Value*, 400 onwards and Hobhouse, *The Metaphysical Theory of the State*.

[60] Rawls, *A Theory of Justice*, 29.

[61] Cf.: 'As the public body is every individual collected, so the public good is the collected good of those individuals' (Thomas Paine, quoted in S. Lukes, *Individualism* (Oxford: Basil Blackwell, 1973), 49). Sidgwick remarks that while we commend 'one man dying for his country ... it would be absurd that all should: there would be no country to die for' (*The Ethics of Green, Spencer, and Martineau*, 79). We might still deny that 'the public good is merely a ... collection of private goods' on the ground that 'men desire for their own sake' irreducibly public goods (J. Plamenatz, *Man and Society*, ii (London: Longmans, 1963), 251). But this claim still appeals to personal desires.

focus less upon the person, the subject of experience, and instead focus more upon the experiences themselves. We may then decide that it is only the nature of what happens which is morally important, not to whom it happens. We may thus decide that it is always right to increase benefits and reduce burdens, whatever their distribution.[62]

'Utilitarianism', Rawls remarks, 'does not take seriously the distinction between persons.'[63] If 'the separateness of persons . . . is *the* basic fact for morals',[64] this is a grave charge. I have tried to show how one view about the nature of persons may provide *some* defence.[65]

---

[62] The Complex View seems also to support other utilitarian claims, such as that the welfare of a person just consists in the quality of his experiences, or (to give a variant) in the fulfillment of his various particular desires. Cf. the remark in R. P. Anschutz, *The Philosophy of J. S. Mill* (Oxford: Clarendon Press, 1953), 19–20, that 'Bentham's principle of individualism', unlike Mill's, 'is entirely transitional', since 'Bentham is saying that . . . as a community is reducible to the individuals who are said to be its members, so also are the individuals reducible, at least for the purposes of morals and legislation, to the pleasures and pains which they are said to suffer.'

[63] Rawls, *A Theory of Justice*, 27; cf. Nagel, *The Possibility of Altruism*, 134.

[64] Findlay, *Values and Intentions*, 393; cf. p. 294.

[65] I have not claimed that it could provide a sufficient defence.

IX

PERSONS, CHARACTER, AND MORALITY

BERNARD WILLIAMS

I

Much of the most interesting recent work in moral philosophy has been of basically Kantian inspiration; Rawls's own work[1] and those to varying degrees influenced by him such as Richards[2] and Nagel[3] are very evidently in the debt of Kant, while it is interesting that a writer such as Fried[4] who gives evident signs of being pulled away from some characteristic features of this way of looking at morality nevertheless, I shall suggest later, tends to get pulled back into it. This is not of course a very pure Kantianism, and still less is it an expository or subservient one. It differs from Kant among other things in making no demands on a theory of noumenal freedom, and also, importantly, in admitting considerations of a general empirical character in determining fundamental moral demands, which Kant at least supposed himself not to be doing. But allowing for those and many other important differences, the inspiration is there and the similarities both significant and acknowledged. They extend far beyond the evident point that both the extent and the nature of opposition to utilitarianism resembles Kant's: though it is interesting that in this respect they are more Kantian than a philosophy which bears an obvious but superficial formal resemblance to Kantianism, namely Hare's. Indeed, Hare now supposes that when a substantial moral theory is elicited from his philosophical premisses, it turns out to be a version of utilitarianism. This is not merely because the universal and prescriptive character of moral judgements lays on the agent, according to Hare, a requirement of hypothetical identification with each person affected by a given decision—so much is a purely

From Bernard Williams, *Moral Luck* (New York: Cambridge University Press, 1981), 1–19. Reprinted by permission of Cambridge University Press and the author.

[1] John Rawls, *A Theory of Justice* (Oxford: Oxford University Press, 1972).

[2] D. A. J. Richards, *A Theory of Reasons for Action* (Oxford: Oxford University Press, 1971).

[3] Thomas Nagel, *The Possibility of Altruism* (Oxford: Clarendon Press, 1970).

[4] Charles Fried, *An Anatomy of Values* (Cambridge, Mass.: Harvard University Press, 1970).

Kantian element. It is rather that each identification is treated just as yielding 'acceptance' or 'rejection' of a certain prescription, and they in turn are construed solely in terms of satisfactions, so that the outputs of the various identifications can, under the usual utilitarian assumptions, be regarded additively.

Among Kantian elements in these outlooks are, in particular, these: that the moral point of view is basically different from a non-moral, and in particular self-interested, point of view, and by a difference of kind; that the moral point of view is specially characterized by its impartiality and its indifference to any particular relations to particular persons, and that moral thought requires abstraction from particular circumstances and particular characteristics of the parties, including the agent, except in so far as these can be treated as universal features of any morally similar situation; and that the motivations of a moral agent, correspondingly, involve a rational application of impartial principle and are thus different in kind from the sorts of motivations that he might have for treating some particular persons (for instance, though not exclusively, himself) differently because he happened to have some particular interest towards them. Of course, it is not intended that these demands should exclude other and more intimate relations nor prevent someone from acting in ways demanded by and appropriate to them: that is a matter of the relations of the moral point of view to other points of view. But I think it is fair to say that included among the similarities of these views to Kant's is the point that like his they do not make the question of the relations between those points of view at all easy to answer. The deeply disparate character of moral and of non-moral motivation, together with the special dignity or supremacy attached to the moral, make it very difficult to assign to those other relations and motivations the significance or structural importance in life which some of them are capable of possessing.

It is worth remarking that this detachment of moral motivations and the moral point of view from the level of particular relations to particular persons, and more generally from the level of all motivations and perceptions other than those of an impartial character, obtains even when the moral point of view is itself explained in terms of the self-interest under conditions of ignorance of some abstractly conceived contracting parties, as it is by Rawls, and by Richards, who is particularly concerned with applying directly to the characterization of the moral interest, the structure used by Rawls chiefly to characterize social justice. For while the contracting parties are pictured as making some kind of self-interested or prudential choice of a set of rules, they are entirely abstract persons making this choice in ignorance of their own particular properties, tastes, and so forth;

and the self-interested choice of an abstract agent is intended to model precisely the moral choice of a concrete agent, by representing what he would choose granted that he made just the kinds of abstraction from his actual personality, situation, and relations which the Kantian picture of moral experience requires.

Some elements in this very general picture serve already to distinguish the outlook in question from utilitarianism. Choices made in deliberate abstraction from empirical information which actually exists are necessarily from a utilitarian point of view irrational, and to that extent the formal structure of the outlook, even allowing the admission of *general* empirical information, is counter-utilitarian. There is a further point of difference with utilitarianism, which comes out if one starts from the fact that there is one respect at least in which utilitarianism itself requires a notable abstraction in moral thought, an abstraction which in this respect goes even further than the Kantians': if Kantianism abstracts in moral thought from the identity of persons, utilitarianism strikingly abstracts from their separateness. This is true in more than one way. First, as the Kantian theorists have themselves emphasized, persons lose their separateness as beneficiaries of the utilitarian provisions, since in the form which maximizes total utility, and even in that which maximizes average utility, there is an agglomeration of satisfactions which is basically indifferent to the separateness of those who have the satisfactions; this is evidently so in the total maximization system, and it is only superficially not so in the average maximization system, where the agglomeration occurs before the division. Richards,[5] following Rawls, has suggested that the device of the ideal observer serves to model the agglomeration of these satisfactions: equivalent to the world could be one person, with an indefinite capacity for happiness and pain. The Kantian view stands opposed to this; the idea of the contractual element, even between these shadowy and abstract participants, is in part to make the point that there are limitations built in at the bottom to permissible trade-offs between the satisfactions of individuals.

A second aspect of the utilitarian abstraction from separateness involves agency.[6] It turns on the point that the basic bearer of value for utilitarianism is the *state of affairs*, and hence, when the relevant causal differences

---

[5] Richards, *A Theory of Reasons for Action*, 87 ff.; cf. Rawls, *A Theory of Justice*, 27; also Nagel, *The Possibility of Altruism*, 134. This is not the only, nor perhaps historically the soundest, interpretation of the device: cf. Derek Parfit, 'Later Selves and Moral Principles', in A. Montefiore (ed.), *Philosophy and Personal Relations* (London: Routledge & Kegan Paul, 1973), 149–50 and nn. 30–4 (Ch. VIII of this volume, pp. 143–69).

[6] For a more detailed account, see 'A Critique of Utilitarianism', in J. J. C. Smart and Bernard Williams, *Utilitarianism, For and Against* (Cambridge: Cambridge University Press, 1973).

have been allowed for, it cannot make any further difference who produces a given state of affairs: if *S*1 consists of my doing something, together with consequences, and *S*2 consists of someone else doing something, with consequences, and *S*2 comes about just in case *S*1 does not, and *S*1 is better than *S*2, then I should bring about *S*1, however prima facie nasty *S*1 is. Thus, unsurprisingly, the doctrine of negative responsibility has its roots at the foundation of utilitarianism; and whatever projects, desires, ideals, or whatever I may have as a particular individual, as a utilitarian agent my action has to be the output of *all* relevant causal items bearing on the situation, including all projects and desires within causal reach, my own and others. As a utilitarian agent, I am just the representative of the satisfaction system who happens to be near certain causal levers at a certain time. At this level, there is abstraction not merely from the identity of agents, but, once more, from their separateness, since a conceivable extension or restriction of the causal powers of a given agent could always replace the activities of some other agent, so far as utilitarian outcomes are concerned, and an outcome allocated to two agents as things are could equivalently be the product of one agent, or three, under a conceivable redistribution of causal powers.

In this latter respect also the Kantian outlook can be expected to disagree. For since we are concerned not just with outcomes, but at a basic level with actions and policies, *who* acts in a given situation makes a difference, and in particular I have a particular responsibility for *my* actions. Thus in more than one way the Kantian outlook emphasizes something like the separateness of agents, and in that sense makes less of an abstraction than utilitarianism does (though, as we have seen, there are other respects, with regard to causally relevant empirical facts, in which its abstraction is greater). But now the question arises, of whether the honourable instincts of Kantianism to defend the individuality of individuals against the agglomerative indifference of utilitarianism can in fact be effective granted the impoverished and abstract character of persons as moral agents which the Kantian view seems to impose. Findlay has said, 'the separateness of persons . . . is . . . the basic fact for morals',[7] and Richards hopes to have respected that fact.[8] Similarly Rawls claims that impartiality does not mean impersonality.[9] But it is a real question, whether the conception of the individual provided by the Kantian theories is in fact enough to yield what is wanted, even by the Kantians; let alone enough for others who, while equally rejecting utilitarianism, want to allow more room than

[7] Findlay, *Values and Intentions* (London: Allen & Unwin, 1961), 235–6.
[8] Richards, *A Theory of Reasons for Action*, 87.
[9] Rawls, *A Theory of Justice*, 190.

Kantianism can allow for the importance of individual character and personal relations in moral experience.

II

I am going to take up two aspects of this large subject. They both involve the idea that an individual person has a set of desires, concerns, or, as I shall often call them, projects, which help to constitute a *character*. The first issue concerns the connection between that fact and the man's having a reason for living at all. I approach this through a discussion of some work by Derek Parfit; though I touch on a variety of points in this, my overriding aim is to emphasize the basic importance for our thought of the ordinary idea of a self or person which undergoes changes of character, as opposed to an approach which, even if only metaphorically, would dissolve the person, under changes of character, into a series of 'selves'.

In this section I am concerned just with the point that each person has a character, not with the point that different people have different characters. That latter point comes more to the fore on the second issue, which I take up in Section III, and which concerns personal relations. Both issues suggest that the Kantian view contains an important misrepresentation.

First, then, I should like to comment on some arguments of Parfit which explore connections between moral issues and a certain view of personal identity: a view which, he thinks, might offer, among other things, '*some* defence'[10] of the utilitarian neglect of the separateness of persons. This view Parfit calls the 'Complex View'. This view takes seriously the idea that relations of psychological connectedness (such as memory and persistence of character and motivation) are what really matter with regard to most questions which have been discussed in relation to personal identity. The suggestion is that morality should take this seriously as well, and that there is more than one way of its doing so. Psychological connectedness (unlike the surface logic of personal identity) admits of degrees. Let us call the relevant properties and relations which admit of degrees, *scalar* items. One of Parfit's aims is to make moral thought reflect more directly the scalar character of phenomena which underlie personal identity. In particular, in those cases in which the scalar relations hold in reduced degree, this fact should receive recognition in moral thought.

Another, and more general, consequence of taking the Complex View is that the matter of personal identity may appear altogether less deep, as

---

[10] Parfit, 'Later Selves and Moral Principles', 160 (p. 169 of this volume). In what follows and elsewhere in this chapter I am grateful to Parfit for valuable criticisms of an earlier draft.

Parfit puts it, than if one takes the Simple View, as he calls that alternative view which sees as basically significant the all-or-nothing logic of personal identity. If the matter of personal identity appears less deep, the *separateness* of persons, also, may come to seem less an ultimate and specially significant consideration for morality. The connection between those two thoughts is not direct, but there is more than one indirect connection between them.[11]

So far as the problems of *agency* are concerned, Parfit's treatment is not going to help utilitarianism. His loosening of identity is diachronic, by reference to the weakening of psychological connectedness over time: where there is such weakening to a sufficient degree, he is prepared to speak of 'successive selves', though this is intended only as a *façon de parler*.[12] But the problems that face utilitarianism about agency can arise with any agent whose projects stretch over enough time, and are sufficiently grounded in character, to be in any substantial sense *his* projects, and that condition will be satisfied by something that is, for Parfit, even *one* self. Thus there is nothing in this degree of dissolution of the traditional self which can help over agency.

In discussing the issues involved in making moral thought reflect more directly the scalar nature of what underlies personal identity, it is important to keep in mind that the talk of 'past selves', 'future selves', and generally 'several selves' is only a convenient fiction. Neglect of this may make the transpositions in moral thought required by the Complex View seem simpler and perhaps more inviting than they are, since they may glide along on what seems to be a mere multiplication, in the case of these new 'selves', of familiar interpersonal relations. We must concentrate on the scalar facts. But many moral notions show a notable resistance to reflecting the scalar: or, rather, to reflecting it in the right way. We may take the case of promising, which Parfit has discussed.[13] Suppose that I promise to A that I will help him in certain ways in three years time. In three years time a person appears, let us say A*, whose memories, character, etc., bear some, but a rather low, degree of connectedness to A's. How am I to mirror these scalar facts in my thought about whether, or how, I am to carry out my promise?

Something, first, should be said about the promise itself. '*You*' was the expression it used: 'I will help *you*', and it used that expression in such a

[11] Parfit develops one such connection in the matter of distributive justice: ibid. 148 ff. (pp. 155 ff. of this volume). In general it can be said that one very natural correlate of being impressed by the separateness of several persons' lives is being impressed by the peculiar unity of one person's life.
[12] Ibid. n. 14.   [13] Ibid. 144 ff. (pp. 150 ff. of this volume).

way that it covered both the recipient of these words and the potential recipient of the help. This was not a promise that could be carried out (or, more generally, honoured) by helping anyone else, or indeed by doing anything except helping that person I addressed when I said 'you'—thus the situation is not like that with some promises to the dead (those where there is still something one can do about it).[14] If there is to be any action of mine which is to count as honouring that promise, it will have to be action which consists in now helping A^*. How am I to mirror, in my action and my thought about it, A^*'s scalar relations to A?

There seem to be only three ways in which they could be so mirrored, and none seems satisfactory. First, the action promised might itself have some significant scalar dimension, and it might be suggested that this should vary with my sense of the proximity or remoteness of A^* from A. But this will not do: it is clearly a lunatic idea that if I promised to pay A a sum of money, then my obligation is to pay A^* some money, but a smaller sum. A more serious suggestion would be that what varies with the degree of connectedness of A^* to A is the degree of stringency of the obligation to do what was promised. While less evidently dotty, it is still, on reflection, dotty; thus, to take a perhaps unfair example, it seems hard to believe that if someone had promised to marry A, they would have an obligation to marry A^*, only an obligation which came lower down the queue.

What, in contrast, is an entirely familiar sort of thought is, last of all, one that embodies degrees of doubt or obscurity whether a given obligation (of fixed stringency) applies or not. Thus a secret agent might think that he was obliged to kill the man in front of him if and only if that man was Martin Bormann; and be in doubt whether he should kill this man, because he was in doubt whether it was Bormann. (Contrast the two analogously dotty types of solution to this case: that, at any rate, he is obliged to wound him; or, that he is obliged to kill him, but it has a lower priority than it would have otherwise.) But this type of thought is familiar at the cost of not really embodying the scalar facts; it is a style of thought appropriate to uncertainty about a matter of all-or-nothing and so embodies in effect what Parfit calls the Simple View, that which does not take seriously the scalar facts to which the Complex View addresses itself.

These considerations do not, of course show that there are no ways of mirroring the Complex View in these areas of moral thought, but they do suggest that the displacements required are fairly radical. It is significant that by far the easiest place in which to find the influence of the scalar considerations is in certain *sentiments*, which themselves have a scalar

---

[14] Parfit, 'Later Selves and Moral Principles', 144 *ad fin.* (pp. 150 *ad fin* of this volume).

dimension—here we can see a place where the Complex View and utilitarianism easily fit together. But the structure of such sentiments is not adequate to produce the structure of all moral thought. The rest of it will have to be more radically adapted, or abandoned, if the Complex View is really to have its effect.

One vitally important item which is in part (though only in part) scalar is a man's concern for (what common sense would call) his own future. That a man should have some interest now in what he will do or undergo later, requires that he have some desires or projects or concerns now which relate to those doings or happenings later; or, as a special case of that, that some very general desire or project or concern of his now relate to desires or projects which he will have then. The limiting case, at the basic physical level, is that in which he is merely concerned with future pain, and it may be that that concern can properly reach through any degree of psychological discontinuity.[15] But even if so, it is not our present concern, since the mere desire to avoid physical pain is not adequate to constitute a character. We are here concerned with more distinctive and structured patterns of desire and project, and there are possible psychological changes in these which could be predicted for a person and which would put his future after such changes beyond his present interest. Such a future would be, so to speak, over the horizon of his interest, though of course if the future picture could be filled in as a *series* of changes leading from here to there, he might recapture an interest in the outcome.

In this connection, to take the language of 'future selves' at all literally would be deeply misleading: it would be to take the same facts twice over. My concern for my descendants or other relatives may be, as Parfit says, to some degree proportional to their remoteness from me; equally, my concern for other persons in general can vary with the degree to which their character is congenial to my own, their projects sympathetic to my outlook. The two considerations, of proximity and congeniality, evidently interact—ways in which they can reinforce or cancel one another are, for instance, among the commonplaces of dynastic fiction. But the proximity of Parfitian 'later selves' to me, their ancestor, just consists of the relations of their character and interests to my present ones. I cannot first identify a later self 'descendant', and then consider the relations of his character to mine, since it is just the presence or lack of these relations which in good part determines his proximity and even his existence as a separate self.

---

[15] Cf. my 'The Self and the Future', in *Problems of the Self* (Cambridge: Cambridge University Press, 1973).

Thus if I take steps now to hinder what will or may predictably be my future projects, as in Parfit's Russian nobleman case,[16] it would be a case of double vision to see this as my treating my future self as another person, since, spelled out, that would have to mean, treating my future self as another person *of whose projects I disapprove*; and therein lies the double vision. To insist here that what I would be doing is to hinder *my own* future projects (where it is understood that that is not necessarily a foolish thing to do) is to keep hold on a number of deeply important facts. One is that to contemplate, or expect, or regard as probable, such changes in my own character is different from my relation to them in someone else (still more, of course, from my attitude to the mere *arrival* of someone else with a different character). The question must arise, how prediction is, in my own case, related to acquiescence, and special and obscure issues arise about the range of methods that it could be appropriate or rational for a man to use to prevent or deflect predicted changes in his own character. Thought about those issues must take as basic the *he* for whom these changes would be changes in *his* character.

Relatedly, there is the question of why I should regard my present projects and outlook as having more authority than my future ones. I do *not* mean by that the question, why I should not distribute consideration equally over my whole life: I shall later touch on the point that it is a mistake of Kantians (and perhaps of some kinds of utilitarians too) to think it a priori evident that one rationally should do that. I mean rather the question of how, in the supposed type of example, I evaluate the two successive outlooks. Why should I hinder my future projects from the perspective of my present values rather than inhibit my present projects from the perspective of my future values? It is not enough in answer to that to say that evidently present action must flow from present values. If the future prospect were of something now identified as a growth in enlightenment, present action would try to hinder present projects in its interest. For that to be so, there indeed would have to be now some dissatisfaction with one's present values, but that consideration just turns attention, in the Russian nobleman case, to the corresponding question, of why the young man is so unquestioningly satisfied with his present values. He may have, for instance, a theory of degeneration of the middle-aged, but then he should reflect that, when middle-aged, he will have a theory of the naïvety of the young.

I am not saying that there are no answers to any of these questions, or that there is no way out of this kind of diachronic relativism. The point is

---

[16] Parfit, 'Later Selves and Moral Principles', 145 ff. (pp. 151 ff. of this volume).

that if it is true that this man will change in these ways, it is only by understanding his present projects *as the projects of one who will so change* that he can understand them even as his present projects; and if he knows that he will so change, then it is only through such an understanding that he could justifiably give his present values enough authority to defeat his future values, as he clear-headedly conceives them to be. If he clear-headedly knows that his present projects are solely the projects of his youth, how does he know that they are not *merely* that, unless he has some view which makes sense of, among other things, his own future? One cannot even start on the important questions of how this man, so totally identified with his present values, will be related to his future without them, if one does not take as basic the fact that it is his own future that he will be living through without them.

This leads to the question of why we go on at all.

It might be wondered why, unless we believe in a possibly hostile after-life, or else are in a muddle which the Epicureans claimed to expose, we should regard death as an evil.[17] One answer to that is that we desire certain things; if one desires something, then to that extent one has reason to resist the happening of anything which prevents one getting it, and death certainly does that, for a large range of desires. Some desires are admittedly contingent on the prospect of one's being alive, but not all desires can be in that sense conditional, since it is possible to imagine a person rationally contemplating suicide, in the face of some predicted evil, and if he decides to go on in life, then he is propelled forward into it by some desire (however general or inchoate) which cannot operate conditionally on his being alive, since it settles the question of whether he is going to be alive. Such a desire we may call a categorical desire. Most people have many categorical desires, which do not depend on the assumption of the person's existence, since they serve to prevent that assumption's being questioned, or to answer the question if it is raised. Thus one's pattern of interests, desires, and projects not only provide the reason for an interest in what happens within the horizon of one's future, but also constitute the conditions of there being such a future at all.

Here, once more, to deal in terms of later selves who were like descendants would be to misplace the heart of the problem. Whether to commit suicide, and whether to leave descendants, are two separate decisions: one can produce children before committing suicide. A person might even choose deliberately to do that, for comprehensible sorts of reasons; or again one could be deterred, as by the thought that one would not be there

---

[17] The argument is developed in more detail in Williams, *Problems of the Self*, 82 ff.

to look after them. Later selves, however, evade all these thoughts by having the strange property that while they come into existence only with the death of their ancestor, the physical death of their ancestor will abort them entirely. The analogy seems unhelpfully strained, when we are forced to the conclusion that the failure of all my projects, and my consequent suicide, would take with me all my 'descendants', although they are in any case a kind of descendants who arise only with my ceasing to exist. More than unhelpfully, it runs together what are two quite different questions: whether, my projects having failed, I should cease to exist, and whether I shall have descendants whose projects may be quite different from mine and are in any case largely unknown. The analogy makes every question of the first kind involve a question of the second kind, and thus obscures the peculiar significance of the first question to the theory of the self. If, on the other hand, a man's future self is not another self, but the future of his self, then it is unproblematic why it should be eliminated with the failure of that which might propel him into it. The primacy of one's ordinary self is given, once more, by the thought that it is precisely what will not be in the world if one commits suicide.

The language of 'later selves', too literally taken, could exaggerate in one direction the degree to which my relation to some of my own projects resembles my relation to the projects of others. The Kantian emphasis on moral impartiality exaggerates it in quite another, by providing ultimately too slim a sense in which any projects are mine at all. This point once more involves the idea that my present projects are the condition of my existence,[18] in the sense that unless I am propelled forward by the conatus of desire, project, and interest, it is unclear why I should go on at all: the world, certainly, as a kingdom of moral agents, has no particular claim on my presence or, indeed, interest in it. (That kingdom, like others, has to respect the natural right to emigration.) Now the categorical desires which propel one on do not have to be even every evident to consciousness, let alone grand or large; one good testimony to one's existence having a point is that the question of its point does not arise, and the propelling concerns may be of a relatively everyday kind such as certainly provide the ground of many sorts of happiness. Equally, while these projects may present *some* conflicts with the demands of morality, as Kantianly conceived, these conflicts may be fairly minor; after all—and I do not want to deny or forget

---

[18] We can note the consequence that present projects are the condition of future ones. This view stands in opposition to Nagel's, as do the formulations used above. But while, as Nagel says, taking a rational interest in preparing for the realization of my later projects does not require that they be my present projects, it seems nevertheless true that it presupposes my having some present projects which directly or indirectly reach out to a time when those later projects will be my projects.

it—these projects, in a normally socialized individual, have in good part been formed within, and formed by, dispositions which constitute a commitment to morality. But, on the other hand, the possibility of radical conflict is also there. A man many have, for a lot of his life or even just for some part of it, a *ground* project or set of projects which are closely related to his existence and which to a significant degree give a meaning to his life.

I do not mean by that they provide him with a life-plan, in Rawls's sense. On the contrary, Rawls's conception, and the conception of practical rationality, shared by Nagel, which goes with it, seems to me rather to imply an external view of one's own life, as something like a given rectangle that has to be optimally filled in.[19] This perspective omits the vital consideration already mentioned, that the continuation and size of this rectangle is up to me; so, slightly less drastically, is the question of how much of it I care to cultivate. The correct perspective on one's life is *from now*. The consequences of that for practical reasoning (particularly with regard to the relevance of proximity or remoteness in time of one's objective), is a large question which cannot be pursued here; here we need only the idea of a man's ground projects providing the motive force which propels him into the future, and gives him a reason for living.

For a project to play this ground role, it does not have to be true that if it were frustrated or in any of various ways he lost it, he would have to commit suicide, nor does he have to think that. Other things, or the mere hope of other things, may keep him going. But he may feel in those circumstances that he might as well have died. Of course, in general a man does not have one separable project which plays this ground role: rather, there is a nexus of projects, related to his conditions of life, and it would be the loss of all or most of them that would remove meaning.

Ground projects do not have to be selfish, in the sense that they are just concerned with things for the agent. Nor do they have to be self-centred, in the sense that the creative projects of a Romantic artist could be considered self-centred (where it has to be *him*, but not *for* him). They may certainly be altruistic, and in a very evident sense moral, projects; thus he may be working for reform, or justice, or general improvement. There is no contradiction in the idea of a man's dying for a ground project—quite the

---

[19] It is of course a separate question what the criteria of optimality are, but it is not surprising that a view which presupposes that no risks are taken with the useful area of the rectangle should also favour a very low risk strategy in filling it: cf. Rawls (on prudential rationality in general), *A Theory of Justice*, 422: 'we have the guiding principle that a rational individual is always to act so that he need never blame himself no matter how things finally transpire'. Cf. also the passages cited in Rawls's footnote. For more on this and the relations of ground projects to rationality, see Williams, *Moral Luck*, ch. 2.

reverse, since if death really is necessary for the project, then to live would be to live with it unsatisfied, something which, if it really is his ground project, he has no reason to do.

That a man's projects were altruistic or moral would not make them immune to conflict with impartial morality, any more than the artist's projects are immune. Admittedly *some* conflicts are ruled out by the projects sincerely being *those* projects; thus a man devoted to the cause of curing injustice in a certain place, cannot just insist on his plan for doing that over others', if convinced that theirs will be as effective as his (something it may be hard to convince him of). For if he does insist on that, then we learn that his concern is not merely that injustice be removed, but that *he* remove it—not necessarily a dishonourable concern, but a different one. Thus some conflicts are ruled out by the project being not self-centred. But not all conflicts: thus his selfless concern for justice may do havoc to quite other commitments.

A man who has such a ground project will be required by utilitarianism to give up what it requires in a given case just if that conflicts with what he is required to do as an impersonal utility-maximizer when all the causally relevant considerations are in. That is a quite absurd requirement.[20] But the Kantian, who can do rather better than that, still cannot do well enough. For impartial morality, if the conflict really does arise, must be required to win; and that cannot necessarily be a reasonable demand on the agent. There can come a point at which it is quite unreasonable for a man to give up, in the name of the impartial good ordering of the world of moral agents, something which is a condition of his having any interest in being around in that world at all. Once one thinks about what is involved in having a character, one can see that the Kantians' omission of character is a condition of their ultimate insistence on the demands of impartial morality, just as it is a reason for finding inadequate their account of the individual.

III

All this argument depends on the idea of one person's having a character, in the sense of having projects and categorical desires with which that person is identified; nothing has yet been said about different persons having different characters. It is perhaps important, in order to avoid misunderstanding, to make clear a way in which difference of character

---

[20] Cf. my 'A Critique of Utilitarianism', sects. 3–5.

does *not* come into the previous argument. It does not come in by way of the man's thinking that only if he affirms these projects will they be affirmed, while (by contrast) the aims of Kantian morality can be affirmed by anyone. Though that thought could be present in some cases, it is not the point of the argument. The man is not pictured as thinking that he will have earned his place in the world, if his project is affirmed: that a distinctive contribution to the world will have been made, if his distinctive project is carried forward. The point is that he wants these things, finds his life bound up with them, and that they propel him forward, and thus they give him a reason for living his life. But that is compatible with these drives, and this life, being much like others'. They give him, distinctively, a reason for living this life, in the sense that he has no desire to give up and make room for others, but they do not require him to lead a *distinctive* life. While this is so, and the point has some importance, nevertheless the interest and substance of most of the discussion depends on its in fact being the case that people have dissimilar characters and projects. Our *general* view of these matters, and the significance given to individuality in our own and others' lives, would certainly change if there were not between persons indefinitely many differences which are important to us. The level of description is of course also vital for determining what is the same or different. A similar description can be given of two people's dispositions, but the concrete detail be perceived very differently—and it is a feature of our experience of persons that we can perceive and be conscious of an indefinitely fine degree of difference in concrete detail (though it is only in certain connections and certain cultures that one spends much time rehearsing it).

One area in which *difference* of character directly plays a role in the concept of moral individuality is that of personal relations, and I shall close with some remarks in this connection. Differences of character give substance to the idea that individuals are not intersubstituable. As I have just argued, a particular man so long as he is propelled forward does not need to assure himself that he is unlike others, in order not to feel substitutable, but in his personal relations to others the idea of difference can certainly make a contribution, in more than one way. To the thought that his friend cannot just be equivalently replaced by another friend, is added both the thought that he cannot just be replaced himself, and also the thought that he and his friend are different from each other. This last thought is important to us as part of our view of friendship, a view thus set apart from Aristotle's opinion that a good man's friend was a duplication of himself. This I suspect to have been an Aristotelian, and not generally a Greek, opinion. It is connected with another feature of his views which seems even stranger to us, at least with regard to any deeply committed friendship, namely that friendship for him has to be minimally *risky*—one of his problems is indeed to reconcile the role of friendship with his unappetizing ideal of self-sufficiency. Once one agrees that a three-dimensional mirror would not represent the ideal of friendship, one can begin to see both how some degree of difference can play an essential role, and, also, how a commitment or involvement with a particular other person might be one of the kinds of project which figured basically in a man's life in the ways already sketched—something which would be mysterious or even sinister on an Aristotelian account.

For Kantians, personal relations at least presuppose moral relations, and some are rather disposed to go further and regard them as a *species* of moral relations, as in the richly moralistic account given by Richards[21] of one of the four main principles of supererogation which would be accepted in 'the original position' (that is to say, adopted as a moral limitation): 'a principle of mutual love requiring that people should not show personal affection and love to others on the basis of arbitrary physical characteristics alone, but rather on the basis of traits of personality and character related to acting on moral principles'. This righteous absurdity is no doubt to be traced to a feeling that love, even love based on 'arbitrary physical characteristics', is something which has enough power and even authority to conflict badly with morality unless it can be brought within it from the beginning, and evidently that is a sound feeling, though it is an optimistic Kantian who thinks that much will be done about that by the adoption of this principle in the original position. The weaker view, that love and similar relations presuppose moral relations, in the sense that one could love someone only if one also had to them the moral relations one has to all people, is less absurd, but also wrong. It is of course true that loving someone involves some relations of the kind that morality requires or imports more generally, but it does not follow from that that one cannot have them in a particular case unless one has them generally in the way the moral person does. Someone might be concerned about the interests of someone else, and even about carrying out promises he made to that person, while not very concerned about these things with other persons. To the extent (whatever it may be) that loving someone involves showing some of the same concerns in relation to them that the moral person shows, or at least thinks he ought to show, elsewhere, the lover's relations will be examples of moral relations, or at least resemble them, but this does not have to be because they are *applications to this case* of relations which

[21] Richards, *A Theory of Reasons for Action*, 94.

the lover, *qua* moral person, more generally enters into. (That might not be the best description of the situation even if he *is* a moral person who enters into such relations more generally.)

However, once morality is there, and also personal relations to be taken seriously, so is the possibility of conflict. This of course does not mean that if there is some friendship with which his life is much involved, then a man must prefer any possible demand of that over other, impartial, moral demands. That would be absurd, and also a pathological kind of friendship, since both parties exist in the world and it is part of the sense of their friendship that it exists in the world. But the possibility of conflict with substantial moral claims of others is there, and it is not only in the outcome. There can also be conflict with moral demands on how the outcome is arrived at: the situation may not have been subjected to an impartial process of resolution, and this fact itself may cause unease to the impartial moral consciousness. There is an example of such unease in a passage by Fried. After an illuminating discussion of the question why, if at all, we should give priority of resources to actual and present sufferers over absent or future ones, he writes:[22]

surely it would be absurd to insist that if a man could, at no risk or cost to himself, save one or two persons in equal peril, and one of those in peril was, say, his wife, he must treat both equally, perhaps by flipping a coin. One answer is that where the potential rescuer occupies no office such as that of captain of a ship, public health official or the like, the occurrence of the accident may itself stand as a sufficient randomizing event to meet the dictates of fairness, so he may prefer his friend, or loved one. Where the rescuer does occupy an official position, the argument that he must overlook personal ties is not unacceptable.

The most striking feature of this passage is the direction in which Fried implicitly places the onus of proof: the fact that coin-flipping would be inappropriate raises some question to which an 'answer' is required, while the resolution of the question by the rescuer's occupying an official position is met with what sounds like relief (though it remains unclear what that rescuer does when he 'overlooks personal ties'—does *he* flip a coin?). The thought here seems to be that it is unfair to the second victim that, the first being the rescuer's wife, they never even get a chance of being rescued; and the answer (as I read the reference to the 'sufficient randomizing event') is that at another level it is sufficiently fair—although in this disaster this rescuer has a special reason for saving the other person, it might have been another disaster in which another rescuer had a special reason

---

[22] Fried, *An Anatomy of Values*, 227. Fried has perhaps now modified the view criticized here. He has himself used the idea of friendship as creating special moral relations, but in a connection where, it seems to me, it is out of place: for criticism, see Williams, *Moral Luck*, ch. 4.

for saving them. But, apart from anything else, that 'might have been' is far too slim to sustain a reintroduction of the notion of fairness. The 'random' element in such events, as in certain events of tragedy, should be seen not so much as affording a justification, in terms of an appropriate application of a lottery, as being a reminder that some situations lie beyond justifications.

But has anything yet shown that? For even if we leave behind thoughts of higher-order randomization, surely *this* is a justification on behalf of the rescuer, that the person he chose to rescue was his wife? It depends on how much weight is carried by 'justification': the consideration that it was his wife is certainly, for instance, an explanation which should silence comment. But something more ambitious than this is usually intended, essentially involving the idea that moral principle can legitimate his preference, yielding the conclusion that in situations of this kind it is at least all right (morally permissible) to save one's wife. (This could be combined with a variety of higher-order thoughts to give it a rationale; rule-utilitarians might favour the idea that in matters of this kind it is best for each to look after his own, like house insurance.) But this construction provides the agent with one thought too many: it might have been hoped by some (for instance, by his wife) that his motivating thought, fully spelled out, would be the thought that it was his wife, not that it was his wife and that in situations of this kind it is permissible to save one's wife.

Perhaps others will have other feelings about this case. But the point is that somewhere (and if not in this case, where?) one reaches the necessity that such things as deep attachments to other persons will express themselves in the world in ways which cannot at the same time embody the impartial view, and that they also run the risk of offending against it.

They run that risk if they exist at all; yet unless such things exist, there will not be enough substance or conviction in a man's life to compel his allegiance to life itself. Life has to have substance if anything is to have sense, including adherence to the impartial system; but if it has substance, then it cannot grant supreme importance to the impartial system, and that system's hold on it will be, at the limit, insecure.

It follows that moral philosophy's habit, particularly in its Kantian forms, of treating persons in abstraction from character is not so much a legitimate device for dealing with one aspect of thought, but is rather a misrepresentation, since it leaves out what both limits and helps to define that aspect of thought. Nor can it be judged solely as a theoretical device: this is one of the areas in which one's conception of the self, and of oneself, most importantly meet.

X

QUANDARY ETHICS

EDMUND PINCOFFS

Ethics is everybody's concern.... Everyone ... is faced with moral problems—problems about which, after more or less reflection, a decision must be reached.

(S. E. Toulmin)

I ask the reader to start by supposing that someone (himself perhaps) is faced with a serious moral problem.

(R. M. Hare)

What is ethical theory about? Someone might propose as an answer: 'Everyone knows what an ethical problem is; ethical theory must be about the solutions to such problems.... But do we really know precisely what an 'ethical problem' is?

(R. M. Brandt)

My ultimate aim is to determine ... how moral judgments can rationally be supported, how moral perplexities can be resolved, and how moral disputes can rationally be settled.

(M. G. Singer)

Only when he has linked these parts together in well-tempered harmony and has made himself one man instead of many, will he be ready to go about whatever he may have to do, whether it be making money and satisfying bodily wants, or business transactions, or the affairs of state. In all these fields when he speaks of just and honourable conduct, he will mean the behaviour that helps to produce and preserve this habit of mind.... Any action which tends to break down this habit will be unjust; and the notions governing it he will call ignorance and folly.

(Plato)

There is a consensus concerning the subject-matter of ethics so general that it would be tedious to document it. It is that the business of ethics is with 'problems', i.e. situations in which it is difficult to know what one should do; that the ultimate beneficiary of ethical analysis is the person

From *Mind*, 80 (1971), 552–71 by permission of Oxford University Press.

who, in one of these situations seeks rational ground for the decision he must make; that ethics is therefore primarily concerned to find such grounds, often conceived of as moral rules and the principles from which they can be derived; and that meta-ethics consists in the analysis of the terms, claims, and arguments which come into play in moral disputation, deliberation, and justification in problematic contexts. It is my purpose in this paper to raise some questions about this conception of ethics, which I shall refer to, for convenience and disparagement, as Quandary Ethics.

I

Before proceeding to more philosophical matters it may be well to attend to rhetorical ones: to present considerations which might at least cause the reader to hesitate before replying. 'Of course ethics is concerned to resolve problems on rational grounds! With what else would it be concerned? To abandon the search for rationally defensible rules and principles is to abandon moral philosophy', etc.

The first and most obvious rhetorical point is that Quandary Ethics is a newcomer: that the quandarist is fighting a very long tradition with which he is at odds. Plato, Aristotle, the Epicureans, the Stoics, Augustine, Aquinas, Shaftesbury, Hume, and Hegel do not conceive of ethics as the quandarists do. If they are read for their 'theories', that is, for the grounds they give for making particular difficult moral decisions, their teachings are inevitably distorted. To give such grounds, such justifications of particular difficult choices, was not their objective. They were, by and large, not so much concerned with problematic situations as with moral enlightenment, education, and the good for man. Again, the shift in emphasis is too patent to require documentation, but we may illustrate the point by means of a brief glance at the ethics of Aristotle.

He, as is well known, thought of ethics as a branch of politics, which in turn he thought of as a very wide-ranging subject having to do generally with the planning of human life so that it could be lived as well as possible. In the *Politics* the question concerns the best political arrangements, and a large and important preliminary is the comparative study of constitutions so that one will know what kind of arrangements there are, with their advantages and disadvantages, so that a choice may be made. Similarly in ethics the leading question concerns the best kind of individual life, and the qualities of character exhibited by the man who leads it. And again, a necessary preliminary is the study of types of men, of characters, as possible exemplars of the sort of life to be pursued or avoided. This study occupies a large part of the *Nicomachean Ethics*. Moral problems are given their due but are by no means stage-centre. The question is not so much how we should resolve perplexities as how we should live. Both the 'we' and the 'perplexity' or 'quandary' must be carefully qualified. The 'we' in question is not a mere placeholder, but refers to those of us who were well brought up, who have had some experience of life, who know something of the way in which the social order operates, who have some control over the direction of our lives in that we are capable of living according to a pattern and are not washed about by emotional tides or pulled hither and yon by capricious whim. So that if Aristotle is presented with a moral quandary he has a right to presuppose a great deal concerning the upbringing, knowledge, and self-control of the persons concerned. But the notion of presenting Aristotle with a quandary is not really clear if looked at through our spectacles. The kind of problems Aristotle's qualified agents typically have concern not so much what is to be done by anyone, qualified or not, in certain sorts of circumstances, as how not to fall into the traps which seize the unwary and convert them into one or another kind of undesirable character. When Aristotle discusses moral deliberation it is not so much in the interest of finding grounds for the solution of puzzles as of determining when we may assign responsibility, not when deliberation was impossible, or of determining what it is that sets off practical from scientific reasoning.

But if Aristotle does not present us with quandaries into which the individual may fall, and which he must puzzle and pry his way out of, this may be just because Aristotle does not value the qualities that allow or require a man to become bogged down in a marsh of indecision. There is, after all, the question when we should and should not be involved in perplexities, when to avoid, as we often should, the *occasion* of perplexity. Men can be perplexed because they are sensitive and conscientious people; because they to not have the sense to avoid perplexity; or because they are pathologically immobilized by moral questions. A well-founded ethics would encourage the development of moral sensitivity, but discourage the entertainment of moral quandaries which arise out of moral ineptness or pathological fixation. The quandarists do not insist upon these distinctions, yet they are as important and obvious as the distinction between preventive and curative medicine. That the moral philosopher can be thought of as prescribing a regimen for a healthy moral life rather than a cure for particular moral illnesses would surely not be news to Aristotle.

The second rhetorical point to be made is that even though there may be philosophers who have thought through their reasons for accepting the present posture of ethics, very little argument can be found in defence of it. In fact it rests, so far as I can tell, on unexamined assumptions which are perpetuated more by scholarly convention than by reasoned agreement. This posture, it may be well to emphasize, is not that of the casuist but one in which the ultimate objective of ethics is conceived to be the resolution of quandaries. It may be felt indeed that the nature of the times dictates what ethics must be, and that therefore no critical examination of the role of ethics is in order. It may be believed that the era in which we live, beset by problems if men ever were, somehow militates in itself against any form of ethics but a problem-oriented one; that in this respect our time differs from all previous less problem-plagued ones; that these problems are loosed upon us by technological and social change; and that since change is so rapid and unpredictable the best we can do for ourselves is to learn how to make decisions as they come along, discover the form of a good decision; and the best we can do for our children is to teach them how to go about making decisions in the tight places into which they are sure to be crowded. This means that the tools for decision-making must be put into their hands: the very general, and quite empty, principles from which rules appropriate to the occasion, whatever it is, may be derived. It may be felt, also, that the kaleidoscopic character of the times rules out an ethics focused, as in most of the long tradition, on qualities of character and their developments, since the inculcation of traits presupposes precisely the social stability which we do not have, because if we cannot count on social stability we cannot know what character traits will be appropriate to the times in which our children will live.

This argument, which I have heard but not read, fails for two reasons, either of which is conclusive. The first is that it rests on a premiss which is historically false. Character Ethics has flourished in times of change comparable in their kaleidoscopic quality to our own. The Stoic ethic was taught and practised over 500 years, during which there were periods of violent change in the ancient world. These changes were often of such scope as to make individual citizens uncertain what kind of world their children were likely to inhabit. Athens, the original home of the movement, fluttered about in the surgings and wanings of empires, now moving forward with a democratic form of government now languishing under tyrants supported by armies of occupation. The form that Stoicism took in Rome during the early empire, with its emphasis on the individual's control of his own soul no matter what the external circumstances might be like, is ample testimony to the insecurity even of the privileged classes in a time of tyranny and corruption.

The second reason is that the argument, even if it were sound, would militate as effectively against Quandary Ethics as against Character Ethics.

Quandary Ethics must, according to the argument, provide some stable means of arriving at decisions, no matter how circumstances may change. This is usually interpreted as requiring that rules and principles (or anyway 'good reasons') of universal application should be provided. But it is not at all clear why rules and principles will transcend change when qualities of character will not. If there are principles which would seem to apply in any conceivable world, why should there not be qualities of character equally universal in scope? If there are character traits of narrower application, then there are principles which would be applicable in some circumstances but not in others. Indeed it would be hard to imagine a world in which we should not make it a principle not to do to others what we would not want them to do to us; but it would be equally hard to imagine a world in which the quality of justice was without relevance. If there could be a world in which there was no place for justice, might there not also be a world in which there was no place for the Silver Rule? The argument works not so much to demonstrate the advantages of principles and rules in an uncertain world as to point up the limits of any form of moral education in times of change.

The rhetorical points, then, are that Quandary Ethics diverges from the main lines of discussion followed through most of the history of ethics; and that there seems to be little offered in justification of this change of orientation, and that little not convincing. Of course, it may well be that there are excellent reasons why ethics should now be focused on disputation, deliberation, and justification to the exclusion of questions of moral character. At best, the rhetorical arguments can challenge the defender of the contemporary trend to produce those reasons.

II

But there are philosophical questions as well, questions which at least have the advantage that they point up some of the presuppositions of Quandary Ethics, and at most reveal that indefensible distortions of ethics result from the contemporary fixation on problems and their resolution. Quandary Ethics, remember, supposes that the ultimate relevance of ethics is to the resolution of the problematic situations into which we fall. The problems in question are, of course, practical and not philosophical. Moral philosophers, like other philosophers, must deal with philosophical quandaries; and these are not escaped, although they may be emphasized or de-emphasized, by changing the focus of ethics. For example, questions about the logical status of 'moral assertions' will present as much of a problem for the non-quandarist as for the quandarist. But the assertions in question are as likely to be about ideal standards as about the duties and obligations that are incumbent upon everyone.

The questions I want to raise are: What is a problematic situation? and Who are 'we' who find ourselves in these situations? But discussion of these questions will require that I rehearse briefly some time-honoured distinctions.

The quandarist typically thinks of the problem-question as: What is the right thing to do? or What would be a good thing to do? or What ought I to do? But these questions are, as is recognized, ambiguous at least in the sense that they fail to distinguish between queries concerning what is the morally *correct* (rule-required, expected, proper, appropriate, fitting) thing to do; and queries concerning the morally *useful* (fruitful, helpful, practical, optimum) thing to do. The questions concerning the rightness, goodness, and oughtness can be questions about correctness, or usefulness, or both. The discussion of these questions is likely to be informed by general theories concerning correctness and usefulness: in particular the theory that the correct thing to do is the thing that it would be correct for any person in similar circumstances to do, and the theory that the useful thing to do is the thing that will, directly or indirectly, increase the happiness and decrease the misery of everyone concerned as much as possible.

Now if we ask the quandarist what a moral problem is, and who 'we' are, who are enmeshed in the problem, certain difficulties arise for the quandarist conception of ethics. The quandarist might hold that a moral problem concerns what it is correct, or what it is useful to do, or both. Whether he holds that correctness entails usefulness or vice versa need not concern us. Let us consider the correctness-question, through examination of a typical quandary.

I have made a promise, one of these promises encountered so frequently in the literature and so infrequently in life. It is to meet a friend to attend a concert. That is to say, I have solemnly averred, using the words, 'I promise', that this time I will not disappoint him, as I did the last time; and that I will indeed be on hand at eight at the theatre. Meantime (back at the ranch) a neighbour calls to remind me of my agreement to attend an eight o'clock school board meeting to argue that a proposed desegregation plan is inadequate. What is the correct thing to do? How shall I decide? What is and is not relevant in my deliberations? Roughly: what is supposedly relevant is the agreements I have made; and what is supposedly not relevant is any personal wants or desires or characteristics I may have. The question is whether a promise of this and this sort may be violated so that I may keep an agreement of that and that sort: whether anyone should violate the promise to keep the agreement whether there is an exception to the rule that one should keep promises, or another more stringent rule which would justify my keeping the agreement and not the promise.

The analogy with the law is never far beneath the surface. A case in which I must decide whether or not to keep a promise is regarded as analogous to a case in which I must decide whether or not I have the right of way at an intersection. I have the right of way if I am approaching from the right. I must keep the promise if it has been made. There are, however, appropriate exceptions in both cases. I do not have the right of way, even though approaching from the right, if I have a 'yield' sign against me. I need not keep the promise, even though made, if to do so would result in my failure to keep an even more binding promise. For example, I need not keep a promise made in passing on a trivial matter, if to do so would result in my violating a promise made in great solemnity on a matter of real importance. In both the moral and the legal case what counts is the rule and its exceptions (or, understood differently, the rule and other rules with which it can conflict). What counts as relevant is differences in the situation; what does not count as relevant is differences in the personal descriptions of the persons involved. In a court of law it is irrelevant to the question whether I have the right of way that I am in a hurry to get home. It is irrelevant to the question whether I should keep the promise to attend the concert that I am very fond of music. What is relevant must have nothing to do with *me*, but only with the situation: a situation in which anyone could find himself. What is right for me must be right for anyone.

On the courtroom board the model cars are moved through the diagramed intersection to represent the movement of the cars which collided. What is relevant is direction, signals given, signs, lighting conditions. Similarly we rehearse promise-breaking. What is relevant is the nature of the emergency, the conflict of agreements, the likelihood of injury or damage if the promise is kept. These are relevant matters in that a general rule can be formulated governing any one of them. For example, it is a general rule that if a promise is a trivial one, and serious injury is likely to result from its being kept, then it need not be kept.

The analogy with law, with respect to the impersonality of the decision whether an action is or is not correct is, I believe, widely accepted. It informs the quandarist conception of what a problematic situation is. According to this conception, it is irrelevant who the person is who is in the situation. It is relevant, at most, what tacit or explicit agreements he has made, and what role, e.g. father, employer, judge, he finds himself playing. The conflicts of rules, or conflicts of duties, are conflicts into which anyone can fall; and the resolution of the conflicts must be such as to be right for anyone who falls into them. This consensus seems to me to hide a confusion.

There is, in fact, an important disanalogy between moral and legal correctness-decisions. There are considerations which are in a sense personal, which would be irrelevant in legal cases, but which are relevant in moral ones. They have to do with what the agent will allow himself to do and suffer in accordance with the conception that he has of his own moral character. The quandarist cannot, I think, ignore these considerations; but to give them their due is to shift the focus of ethics away from problematics toward character: away from Hobbes and toward Aristotle.

The moral question, inevitably, is: What would it be correct for me to do? It may be, indeed, that I cannot both keep my promise to my friend and my agreement with my neighbour. So I will have to decide. Say I decide to keep the agreement. How can I justify this decision to my friend? If I can do so at all, I must make use of principles I set for myself but not necessarily for other people, and of moral ideals I have, but do not necessarily attribute to other people. I must justify myself to him for what I have done. I cannot do this by talking only about what anyone should have done in the circumstances. Indeed, if what I did would have been wrong for anyone in the same circumstances to do, then it would have been wrong for me. If there had been no conflicting agreement, and I simply broke the promise to avoid the perturbation of my soul likely to be caused by rushing to be on time, then I decided incorrectly. But *it does not follow that because my decision would have been right for anyone in the same circumstances it would have been right for me.* It follows only that almost no one could rightly blame me for what I did: that what I did was permissible. But I can blame myself. Those persons close enough to me to understand and share my special moral ideals can blame me, too.

Suppose that I have devoted my life to the cause of desegregation: that all of my spare time and energy and means are devoted to it. Suppose that I have taken a particular interest in the development of school policy in my town. Suppose that it is simply a part of my self-conception, and a part of the conception that others have of me, that I could not miss an opportunity to press the cause of desegregation: that if I did so I would have to question my own integrity as a person. Suppose that I know that this particular meeting of the school board is a crucial one: one at which the final decision on a plan will be made. Suppose that I am recognized as the chief spokesman for the cause of meaningful desegregation. Suppose that I have built a deserved reputation with others and with myself for persistence and courage in the face of obstacles, for being a man of principle, for sensitivity to the needs of others. Then what would be right for anyone in a situation in which a solemnly given promise conflicts with an agreement to attend a meeting might well not be right for me. If my personal ideals and my conception of myself as a moral person are to be excluded from consideration as merely personal; if nothing is to remain but considerations which have to do with the situation as it would appear to anyone regardless of his former character; then the decision process has been distorted in the interest of a mistaken conception of ethics. The legal analogy has been taken too seriously.

It is easy to be misunderstood here. I am not glorifying the prig, nor do I intend to offer him comfort. I am not suggesting that the person who takes into account his ideals of character should agonize in public over them, nor that he should be pointedly or even obnoxiously rigid in his adherence to his standards. In fact, his ideals of character may rule out priggishness, too. Nevertheless, even though he should not take his ideals inappropriately into account, he should take them into account.

But suppose the quandarist is quite willing to allow all of the sorts of considerations I have mentioned in the previous paragraph. Suppose he insists that there is nothing inherent in his conception of ethics as focused upon the resolution of moral difficulties which prevents him from taking these matters into account. Well, fine! That is all that I am arguing for. Then ethics must take seriously the formation of character, and the role of personal ideals. And these matters must be discussed at length before decision-making is discussed. Moral decision-making will no longer appear in the literature as an exercise in a special form of reasoning by agents of undefined character. But the quandarist might take a different tack, arguing that the distinction between considerations having to do with the situation and considerations having to do with the character of the agent breaks down. 'Why should not my formed character be a part of the situation?' he might ask. My response must be a qualified one. In courts of law such a distinction is maintained, even though it may not always be clear what is and is not relevant to the issue of guilt (that is one reason we must have judges). In the 'court of morals' we maintain it fairly well, although there is a wide twilight zone between the two. But, again, this is an objection which works more in my direction than in his. To whatever extent it is impossible to maintain the distinction, to that extent we must pay more attention in ethics to character and its formation.

The general point I have made is that what would be right for anyone in the same circumstances (understanding 'circumstances' to refer to what in law would be the 'collision situation' only: and not to refer to what is 'merely personal') is not necessarily right for me. Because what I have to take into account as well as the situation is the question what is worthy of me: What may I permit myself to do or suffer in the light of the conception I have of my own so far formed, and still forming, moral character?

It may be useful in expanding this point to return for a time to the concept of rules. It is here that the legal analogy has the strongest grip on the imagination. We say to ourselves: If I want to know what is the correct thing to do, then I must know whether there is a rule that covers this situation, or two rules, or a rule and an exception. But even if, as I would deny, we are tied by some kind of logical necessity to the concept of rule-abiding in thinking what is and is not correct, we would still have to let in considerations of character by the back door. Let me explain.

To do so, it is necessary to distinguish between different ways in which a rule may come to bear upon an agent. An analogous distinction could be made for prescriptions. In the armed services, as I remember dimly form an ancient war, it is customary to distinguish between orders and commands. A command tells us what to do or refrain from doing in such explicit terms that there is no, or very little, room for variation in the way in which it is obeyed or disobeyed. An order, on the other hand, does not so much specifically tell us what to do as what to accomplish, or at what we should aim. 'Report at ten' is a command; 'Provide protective screen for the convoy' is an order. There can, or course, be general and standing orders and commands. A general command would be, 'All hands report at ten tomorrow morning', and a general standing command would require all hands to report every morning at ten. 'Exercise extreme caution when in enemy waters' can serve as a general standing order. General commands and orders apply to everyone; standing orders and commands apply to recurrent situations. Rules may be like general standing commands or like general standing orders; analogously they may be like general standing specific and non-specific prescriptions. They may allow no leeway in compliance, or they may allow a great deal.[1]

Some moral rules are more like general standing orders than like general standing commands, e.g. 'Love thy neighbour' or 'Do not cause suffering'. They say what is wanted, but not what to do. If, however, we concentrate upon moral rules that are like commands, such as 'Do not kill' or 'Never break promises', we are likely to think of moral rules much like criminal laws, in that they will consist, for us, largely of specific injunctions and directions. But if we recognize that they can also be like orders, we will

---

[1] The distinction is very similar to Kant's distinction between perfect and imperfect duties. I have avoided making it in Kant's terms because of the possibilities for confusion inherent in Kant's association of the former with one form of ethics 'the doctrine of right', and the latter with another.

be more aware of the discretion they sometimes allow. They do not tell us exactly what to do so much as indicate what we should struggle toward in our own way. But, since we are already moral beings with characters formed, the way in which I will abide by an order-rule is not the same as the way in which you will. In fact, I have to decide not just what the rule is which governs the case, but how to go about honouring it. In deciding this, it is inevitable that I will not approach the problem in a vacuum, as any anonymous agent would, but in the light of my conception of what is and is not worthy of me. So considerations of character, or my own character, do enter in by the back door, even if, as I have assumed for the sake of argument, the notion is that being moral is nothing but following a set of moral rules.

Personal considerations, then, in moral decisions, as opposed to legal decisions, need not be merely personal. It is often not irrelevant to the correctness of my moral decision that I take into account what I am: the conception that I have of myself as a moral being. In fact, the recognition of these considerations of worthiness leads us away from the typical examples of Quandary Ethics. We may now also consider examples in which the individual is not so much faced with a quandary concerning what he should do, as one in which he is reacting as an admirable moral character would to a situation which might call forth less admirable responses on the part of another. He turns the other cheek, walks the second mile, storms the impossible bastion, exhibits his finely tuned sense of justice by his decision, refrains from pleasurable recreation until the last job of his work is done. He exhibits his character in doing these things: shows forth the kind of man that he is.

Now it might be said, in weary professional tones, that I have simply insisted upon a distinction which is quite familiar to the contemporary moral philosopher: the distinction, with us at least since Aristotle, between the rightness of the act and the praiseworthiness of the agent. The act, it will be said, may be right even though the agent is not praiseworthy for having done it. Or it will be said that I have failed to distinguish between obligation and supererogation: that what a man is obliged to do is one thing, but that if he is a saint or a hero he may of course exceed the demands of duty and be accorded a halo or garland as the case may be.

In response, I want to say that both of these distinctions, while in other ways useful, may lead us to miss the point I want to make. Consider first the distinction between the rightness of the act and the praiseworthiness of the agent. I want to insist that the question whether the act is right may only with care be severed from the question whether the agent is praiseworthy. The agent earns praise by doing what in his lights in only right, by doing what he could not conceive of himself as not doing. In considering whether the action is right he brings in considerations beyond those of the generalizability of a rule. He wants to know not merely whether anyone may do it, but whether he may. Indeed we would not blame him for failing to go the second mile, but from his standpoint he is convinced that this is what it was right for him to do. He in fact exhibits himself as the moral character that he is by the demands that he makes upon himself, and by his taking it for granted that these demands must be met.

Now take the distinction between obligation and supererogation. Again: it does not follow that, since a man has more guide-rails than the rules that in his opinion should apply to everyone, that he is either a saint or a hero: that he is morally extraordinary. In fact a man's character is likely to exhibit itself in his making obligatory for himself what he would not hold others obliged to do. A man does not attain moral stature by what he demands of others but by what he demands of himself; and that he demands more of himself than others is not something in itself admirable, but is what is to be expected if he is to have a distinct moral character. The question whether an act would be right for anyone in the same circumstances can show only that it would be permissible for everyone, or that it would be mandatory for everyone. What is permissible or mandatory for everyone is so for the moral man, but, even leaving aside the question of leeway discussed above, he may not consider it right for him to do what would be permissible for anyone, or he may regard it as mandatory for him to go the second mile rather than merely the first which is mandatory for everyone. The question what is right for anyone in the same circumstances therefore provides the agent with but the beginnings of an answer to the question what he should do.

The special requirements I place upon myself in virtue of the conception I have of what is and is not worthy of me must not be confused, either, with the special requirements incumbent upon me in virtue of 'my station and its duties'. These requirements deal with duties I have as a father, a judge, a village lamplighter, a sergeant-at-arms, or what have you. These are again in the realm of the minimal requirements which should be met by anyone: anyone, this time, who falls into the same role as I do.

Quandary Ethics, then, conceives of a quandary which arises because I fall into a certain situation. The situation is such that it can be described in perfectly general terms, without any reference to me as an individual, including my personal conceptions of what are and are not worthy deeds and attitudes and feelings: worthy of me. I may, according to this conception, fall into the situation in virtue of my falling under a rule which would apply to any person, or in virtue of my falling under a rule which would apply to any person playing a particular role. The general situation is what gives rise to the quandary; and it is only by reference to the features of the situation that I may deliberate concerning what I should do, or justify my action. Just as I may refer only to the position of my automobile at the intersection and not to my personal standards or ideals, so I may refer only to the promising and to the nature of the emergency which caused its violation: with no reference to my standards or ideals. But, I contend, reference to my standards and ideals is an essential, not an accidental feature of my moral deliberation. An act is or is not right from my standpoint, which is where I stand when I deliberate, not merely as it meets or fails to meet the requirements of an ideal universal legislation, but also as it meets or fails to meet the standards I set for myself. I am not judged morally by the extent to which I abide by the rules (those which are like general standing commands) which set the minimal limits anyone should observe in his conduct, even though it may be a necessary condition of my having any degree of moral worth that I should abide by such rules.

The man who is concerned in non-stupid and non-pathological ways over what he should and should not do is, to that extent, a conscientious man. Quandary Ethics is addressed to the conscientious man. He is its ultimate customer. But two things should be said here: that the truly conscientious man is concerned not just with what anyone should do but with what he should do, this I have discussed; and that conscientiousness is but one feature of moral character. Loyalty, generosity, courage, and a great many other qualities may figure as well. We cannot identify morality with conscientiousness. This, I charge, is what Quandary Ethics does. By starting from problems and their resolution, and by confining the description of problematic situations to those features of which a general description can be given, the whole of the question of morality of character is restricted to judgements concerning the conscientiousness of the agent. Since it may be somehow possible to reduce being moral to being conscientious, we should examine the plausibility of such a reductivist claim. But it is worth mentioning that the question what gives conscientiousness the sole claim to moral worth is not so much as recognized as such by the quandarists. It is worth repeating that in speaking of conscientiousness we do not speak of those degenerate forms, seldom recognized by the quandarist, in which there is mere moral dithering (the Buridan's Ass Complex) or in which there is a seeking out of occasions for moral puzzlement when there is no real ground for such puzzlement (pathological conscientiousness).

Why is it, then, that conscientiousness gets the nod from contemporary moral philosophers over such qualities as loyalty, integrity, and kindness?

Why would not honesty have equal claim to consideration? Or sensitivity to suffering? The answer may be obvious to others, but it is not so to me. I suspect that the best answer would take the form of a historico-sociological disquisition upon the increasing complexity of the social order, the increase in the possibilities of breakdown and disorder, the resultant need for more and more complex rules, and, finally, the consequent demand for the kind of individual who will not only be rule-abiding but also 'rule-responsible': in that he does not flap, panic, or throw up his hands when—as is inevitable—the rules conflict in a given situation in which he may find himself. He should be rule-responsible also in that where there is no rule to govern a given choice he will create a rule consistent with the other rules which he accepts; and in that he has at heart the attainment of a community governed by a set of rules which is ideal; and that he evinces this interest in the legislation for himself of rules which would be consistent with the rules governing such a community. Such a man would have an intense regard for rules: for their enactment, interpretation, and application. This regard would extend not only to 'public' rules: rules which govern everyone's action in recurrent situations, but to 'private' rules as well: rules which result from particular relationships with other persons into which he voluntarily enters. There rules, which might be distinguished from others by being called 'obligations', resting on tacit or explicit commitment to do or refrain, require constant interpretation, since the implications of our commitments in future contingencies is often far from clear at the time that we make them ('Love, honour, and obey', '. . . help you get started').

Surely the disquisition need not extend farther. It could easily be expanded into a convincing case for the importance of rule-responsibility in our culture. But it would show at best that one desirable, even socially necessary, quality in men is rule-responsibility or conscientiousness. It does not have the consequence that we must confine our assessments of moral character to judgements of the extent to which the individual is rule-responsible.

Suppose that a man wants to know what he should do about the moral education of his children. What will he learn from the quandarists? He will learn, as might be expected, that he should teach them how to make decisions: that is, according to one popular version, he will impart to his children as stable a set of principles as is possible in the changing circumstances in which he lives; but he will also give them the idea that they must learn to make their own decisions of principle when the occasion arises, even though he cannot teach them how to do so. We later learn that the principles in question must be universalizable prescriptions applicable to any persons similarly situated. But is moral education best understood as the teaching of children how to make moral decisions? One might almost reply that the problem of moral education is not so much teaching children how to make moral decisions as giving them the background out of which the demands that decisions be made arise. The focus of moral education might well be not so much decisions as the inculcation of excellences of character. The adult of good moral character must indeed be able to handle difficult situations as they arise, and to reason about problems unforeseeable by his parents; but to reason well he must already be an adult of good moral character: loyal, just, honest, sensitive to suffering, and the rest. Everything is not up for grabs! Unless he has these qualities, moral dilemmas will not arise for him. Unless he has a well-formed character his prescriptions for himself and others are not likely to be morally acceptable. It is, as Aristotle notes, the prescriptions of qualified moral agents to which we should bend our ears.

An aim of moral education, likely to be overlooked by quandarists, is the development of the sense of the moral self as the product of continuous cultivation. It is as a formed and still forming self that one confronts, or properly avoids, moral problems. There are no moral problems for the child whose character is yet to be formed. For the quandarist, problems may arise for anyone at whatever stage of development he may be, when there is a conflict of rules or principles. What is socially essential is that there should be a workable and working set of rules and that there should be principles which serve as arbitrators between them. The argument that there is a need for such rules and principles is inevitably a Hobbesian one. But it was precisely the source of the discomfort with Hobbes that he approached ethics from this administrative point of view. He abandoned the cultivated moral self and insisted on reducing ethics to a code of minimal standards of behaviours: standards which cannot be ignored without social disaster.

There is very close to the surface in Quandary Ethics the presupposition that there is an essence of morality: that being moral can be reduced to being rule-responsible. But there is no more reason to believe that there is an essence of morality than that there is an essence of beauty. The suspect notion that there is an essence of morality is confused with the defensible idea that some moral rules are socially essential. However men may conceive their moral characters, whatever moral education they may have had, whatever moral models they may hold dear, whatever may be their religious beliefs, whatever virtues they may consider paramount—it is socially essential that they should be rule-responsible. But to grant that rule-responsibility is socially essential is not to grant that it is the essence of morality, in that all other moral character traits can be reduced to or derived from some form of this one. We may, even if we hold to the administrative point of view, expand our list of socially necessary character traits beyond rule-responsibility. Chaos also threatens in the absence of tolerance, temperance, and justice, for example. These too are socially essential virtues.

To say that they are socially essential is of course to speak elliptically. What is essential is that everyone should exhibit some virtues to a certain degree, and that some persons should exhibit others to a certain degree. It is not essential that all be as honest as Lincoln, nor is it essential that any but judges or others who have something to distribute should be just in any degree, since the opportunity for justice or injustice does not otherwise arise. It is clearly socially essential that all should be rule-responsible to a degree commensurate with the complexity of the society; and it is socially desirable that all should be rule-responsible to as high a degree as possible, and that moral models or prophets should show the way. But it does not follow from any of this that morality can be reduced to rule-responsibility. The attempt to reduce moral character to any given trait by philosophical fiat is open to suspicion. Individuals may, and perhaps should, give focus to their moral lives by centring them around some particular virtues, for example sensitivity to suffering, or honesty. But to contend that morality is nothing but sensitivity to suffering or honesty is to attempt to legislate for everyone what cannot be legislated. We may encourage children and ourselves in the development of certain virtues, but the form which each person's character assumes will inevitably be the result of his own selective cultivation and his own conception of what is and is not worthy of himself. It is, once we move beyond the minimal needs of society, his problem, peculiar to him, his training, and his ideals. To insist otherwise is to espouse the cause of the moral Leveller.

The remark that certain virtues are socially essential is elliptical, also, in that it fails to distinguish between virtues which are essential, to a certain degree, in all or some men, to the very existence of any social order, and those which are essential to the continued existence of a particular social order. The distinction is, as Hobbes recognized, a crucial one. 'Gentility', as that term was understood in the pre-Civil War South, was necessary to the existence of the social order created by white landholders. When the non-gentile Snopeses appeared, that social order collapsed. It may be that men are so attached to a particular social order, or so averse to another, that they are willing to entertain the possibility of the absence of any social order rather than see the one collapse or the other prevail. This is social nihilism, but it does not entail moral nihilism. The individual may prize non-socially essential virtues over socially essential ones. In the interest of the continued existence of society, we cannot allow such moralities to prevail.

III

Earlier I distinguished between questions of correctness and questions of usefulness. I have confined my discussion to the former sort of question, but it could be extended with little difficulty to the latter. Suppose that the conception of decision-making is that it has to do with the best way to use the circumstances, to take advantage of the situation, to maximize the happiness of everyone concerned. Again, the question will be not, What should I—in the light of my moral character and ideals—do? but, What might anyone who finds himself in this situation most usefully do? It is a question about means to ends; not a question about how I might be most useful in the circumstances, but about how anyone might increase happiness. Conceived this way, and supposing the goal of happiness to be one that we all understand in the same way, then the question what I should do is not a moral question at all; but one that could best be answered by a social engineer familiar with the circumstances. Even if the question what would be most useful does not trail behind it a general theory to the effect that there is only one kind of thing which is ultimately useful, and if the possibility that there are a great many useful kinds of things that one may do is left open, as it should be, there is still a tendency to regard the question what 'one' may do which is most useful in a given 'situation' as if it could be answered without regard to the moral character of the agent. Again: granting that the promotion of a given state of affairs would be useful, and that a given line of action would promote that state of affairs, it might seem to follow that I should undertake that line of action. It does not. All that follows is that it would be generally desirable if I, or anyone, should. But, in the light of the commitments, interests, and tendencies which I have already developed, it might seem a great deal more desirable that I should follow some alternative course of action. It might be generally desirable that I, and others, should join in a general demonstration against a war; but it might be more desirable that I should follow my already developed moral commitment to the abolition of capital punishment. I cannot decide what would be most useful without taking into account my own conception of myself as a committed moral agent who has already for some time been active in the world.

Hegel suggests that an approach to understanding a philosophical view may be to find out what, on that view, are the chief obstacles to overcome. The chief obstacle for the quandarist faced with a moral perplexity is, I think, the void. It is the nightmare realm in which we can find no ground as heavier and disconcertingly heavier burdens descend upon us. The chief problem is how to find footing. The existentialists create it: harden thin air. The naturalists and intuitionists claim to discover it where intelligent men had somehow missed it before. The subjectivists fashion it out of their own approval. None of this is very plausible. We must ask, not how we find ground in the void, but why we think that we are in one. Who are 'we' who are supposed to be in a void? Are we not concerned to find answers to our repeated demands for ground? We are not then morally featureless, but we have concerns. The intuitions are ours, the discoveries ours, the intro-spection ours. We are not disembodied, historyless, featureless creatures. We are beings who have developed to a point, have even cultivated our-selves. The problems which we face must qualify as problems for us, be our problems: it makes a difference who we are. We cannot describe the problem by describing an anonymous collision situation. Aristotle did not give open lectures; St Paul did not write open letters. When they used the word 'we', they spoke from within a community of expectations and ideals: a community within which character was cultivated.

In part, the problem of the featureless 'we' arises out of the sense that somehow a universal ethic must be created. The 'must' is, of course, a Hobbesian one: it is socially essential. But if we create a universal ethic it must, it seems, be for abstract, general man: the man who has no special features, moral or otherwise. But of course it does not follow that an ethic which is for the man who has no special features is for the man who has none. It is precisely these special features which are likely to give form to the perplexities which arise. They arise for us, not in a void.

It might seem as if they could arise in a void, in which considerations of our own character-defined possibilities and impossibilities are irrelevant, if we fix our gaze on quasi-legal, collision-situation paradigms: on what seem to be moral general standing commands, 'Keep promises', 'Don't kill'. But even if these bare rules be admitted as moral, one could hardly give an acceptable account of moral quandaries by reference to them alone. For, in the first place, there are also general standing moral orders, which give us vast scope in application; and, secondly, there are the perplexities which arise quite outside of the supposedly rule-governed realm of morals: per-plexities which come about because of the conflict of commitments and ideals that I as a moral agent have.

To take the resolution of problems as central, and to conceive of prob-lems on the collision model is indefensibly reductivist. It reduces the topic of moral character to the topic of conscientiousness or rule-responsibility. But it gives no account of the role of the character as a whole in moral deliberation; and it excludes questions of character which are not directly concerned with the resolution of problems.

It may be useful, in closing, to mention some things that I am not claiming. My position is not the subjectivist one that whatever seems right to me is right. Universalizability does provide a test for the rightness of my action, but it sets only minimal requirements, and these often in such fashion as to leave me a range of ways in which I can meet them. I am not claiming that an interest in finding grounds for the resolution of moral problems is the wrong door through which to enter ethics. But there can be more than one door; and the house is a larger one than the quandarists would lead us to believe. I am not insisting that every moral agent must be a saint or a hero, or some combination of both; but only that his moral character cannot be defined solely by reference to his conscientiousness in finding the appropriate rules of the road, or the appropriate means to a common end. I do not contend that all that should count in moral deliberation is whether the proposed action would be acceptable to me in the light of the moral conception that I have of myself. I must first ask what would, in this or any similar situation, be mandatory or permissible for anyone. But this is not all that I must ask. To hold, or presuppose, that it is, is to adopt an indefensibly narrow conception of the subject of ethics.

XI

SUPEREROGATION, WRONGDOING, AND VICE: ON THE AUTONOMY OF THE ETHICS OF VIRTUE

GREGORY VELAZCO Y TRIANOSKY

It is agreed by most philosophers that an adequate ethical theory must include both a theory of right conduct and a theory of virtue. Yet there has been surprisingly little discussion of what forms the connections between these two theories may take. In this paper I will try to show that the fit between the two may be fairly loose. In particular, I will try to show that there need be no close relationship between views about what motives are vicious and views about what conduct is wrong.[1]

I first establish that judgements of the viciousness of particular motives do not necessarily presuppose judgements of the wrongness of particular acts. Then I turn to a discussion of the general looseness of fit between standards of vice and principles of wrongdoing. Here I suggest a contrast between the intimate and personal nature of vice, on the one hand, and the public and social nature of wrongdoing, on the other. Taken as a whole, I hope that this paper will help to encourage a fuller discussion of the complex relations between the theory of the right and the theory of virtue.

I will approach the issue of the relation between wrongdoing and vice indirectly, via a discussion of supererogation and its connections with virtue and vice.

From *Journal of Philosophy*, 83 (1986), 26–40. Reprinted by permission of the *Journal of Philosophy* and the author.

I would like to thank Susan Wolf, Gerald Postema, Thomas E. Hill, Jr., and Arne Gray for very helpful discussion on this and related topics. I am grateful to Laurence Thomas for suggesting to me the need for the comments at the beginning of Sect. IV. Finally, I would like to thank Stephanie Talbott, without whose contributions this paper would not have been written.

[1] For want of a better term, I will use 'vicious' as the contrary of 'virtuous', as 'vice' is the contrary of 'virtue'. As I emphasize below in Sect. III, not every shortcoming in motivation is so great as to be vicious, any more than every shortcoming in character is so great as to be a vice.

I

It might be thought that the contrast between those acts which are obligatory and those which are supererogatory, or good to do but not required, could be drawn roughly in the following way:

(O) An obligatory act is an act whose performance is required and whose omission is forbidden.

(S) A supererogatory act is an act whose performance is recommended but not required and whose omission is permitted rather than forbidden.

Now, given such *deontic* characterizations, it is plausible to think that blame for failure to perform is appropriate only when the act in question is obligatory and not when it is merely supererogatory.[2] It is also plausible to think that there is an essential connection between *blame* and *excuse* of roughly this sort: excuses function essentially to deflect blame for failure to perform. Given these assumptions, it follows that excuses are never appropriately made for failure to perform a supererogatory act. They are inappropriate because no excuse is ever necessary for omitting to do what is merely good to do but not required.

II

There is a certain phenomenon in our shared, common-sense morality which seems puzzling in light of this conclusion. I will describe it and then show how the puzzle may be resolved. This puzzle is of interest primarily because its resolution allows us, first, to identify and explore some of the deeper connections between supererogation and vice, overlooked by the purely deontic characterizations, and, second, because its resolution then encourages us to examine more carefully the relation between wrongdoing and vice.

Sometimes we are challenged to perform acts that are good to do but not required, by individuals who plainly are already committed to performing them. Challenges to join in the support of a charitable enterprise are often of this sort: 'Would you help us with the telethon this year?' or, 'Would you join us in a march against birth defects?' More dramatic challenges, challenges to take up the life of commitment to others, may also be of this

---

[2] I do not claim that if an act is obligatory then it must always be appropriate publicly to *express* blame for failure to perform it. Who has a right to express blame, and when, is a distinct moral question.

sort: 'Why don't you join the Peace Corps with me?' or 'Join the Lincoln Brigade with me, and we'll fight the Fascists together'.

Although the line between supererogation and obligation in common-sense morality is vague and imprecise, I assume that none of these actions is such that morality would ordinarily be said to require its performance and forbid its omission. Instead, these actions are commonly regarded as supererogatory.

However, even though what we are challenged to do is supererogatory, we frequently respond by offering what seem to be *excuses*: 'Sorry, I'm busy that day', 'I'm afraid I don't have any cash on me', 'I'm already tied down to a job'. We seem often to feel uncomfortable or even ashamed that we are unwilling to do more than is required of us, to 'go the extra mile'. So much so, in fact, that we often make one of the above excuses even when it isn't true.

But if what we are challenged to do is supererogatory, it would suffice to say, politely, 'No thanks, I'm not in the mood' or 'No thanks, I'm interested in saving up for a new tennis-racket' or 'No thanks, I like my current job too much'. Yet these replies seem somehow infelicitous.

The puzzle is simply that, on the assumptions I made is Section I, excuses of the former, more felicitous sort must be inappropriate because unnecessary. Yet they seem perfectly in order. How can this be?

There are of course a number of ways of discounting this putatively puzzling phenomenon, but none of them seems entirely convincing. For example, one might insist that these excuses are in fact appropriate because the acts we are challenged to do are instances of *imperfect* duties. The excuses described above thus serve to show that nothing can be inferred from this failure to act about whether I will on sufficiently many other occasions act charitably. But the same sort of puzzle arises when the agent has obviously done even more than is necessary to fulfil the common-sense requirements of imperfect duty. Perhaps the neighbourhood 'organizer' challenges me, knowing full well how much volunteer work I'm doing already. Yet 'I gave last week' or 'I'm too tired' or even 'I've already done all I'm required to do' still may seem inadequate and infelicitous as replies. One may still feel embarrassed to use them, and be inclined to offer the other, more felicitous 'excuses' I have described instead. This is especially true when the challenger himself is plainly going beyond the call of duty.

In short, we seem often to be concerned that morally significant others not disapprove or think less well of us. The 'excuses' I have described thus do seem to function, at least in part, as excuses: they seem to serve, paradoxically, as attempts to deflect imputations of blame for failure to act.

III

I conclude that the phenomenon I have described is indeed puzzling. In this section I propose a resolution of the puzzle which will serve ultimately to reveal the looseness of some of the connections between wrongdoing and vice.

There are at least two types of negative moral judgements that take persons as their objects: negative *deontic* judgements of the person and negative *aretaic* judgements of the person. The former logically presuppose judgements about the wrongness of some particular act of the agent's. Judgements of blameworthiness are paradigm examples: they logically presuppose a judgement of the wrongness of the act for which the agent is held blameworthy. Judgements of culpability, fault, or negligence, and judgements of responsibility for reparations, are also deontic judgements of the person.

Negative aretaic judgements of the person presuppose a judgement about the viciousness of some conative or affective state of the agent's. They are of two kinds: those which presuppose judgements about the viciousness of standing traits or dispositions, and those which presuppose judgements about the viciousness of occurrent motives or states. Judgements about what a bad person someone is, or about how cowardly or dishonest a person he is, are aretaic judgements of the first sort. Judgements about how inconsiderate someone was on a certain occasion or about how insensitive, dishonest, or cowardly it was *of him* to do what he did are aretaic judgements of the person of the second sort. A judgement about the viciousness of some standing trait is a judgement about a vice, or a general flaw in the agent's moral *character*. A judgement about the viciousness of some occurrent motive is a judgement only about a flaw in what I call the agent's *motivational structure* on some particular occasion.[3]

The judgement that there are vicious elements in an agent's motivational structure on a given occasion of course does not imply that his character is vicious in some respect. One may act insensitively on a given occasion (when under great stress, for example) and yet be acting entirely out of character. In what follows, I will focus primarily on those aretaic judgements of the person which presuppose attributions of viciousness to

---

[3] A description of the agent's moral *character* includes a description of the agent's standing traits or dispositions to choose, act, and feel in various ways. A description of the agent's *motivational structure* on a given occasion is a description of what occurrent motives, feelings, etc. were at work in the agent on that occasion, what their relative strengths were, and how they were related to each other. I will sometimes use 'motives' as shorthand for 'motives, feelings, attitudes, etc.'.

the agent's motivational structure on a given occasion; and I will use phrases like 'aretaic judgements', or judgements of vice' to refer only to these. It is an interesting question, which I will not discuss here, to what extent my conclusions can be generalized to aretaic judgements about traits and the judgements of the person based on these.

Now it is easy to resolve the puzzle. If an act is supererogatory, then, I suppose, no negative *deontic* judgements can appropriately be made of the person who fails to perform it. In particular, the agent cannot appropriately be blamed. But it does not follow that no negative *aretaic* judgement can appropriately be made; for the agent may still have acted from a less-than-virtuous motive or, it seems, even a vicious motive. In the cases of 'excuse'-making I have described above, for example, we seem to be concerned that we not appear to lack a certain moral seriousness: we do not want to appear to be acting frivolously, insensitively, or callously. The felicitous 'excuses' I have described function to deflect such negative judgements about our motives and the aretaic judgements of the person grounded in them, rather than to deflect blame or other deontic judgements of the person.[4]

This resolution indicates that the deontic characterization of supererogatory action may be both misleading and incomplete. It is misleading if it is taken (together with the two assumptions I mentioned at the end of Section I) to imply that no negative judgement of the person of any sort can be grounded on the omission of a supererogatory act. Negative aretaic judgements may be quite in order, as I have suggested.[5]

---

[4] Aretaic excuses seem to function differently from deontic excuses in some respects. Generally a deontic excuse functions to deflect blame by disrupting the inference from the wrongness of the *act* to the blameworthiness of the agent. One way in which this may be done is by claiming that the act was radically out of character: the agent was too upset, or too angry, or under too much stress, perhaps, to appreciate what he was doing. He would never have done such a thing had he 'been himself', we say.

If aretaic excuses were to function in a parallel fashion, they would generally function to deflect an attribution of viciousness to the person by disrupting the inference from the viciousness of his *motive* to the viciousness of the agent. But, as I indicate below in my discussion of the liberal model (Sect. V), the connection between a person's motives and his self is generally too close to make such a disruption very plausible. We do not seem to think that it was any the less vicious, insensitive, or cruel of the agent to do what he did just because he was too upset or too angry to think clearly about it. (Such excuses may, however, function to block the rather different inference, from a vicious motivational structure on a given occasion to a general flaw of character.)

There is another strategy which may work equally well in both cases: redescribing the object of the original judgement (act or motive) so that it is no longer reasonable to regard it as wrong or vicious. If we become convinced that the agent acted or spoke in ignorance, for example, we may withdraw the judgement that his act was wrong, or that his motive was vicious. Here the judgement of the person is deflected because the very judgement of act or motive on which it was grounded is defeated.

[5] Even in the privacy of our own conscience, we are sometimes hesitant to refrain from what

The deontic characterization of *obligation* is at least complete in this respect: it is possible to see how failure to do what is obligatory, on this characterization, may provide grounds for some critical judgement of the person, viz. a deontic judgement. The deontic characterization of supererogatory action, on the other hand, provides no such connection with judgements of the person. It is incomplete, as any deontic characterization of such acts must be, precisely because it disregards the way in which negative aretaic judgement is connected with failure to do what is supererogatory.

Moral saints and moral heroes are typically people who are always willing to help those in need, even at great risk or inconvenience to themselves. They are responsive to moral considerations in general, and usually to altruistic considerations in particular, even when they don't have to be. They are always willing to go the extra mile.

We may think of such noble and selfless individuals as more or less faithful renditions of an ideal type, which I will call *the fully virtuous person*. The fully virtuous person is willing to do both what morality requires and what it only recommends, and has whatever supporting traits are sufficient to maintain this commitment in human beings.[6]

Now, on this characterization, there is a straightforward connection between supererogation and virtue, since the fully virtuous person is always willing to do more than just what's required. It is the deeper connections between vice and failure to do what is supererogatory to which I wish to draw attention.

To begin with, it seems clear that the deliberate omission of a supererogatory act on a given occasion entails that the agent's motivational structure on that occasion falls short of that which the ideal, fully virtuous person would display. I will say that such an omission reveals a

---

is supererogatory because of what we think that choice would say *to ourselves* about the depth and sincerity of our moral commitment. Notice that this hesitation comes from a concern with character and motive, and not just from a concern over the act, conceived independently of motive, and our culpability for it. This issue requires much more discussion. See, for example, Thomas E. Hill, Jr.'s very interesting paper 'Ideals of Human Excellence and Preserving Natural Environments', *Environmental Ethics*, 5 (Fall 1983), 211–24.

[6] Such traits might include: self-discipline, strength of will, optimism in the face of difficulties, and resilience in the face of failure. I should note that it may well not be possible to do *all* that morality recommends. The fully virtuous person, I take it, is willing to perform some maximally compossible subset of all such acts. I will ignore this qualification in what follows. On pain of circularity, my characterization of this ideal type does presuppose that supererogatory and obligatory actions may be identified without reference to what a fully virtuous person would do. This seems plausible as an assumption about common-sense morality. (But see John Kekes, 'Moral Sensitivity', *Philosophy*, 59, 227 (Jan. 1984), 3–19.) I do not claim that this characterization constitutes a complete account of the common-sense conception of a fully virtuous person, however.

shortcoming in the agent's motivational structure on that occasion. Not every shortcoming is actually vicious, however.

Moreover, if my earlier account of excuses was correct, then whether a shortcoming is so great as to constitute a genuine *defect*, a vicious flaw in motivation, depends in large part on the sorts of reasons the agent has for omission. The more felicitous excuses I have described above seem to be those which, if true, serve to deflect the imputation of a vicious or genuinely defective motive. The more infelicitous excuses that we are embarrassed to give are precisely those which would reveal such a defect in motivation on the occasion in question.

IV

I have argued that there is a deeper, negative connection between supererogation, on the one hand, and virtue and vice, on the other: The choice to refrain from doing what is good but not required may reveal not merely a shortcoming but a genuine defect, a vicious shortcoming, in the agent's motivational structure on the relevant occasion. My first claim about the looseness of fit between wrongdoing and vice follows directly: a particular motive may be vicious even though the action to which it gives rise is entirely permissible. Not every judgement of viciousness presupposes a judgement that the agent has done wrong; and not every negative aretaic judgement of the person need also be a negative deontic judgement of the person.

Now it might be thought that this first claim about the looseness of fit between wrongdoing and vice was trivial. After all, it might be said, it has always been obvious that one could do the right things for the wrong reasons. I may intend to ruin Ralph's reputation by telling others of his sordid past, for example, and succeed only in procuring him their sympathy and support. Or Mayor Daley may donate money to an orphanage, intending only to manipulate public opinion before the upcoming election. Or again, by my refusal to rush into a burning building to save a child, I may reveal that, on this occasion, anyway, I place my own welfare above that of the helpless victims of ill fortune.

In point of fact, however, none of these standard cases of 'doing the right thing for the wrong reasons' provides any support for my claim at all.

This is clearest in the third case. I claim that a permissible act may reveal a *vice*. But my refusal to save the child shows not a genuine *defect* in my motivational structure, but only a shortcoming. I have failed to do what the fully virtuous person would do; and so, more or less trivially, my motivation falls short of the ideal. But my priorities are still not *viciously* ordered.

In the other two cases there is still a connection below the surface between the vicious motive and some wrongful act. In the first case, the viciousness of the motive seems plainly to be borrowed from the wrongness of the act *intended*, even if, through no fault of the agent's, so to speak, this intended act is never completed. In the second case, the agent does what is permissible (donating money) as a means to performing some wrongful action (deceiving the public about his virtue, or, perhaps, manipulating public opinion). I suggest that virtually all the standard cases of doing the right thing for the wrong reason are cases in which the viciousness of the motive (if it really is vicious and not just short of perfect) is borrowed in some such way from the wrongness of some action the agent does or intends. In the standard cases, therefore, the incongruity between the positive deontic status of the action and the negative aretaic status of the motive is only apparent. The existence of such cases does not help to establish my first claim.

What would cases look like which did support my claim, cases in which there was no direct connection at all between vice and wrongdoing? Cases of one sort I have already mentioned: I may refuse to join in some charitable effort, giving as my reason a complete lack of interest in the particular cause in question, or perhaps my concern to pursue some comparatively trivial personal desire instead. Or, I may refuse brusquely or rudely, slamming the door in your face. In such cases as these, you may well judge that my *motive* for choosing not to help is vicious—a callous, insensitive, and uncaring attitude toward those in need; and indeed that it was callous, insensitive, and uncaring *of me* to refrain for the reasons I did. Yet by hypothesis my choice not to help out was permissible.

Of course it may be that rudely *expressing* my refusal to help is wrong, Indeed, perhaps any public statement, however polite, of my true, selfishly trivial reasons for not helping is wrong because it is belittling or offensive to my challenger.[7] But my refusal to help is itself permissible; and the crucial point here about my public statement (wrongful or not) is what it reveals about my motives for the entirely permissible choice not to help in the first place. Your judgement about my viciousness in publicly stating my refusal may be a deontic judgement of the person; but your judgement about my viciousness in choosing not to help in the first place, is not. The

---

[7] I am grateful to Stephen Darwall for pointing this out.

motive that gave rise to my negative choice is vicious, even though *the choice itself* is not wrong, intended to be wrong, a means to what is wrong, etc.

Parenthetically it is worth pointing out that, if this defect in motivational structure reflects a standing trait, then the agent may well also be guilty of a certain *hypocrisy*. Imagine that his concern for the well-being of others regularly vanishes when his obligations come to an end, to be replaced by a disposition to coldly calculated self-interest. Then we may reasonably suspect that what altruistic concern he seems to display in fulfilling his obligations is itself really a sham. In all likelihood, real concern for others is not defined by the same boundaries that define our obligations. Conscientious such an agent may be. But, we suspect, he is conscientious as the Pharisees described in the New Testament were conscientious. He swerves not one jot from what the law requires, but has no real human concern in his heart. This hypocrisy is also a vice, a genuine defect of *character*, which might be revealed in—and perhaps only in—the consistent refusal to do what is beyond duty. On the other hand, if the agent continues to exhibit altruistic concern (e.g. in the form of expressions of sympathy or feelings of regret) despite regular refusals to do what is supererogatory, we may suspect that his concern, though genuine, is weak or superficial, insufficient to move him to action without the additional spur of moral obligation. This superficiality seems to me also to be something we commonly regard as a vice, primarily displayed in the failure to do what is supererogatory.

Yet another sort of case that supports the divorce of vice from wrongdoing is the case in which I stand on my rights. I take it that when I say 'I had every right to act as I did', or, 'I was within my rights', what I say is true only if what I have done was not forbidden, and so only if what I might have done instead was not obligatory.[8] None the less, when our moral obligations are highly conventionalized, such assertions may function to deflect moral criticism. Suppose, for example, that I refuse to forgive you a debt, even though I know you need the money a good bit more than I do; or suppose that I decide to sell my house to the highest bidder rather than to the people who need it most, when their bid is only a few thousand dollars less. Our shared moral convictions indicate that these are surely permissible choices. In response to criticism, I might correctly point out, 'I had every right to do what I did'.

[8] The quoted claims are in one respect ambiguous: they mean 'I was not obligated to do anything else', or they may mean 'Others were obligated not to interfere with my doing as I did'. Meant in the former way, such claims entail that I was morally permitted to do as I did. Meant in the latter way, they probably do not. I suggest that, when these claims are made defensively, in response to moral criticism of what was done, they are meant in the former way. The agent seeks to deflect criticism by saying, in effect, 'I don't *have* to do that if I don't want to'.

Here, as in Section II above, however, I suggest that such a response blocks only negative *deontic* judgement of the person and his motivational structure. If I really am within my rights to do these things, you cannot correctly say of me what you can say of Shylock: that what he proposes to do is really wrong, but that he has chosen to ignore his real obligations when his desire for revenge is thereby served; or, perhaps, that he is twisting the moral rules to serve his own impermissible ends. What is objectionable in the two cases I mentioned above is that the agent expresses a narrowly legalistic attitude toward morality by asserting his rights in such cases. It is not that what he *does* is wrong, considered independently of its motive; for our common-sense principles of moral obligation *are* narrow and legalistic here. Nevertheless, the agent reveals a genuinely vicious motivation in his coldly calculated insistence on what is rightfully his.[9]

This particular defect in the agent's motivational structure, again, is especially striking because it can be revealed *only* in a refusal to do what is supererogatory. The agent I have in mind reveals a vicious or defective motivational structure precisely because he is willing on the occasion in question to do only what morality requires him to do, and no more. If he is challenged to do any more on that occasion, he stands on his rights.

In the cases I have described, the incongruity between deontic and aretaic judgements is deep. There is no underlying connection here between the viciousness of the agent's motive and the wrongness of any act that he performs or intends, now or in the future.

V

Thus far I have argued only that there is a fairly loose fit between particular aretaic judgements of motive and judgements about the wrongness of particular acts. Perhaps there is still a general but indirect connection between wrongdoing and vice. Perhaps what makes a motive vicious is that it is the *type* of trait which either involves or tends to produce acts that are wrong. This view, after all, is compatible with my claim that in a particular case a vicious motive may manifest itself in a permissible act. A certain

[9] One might be inclined to say that the agent ought not assert his rights in such a case. This raises some difficult issues. It seems to me that this may just be a way of saying that only a viciously motivated person would do so. If this is right, then if there is a judgement of wrongdoing here, it is itself derivative from a prior judgement of vice, rather than the converse. I think the same point may be made, *mutatis mutandis*, about a possibility suggested to me by Gerald Postema: that what is impermissible here is something like 'doing-what-one-has-a-right-to-do-for-cold-hearted-reasons'. I have discussed the notion of derivative judgements of wrongdoing, in my 'Virtue, Action, and the Good Life: Toward a Theory of the Virtues', MS.

degree of insensitivity may motivate me to refuse to go beyond my duty. But, on the view at hand, insensitivity of that degree may actually be a vice only if in general it is also connected with doing wrong, and not merely with omitting to do what is supererogatory. This view allows, of course, that mere shortcomings in motivation need have no special connection with wrongdoing. What it insists on is that no shortcoming may be so objectionable as to be vicious unless it has some general if indirect connection with wrongdoing.[10]

In this section I will argue that the view I have just described is mistaken. There is in fact an important looseness in the general fit between standards of vice and principles of wrongdoing as well.

I assume that there are various motivational structures that a given agent might display on a certain occasion of choice. I assume further that these structures can be arranged in rough order along a continuum, beginning with the fully virtuous motivational structure, and proceeding down through structures with ever greater shortcomings.[11] A *standard of vice* then indicates for a broad range of occasions at what points along these continua that agent's shortcomings become so great as to become genuine defects, vicious motivational flaws.

Now intuitively it seems as though with the description of a given set of fully virtuous motivational structures and the corresponding continua of shortcomings there could be associated any one of a number of standards of vice, ranging from the harsh and demanding to the tolerant, if not lax. A harsh standard of vice might insist that almost any shortcoming, however slight, was vicious. A tolerant standard might hold that only very substantial shortcomings, far along the continua, were vicious.

Principles of wrongdoing indicate what sorts of action under what sorts of circumstance are wrong, forbidden by morality. Now it also seems plausible to think that principles of wrongdoing may vary in degree of harshness, and so some will require what others merely recommend; but I will not pursue this more complex matter here. What I want to show is rather that *standards of vice may legitimately vary in degree of harshness even if principles of wrongdoing remain fixed.*

[10] In what follows I am adopting a relatively 'fine-grained' criterion for individuating motives, so that different degrees of, e.g., insensitivity or cruelty count as qualitatively distinct motives. This sort of criterion is the most useful in the present context, given my characterizations of the fully virtuous person, the fully virtuous motivational structure, and the relevant continua.

[11] The description of the set of all possible fully virtuous motivational structures for a given agent can for our purposes be regarded as identical with the description of the fully virtuous person which is relevant for that agent. If there are many ways to fall short of the relevant ideal, then there will be many such continua for any given agent and occasion; and the standard of vice will correspondingly be multi-branched.

Consider what I will call a *liberal model* of social morality. On this model, valid deontic principles must all be public and conventional; but valid standards of vice are to a large extent private or personal.[12] More precisely, this model endorses the following principles:

1. Conventionalism with respect to the deontic realm. On the liberal model of social morality I have in mind, an act is wrong only if the conventions of the relevant society identify its performance as blameworthy. An act is supererogatory only if those conventions exempt failure to perform it from blame. Deontic principles of wrongdoing, other deontic principles of action, and the standards for deontic judgements of the person are, on this model of social morality, all conventional in analogous ways.

2. Liberalism with respect to the aretaic realm. On the liberal model, the ideal of the fully virtuous person and the related ideal of a fully virtuous motivational structure are both fixed by deontic principles in the manner described above, and shortcomings in motivation are to be arranged along suitable continua. Within these broad, socially established parameters, however, individuals are free to accept harsh or tolerant standards of vice for themselves, as they see fit. The ideal of virtue is public, on this model, but the standard of vice is largely private.

The liberal model I am describing supports these views by making the following two assumptions:

(A) Outward action is public. The question of how to treat outward actions, the model claims, is a social question. Outward actions are in principle and usually in practice public. Hence the question can always be raised of how others should react to them: are they to blame the agent for what has been done? encourage him? say to him and to each other that he has only done what can in reason be expected? tolerate what he has done? condemn it? praise it? adopt an indifferent attitude toward it?[13]

(B) Inward motives are private. Judgements of viciousness (and the aretaic judgements of the person grounded on them), it is supposed, have a peculiarly intimate character which judgements of wrongdoing (and the deontic judgement of the person based on them) lack. Judgements of vice

[12] So far as I can see, nothing in my discussion of the liberal model turns on whether it is interpreted as involving an actual-conventionalist view or an ideal-conventionalist view like ideal rule-utilitarianism. So long as the model maintains that valid deontic principles must be social or conventional, but that valid standards of vice need not be, it won't matter for my argument whether it maintains that the relevant conventions must be actual or that they must be ideal.

[13] Some of these are questions to be settled by reference to deontic principles (e.g. principles of wrongdoing or of supererogation), whereas others can be settled only by reference to standards for deontic judgements of the person.

are not simply judgements about *what one does*, publicly; so aretaic judgements of the person are not grounded simply on judgements of one's public behaviour. Judgements of viciousness and the attendant judgements of the person are, unavoidably, deeper judgements about *what one is*.

This assumption seems plausible. After all, it may be possible to discover or create a distance between veridical deontic judgements, based as they are on outward action, and one's conception of one's 'true self'. Then judgements of wrongdoing or even of blameworthiness won't necessarily reflect badly on what one 'truly is', inwardly. 'That's only how I am on the outside', one may say to oneself.[14]

Indeed, it becomes even more plausible if deontic judgements of the person are conceived simply as judgements about one's liability to further social 'punishment' or one's obligations to compensate the victims of one's wrongdoing; or perhaps just as expressions of social disapproval of one's unexcused behaviour. Judgements of wrongdoing and the attendant deontic judgements of the person thus may indeed fail always to catch hold of 'the true self'.[15]

The case seems quite different on any reasonable view of judgements of viciousness and the consequent aretaic judgements of the person. It would be very difficult for a sane human being systematically to discover or to create any such distance between veridical judgements of these types and his view of his own inner self.

On the liberal model, then, judgements of wrongdoing and blameworthiness are seen as superficial; whereas judgements of viciousness, both of motives and of persons, are seen as typically cutting deep with respect to one's conception of 'one's true self'.

Given assumption (A), the liberal model asserts, it is plausible to conceive of deontic standards and principles as conventional guides which tell us how to respond to the overt behaviour of others. Likewise, given assumption (B), the liberal model conceives of judgements and standards of vice as by and large too intimate a matter for public scrutiny.[16] In a society that instantiated this model, one might say to a close friend, 'What you did

---

[14] Cf. B. F. Skinner's discussion of 'the inner man' in *Beyond Freedom and Dignity* (New York: Knopf, 1971).

[15] However deontic judgements of the person are understood, obviously judgements of blameworthiness must not entail judgements of viciousness if the liberal model is to be coherent. It seems reasonable enough to take this for granted, however, since some of the 'excuses' that serve to deflect judgements of viciousness do not necessarily serve also to deflect judgements of blameworthiness. See above, n. 4.

[16] The objection may be raised that, although the mere having of a motive is not necessarily public, its expression in action is. But standards of vice are first and foremost standards for evaluating motives, although (as Hume insisted) they certainly can support derivative judgements of action. Moreover, so long as a relatively complete set of deontic principles is already in place, the actions in which moral or immoral motives are expressed may be judged publicly

was certainly within your rights; but I have to say that your motives were far from ideal. You can even call them vicious, if you think that; but it's not for me to judge.'[17]

This is the most extreme liberal model of wrongdoing and vice. There is a more attractive version of the model which is a bit more conservative and yet retains the substance of the liberal notions. This more conservative model assumes, to use the language of the law, that there is an 'overriding public interest' in setting a *lower limit* to private standards of vice, such that, at the very least, any trait suitably connected with serious wrongdoing must count as a vice.

Perhaps there really is an overriding public interest in this close a tie between judgements linked directly to one's self-concept, and acts of wrongdoing. But even if this is so, defenders of liberal notions may still maintain that whether one is committed to any standard of vice harsher than this minimalist standard, is—and should remain—an entirely private matter.

I do not think that the liberal model is accurate as a *descriptive* model for our current shared morality. Nevertheless, there are certainly liberal strands in our shared moral thought.[18] Indeed, I believe that the liberal model may have significant explanatory power.[19]

according to these principles. A single, socially established standard of vice is not necessary *in addition to* public deontic principles in order to settle the question of how it is appropriate to treat behaviour that expresses moral motives. Of course a morality that included only such deontically grounded judgements about actions would be highly impoverished, for it would address acts largely without reference to the moral quality of their motives. This was Mill's criticism of Bentham's moral theory in his 'Essay on Bentham'.

[17] The objection may also be raised that there is no rational basis for choosing one standard of vice over another once these standards are cut loose from principles of wrongdoing. But I suspect that, if legitimate standards of vice are individualized as the liberal model maintains they are, it is a matter of discovery rather than of choice which standard commands one's allegiance. How demanding a standard one holds oneself to, here as elsewhere in life, probably depends on how invested one is in the projects in question and how tolerant one tends to be of one's own failings. To the extent that finding a standard of vice for oneself involves choice, therefore, it probably involves the choice to try to modify one's attitudes toward and investments in morality.

[18] If the liberal model were adopted as a bit of revisionary theory, then of course certain of the aretaic judgements I discussed in earlier sections could appropriately be made only by the agent himself. Although this would complicate my exposition in those sections considerably, I do not believe it would materially affect the points I make there. See above, n. 5.

[19] For example, it may explain the asymmetry between the harsh judgements that saintly and heroic people tend to make of their own failures to live up to very high ideals of virtue, on the one hand, and the inclination that the rest of us have respectfully to refrain from judging these failures at all, on the other. There are undoubtedly other explanations for why we are generally reluctant to express or even to make negative aretaic judgements of saintly and heroic people. (Cf. e.g. the higher-order deontic principle suggested by Matt. 8: 3, 'Why beholdest thou the mote that is in thy brother's eye but considerest not the beam that is in thy own eye?', and other similar New Testament passages.) But at most these explanations account for only one half of the asymmetry in negative judgements.

Any explanation that accounts for both halves of the phenomenon must show how it is that saints and heroes may legitimately evaluate their motives and conduct by a standard that

The liberal model, however, relies essentially on the notion of a private aretaic standard. If this notion seems unacceptable, we can drop it and still retain the fundamental insight that the liberal model expresses about the looseness of fit between vice and wrongdoing. I will call the model I have in mind here *the moralistic model*, for it insists that not just outward conduct but also inward vice and virtue can appropriately be subjected to public scrutiny. On this model, deontic principles, deontic standards, and standards of vice are all conventional. Nevertheless, the liberal model and the moralistic model agree that fixing the first two does not necessarily fix standards of vice.

On the moralistic model, therefore, these standards may vary in degree of harshness from society to society, while the deontic principles and standards remain unchanged. Using the moralistic model allows us to express the liberal insight in a more general way: principles of wrongdoing and standards of vice may be conceived as serving very different functions. Principles of wrongdoing tell us when we are permitted to disregard the pronouncements of morality and when we are forbidden to do so, and what the social moral consequences of our respecting or ignoring these pronouncements will be. Standards of vice tell us how our motives in doing these things are to be assessed and, by implication, how these motives reflect on what we are. Nor need these functions be related in any simple way, such that, e.g., one's motives are virtuous so long as one is inclined to do only what is permissible, and one's motives are vicious only if one is inclined to do what is wrong. How good one's motives are, and how good it is *of one* to act on them, depends not simply on the deontic status of what one is moved to do, but on what kind of sensitivity to moral considerations one's motives express. On either the liberal model or the moralistic model, therefore, standards of vice and principles of wrongdoing need not fit closely together.

In this paper I have argued that judgements of vice, and perhaps even general standards of vice, may have a life of their own: a life which is to a significant extent independent of the guide-lines mapped out by judgements and principles of wrongdoing. It should be clear from my argument

is plainly harsher than that which the rest of us recognize as legitimate in our own case. It is difficult to see how any explanation can do this without assuming that legitimate moral standards or principles can be private at least some of the time. The liberal model, in its less extreme form, shows, as well as any other I can think of, how and when to draw the line between the public and the private domains in moral judgement. A fuller discussion of the differences between the saintly life and the life of commitment to a merely personal ideal, including some remarks on the continuity between the lives we ordinary people try to lead and the lives saints and heroes try to lead, is contained in my 'Supererogation and the Moral "Must" ', MS.

that I do not here suggest, as some have, that an ethic of virtue can operate with full autonomy, entirely independent of a theory of the right. Nevertheless, I do claim for virtue and vice at least partial autonomy from such a theory.

XII

ALIENATION, CONSEQUENTIALISM, AND THE DEMANDS OF MORALITY

PETER RAILTON

INTRODUCTION

Living up to the demands of morality may bring with it alienation—from one's personal commitments, from one's feelings or sentiments, from other people, or even from morality itself. In this article I will discuss several apparent instances of such alienation, and attempt a preliminary assessment of their bearing on questions about the acceptability of certain moral theories. Of special concern will be the question whether problems about alienation show consequentialist moral theories to be self-defeating.

I will not attempt a full or general characterization of alienation. Indeed, at a perfectly general level alienation can be characterized only very roughly as a kind of estrangement, distancing, or separateness (not necessarily consciously attended to) resulting in some sort of loss (not necessarily consciously noticed).[1] Rather than seek a general analysis I will rely

Railton, Peter 'Alienation, Consequentialism, and the Demands of Morality'. Copyright © 1984 by Princeton University Press. Reprinted by permission of Princeton University Press.

I am grateful to a number of people for criticisms of earlier drafts of this paper and helpful suggestions for improving it. I would especially like to thank Marcia Baron, Stephen Darwall, William K. Frankena, Allan Gibbard, Samuel Scheffler, Rebecca Scott, Michael Stocker, Nicholas Sturgeon, Gregory Velazco y Trianosky, and Susan Wolf.

[1] The loss in question need not be a loss of something of value, and *a fortiori* need not be a bad thing overall: there are some people, institutions, or cultures alienation from which would be a boon. Alienation is a more or less troubling phenomenon depending upon what is lost; and in the cases to be considered, what is lost is for the most part of substantial value. It does not follow, as we will see in Sect. V, that in all such cases alienation is a bad thing on balance. Moreover, I do not assume that the loss in question represents an actual *decline* in some value as the result of a separation coming into being where once there was none. It seems reasonable to say that an individual can experience a loss in being alienated from nature, for example, without assuming that he was ever in communion with it, much as we say it is a loss for someone never to receive an education or never to appreciate music. Regrettably, various relevant kinds and sources of alienation cannot be discussed here. A general, historical discussion of alienation may be found in Richard Schacht, *Alienation* (Garden City, NY: Doubleday, 1971).

upon examples to convey a sense of what is involved in the sorts of alienation with which I am concerned. There is nothing in a word, and the phenomena to be discussed below could all be considered while avoiding the controversial term 'alienation'. My sense, however, is that there is some point in using this formidable term, if only to draw attention to commonalities among problems not always noticed. For example, in the final section of this article I will suggest that one important form of alienation in moral practice, the sense that morality confronts us as an alien set of demands, distant and disconnected from our actual concerns, can be mitigated by dealing with other sorts of alienation morality may induce. Finally, there are historical reasons, which will not be entered into here, for bringing these phenomena under a single label; part of the explanation of their existence lies in the conditions of modern 'civil society', and in the philosophical traditions of empiricism and rationalism—which include a certain picture of the self's relation to the world—that have flourished in it.

Let us begin with two examples.

I. JOHN AND ANNE AND LISA AND HELEN

To many, John has always seemed a model husband. He almost invariably shows great sensitivity to his wife's needs, and he willingly goes out of his way to meet them. He plainly feels great affection for her. When a friend remarks upon the extraordinary quality of John's concern for his wife, John responds without any self-indulgence or self-congratulation. 'I've always thought that people should help each other when they're in a specially good position to do so. I know Anne better than anyone else does, so I know better what she wants and needs. Besides, I have such affection for her that it's no great burden—instead, I get a lot of satisfaction out of it. Just think how awful marriage would be, or life itself, if people didn't take special care of the ones they love.' His friend accuses John of being unduly modest, but John's manner convinces him that he is telling the truth: this is really how he feels.

Lisa has gone through a series of disappointments over a short period, and has been profoundly depressed. In the end, however, with the help of others she has emerged from the long night of anxiety and melancholy. Only now is she able to talk openly with friends about her state of mind, and she turns to her oldest friend, Helen, who was a mainstay throughout. She'd like to find a way to thank Helen, since she's only too aware of how much of a burden she's been over these months, how much of a drag and a bore, as she puts it. 'You don't have to thank me, Lisa,' Helen replies, 'you deserved it. It was the least I could do after all you've done for me. We're friends, remember? And we said a long time ago that we'd stick together no matter what. Some day I'll probably ask the same thing of you, and I know you'll come through. What else are friends for?' Lisa wonders whether Helen is saying this simply to avoid creating feelings of guilt, but Helen replies that she means every word—she couldn't bring herself to lie to Lisa if she tried.

II. WHAT'S MISSING?

What is troubling about the words of John and Helen? Both show stout character and moral awareness. John's remarks have a benevolent, consequentialist cast, while Helen reasons in a deontological language of duties, reciprocity, and respect. They are not self-centred or without feeling. Yet something seems wrong.

The place to look is not so much at what they say as what they don't say. Think, for example, of how John's remarks might sound to his wife. Anne might have hoped that it was, in some ultimate sense, in part for *her* sake and the sake of their love as such that John pays such special attention to her. That he devotes himself to her because of the characteristically good consequences of doing so seems to leave her, and their relationship as such, too far out of the picture—this despite the fact that these characteristically good consequences depend in important ways on his special relation to her. She is being taken into account by John, but it might seem she is justified in being hurt by the way she is being taken into account. It is as if John viewed her, their relationship, and even his own affection for her from a distant, objective point of view—a moral point of view where reasons must be reasons for any rational agent and so must have an impersonal character even when they deal with personal matters. His wife might think a more personal point of view would also be appropriate, a point of view from which 'It's my wife' or 'It's Anne' would have direct and special relevance, and play an unmediated role in his answer to the question '*Why* do you attend to her so?'

Something similar is missing from Helen's account of why she stood by Lisa. While we understand that the specific duties she feels toward Lisa depend upon particular features of their relationship, still we would not be surprised if Lisa finds Helen's response to her expression of gratitude quite distant, even chilling. We need not question whether she has strong feeling for Lisa, but we may wonder at how that feeling finds expression in Helen's thinking.[2]

John and Helen both show alienation: there would seem to be an estrangement between their affections and their rational, deliberative selves; an abstract and universalizing point of view mediates their reponses to others and to their own sentiments. We should not assume that they have been caught in an uncharacteristic moment of moral reflection or after-the-fact rationalization; it is a settled part of their characters to think and act from a moral point of view. It is as if the world were for them a fabric of obligations and permissions in which personal considerations deserve recognition only to the extent that, and in the way that, such considerations find a place in this fabric.

To call John and Helen alienated from their affections or their intimates is not of itself to condemn them, nor is it to say that they are experiencing any sort of distress. One may be alienated from something without recognizing this as such or suffering in any conscious way from it, much as one may simply be uninterested in something without awareness or conscious suffering. But alienation is not mere lack of interest: John and Helen are not *uninterested* in their affections or in their intimates; rather, their interest takes a certain alienated form. While this alienation may not itself be a psychological affliction, it may be the basis of such afflictions—such as a sense of loneliness or emptiness—or of the loss of certain things of value— such as a sense of belonging or the pleasures of spontaneity. Moreover, their alienation may cause psychological distress in others, and make certain valuable sorts of relationships impossible.

However, we must be on guard lest over-simple categories distort our diagnosis. It seems to me wrong to picture the self as ordinarily divided into cognitive and affective halves, with deliberation and rationality belonging to the first, and sentiments belonging to the second. John's alienation is not a problem on the boundary of naturally given cognitive and affective selves, but a problem partially constituted by the bifurcation of his psyche into these separate spheres. *John*'s deliberative self seems remarkably divorced from his affections, but not all psyches need be so divided. That there is a cognitive element in affection—that affection is not a mere 'feeling' that is a given for the deliberative self but rather involves as well certain characteristic modes of thought and perception—is

---

[2] This is not to say that no questions arise about whether Helen's (or John's) feelings and attitudes constitute the fullest sort of affection, as will be seen shortly.

suggested by the difficulty some may have in believing that John really does love Anne if he persistently thinks about her in the way suggested by his remarks. Indeed, his affection for Anne does seem to have been demoted to a mere 'feeling'. For this reason among others, we should not think of John's alienation from his affections and his alienation from Anne as wholly independent phenomena, the one the cause of the other.[3] Of course, similar remarks apply to Helen.

III. THE MORAL POINT OF VIEW

Perhaps the lives of John and Anne or Helen and Lisa would be happier or fuller if none of the alienation mentioned were present. But is this a problem for *morality*? If, as some have contended, to have a morality is to make normative judgements from a moral point of view and be guided by them, and if by its nature a moral point of view must exclude considerations that lack universality, then any genuinely moral way of going about life would seem liable to produce the sorts of alienation mentioned above.[4] Thus it would be a conceptual confusion to ask that we never be required by morality to go beyond a personal point of view, since to fail ever to look at things from an impersonal (or non-personal) point of view would be to fail ever to *be* distinctively moral—not immoralism, perhaps, but amoralism. This would not be to say that there are not other points of view on life worthy of our attention,[5] or that taking a moral point of view is always appropriate—one could say that John and Helen show no moral defect in thinking so impersonally, although they do moralize to excess.

[3] Moreover, there is a sense in which someone whose responses to his affections or feelings are characteristically mediated by a calculating point of view may fail to know himself fully, or may seem in a way unknowable to others, and this 'cognitive distance' may itself be part of his alienation. I am indebted here to Allan Gibbard.

[4] There is a wide range of views about the nature of the moral point of view and its proper role in moral life. Is it necessary that one actually act on universal principles, or merely that one be willing to universalize the principles upon which one acts? Does the moral point of view by its nature require us to consider everyone alike? Here I am using a rather strong reading of the moral point of view, according to which taking the moral point of view involves universalization and the equal consideration of all.

[5] A moral point of view theorist might make use of the three points of view distinguished by Mill: the moral, the aesthetic, and the sympathetic. 'The first addresses itself to our reason and conscience; the second to our imagination; the third to our human fellow-feeling' ('Bentham' (1838), repr. in *John Stuart Mill: Utilitarianism and Other Writings*, ed. Mary Warnock (New York: New American Library, 1962), 121). What is morally right, in his view, may fail to be 'lovable' (e.g. a parent strictly disciplining a child) or 'beautiful' (e.g. an inauthentic gesture). Thus, the three points of view need not concur in their positive or negative assessments. Notice, however, that Mill has divided the self into three realms, of 'reason and conscience', of 'imagination', and of 'human fellow-feeling'; notice, too, that he has chosen the word 'feeling' to characterize human affections.

But the fact that a particular morality requires us to take an impersonal point of view could not sensibly be held against it, for that would be what makes it a morality at all.

This sort of position strikes me as entirely too complacent. First, we must somehow give an account of practical reasoning that does not merely multiply points of view and divide the self—a more unified account is needed. Second, we must recognize that loving relationships, friendships, group loyalties, and spontaneous actions are among the most important contributors to whatever it is that makes life worth while; any moral theory deserving serious consideration must itself give them serious consideration. As William K. Frankena has written, 'Morality is made for man, not man for morality.'[6] Moral considerations are often supposed to be overriding in practical reasoning. If we were to find that adopting a particular morality led to irreconcilable conflict with central types of human well-being—as cases akin to John's and Helen's have led some to suspect—then this surely would give us good reason to doubt its claims.[7]

For example, in the closing sentences of *A Theory of Justice* John Rawls considers the 'perspective of eternity', which is impartial across all individuals and times, and writes that this is a 'form of *thought and feeling* that rational persons can adopt in the world'. 'Purity of heart', he concludes, 'would be to see clearly and act with grace and self-command from this point of view.'[8] This may or may not be purity of heart, but it could not be the standpoint of actual life without radically detaching the individual from a range of personal concerns and commitments. Presumably we should not read Rawls as recommending that we adopt this point of view in the bulk of our actions in daily life, but the fact that so purely abstracted a perspective is portrayed as a kind of moral ideal should at least start us wondering.[9] If to be more perfectly moral is to ascend ever higher toward *sub*

---

[6] William K. Frankena, *Ethics*, 2nd edn. (Englewood Cliffs, NJ: Prentice-Hall, 1973), 116. Moralities that do not accord with this dictum—or a mordified version of it that includes all sentient beings—might be deemed alienated in a Feuerbachian sense.

[7] Mill, for instance, calls the moral point of view 'unquestionably the first and most important', and while he thinks it the error of the moralizer (such as Bentham) to elevate the moral point of view and 'sink the [aesthetic and sympathetic] entirely', he does not explain how to avoid such a result if the moral point of view is to be, as he says it ought, 'paramount'. See his 'Bentham', 121–2.

Philosophers who have recently raised doubts about moralities for such reasons include Bernard Williams, in 'A Critique of Utilitarianism', in J. J. C. Smart and B. Williams, *Utilitarianism, For and Against* (Cambridge: Cambridge University Press, 1973), and Michael Stocker, in 'The Schizophrenia of Modern Ethical Theories', *Journal of Philosophy*, 73 (1976), 453–66.

[8] John Rawls, *A Theory of Justice* (Cambridge, Mass.: Harvard University Press, 1971), 587 (my italics).

[9] I am not claiming that we should interpret all of Rawls's intricate moral theory in light of these few remarks. They are cited here merely to illustrate a certain tendency in moral thought, especially that of a Kantian inspiration.

specie aeternitatis abstraction, perhaps we made a mistake in boarding the moral escalator in the first place. Some of the very 'weaknesses' that prevent us from achieving this moral ideal—strong attachments to persons or projects—seem to be part of a considerably more compelling human ideal.

Should we say at this point that the lesson is that we should give a more prominent role to the value of non-alienation in our moral reasoning? That would be too little too late: the problem seems to be the way in which morality asks us to look at things, not just the things it asks us to look at.

IV. THE 'PARADOX OF HEDONISM'

Rather than enter directly into the question whether being moral is a matter of taking a moral point of view and whether there is thus some sort of necessary connection between being moral and being alienated in a way detrimental to human flourishing, I will consider a related problem the solution to which may suggest a way of steering around obstacles to a more direct approach.

One version of the so-called 'paradox of hedonism' is that adopting as one's exclusive ultimate end in life the pursuit of maximum happiness may well prevent one from having certain experiences or engaging in certain sorts of relationships or commitments that are among the greatest sources of happiness.[10] The hedonist, looking around him, may discover that some of those who are less concerned with their own happiness than he is, and who view people and projects less instrumentally than he does, actually manage to live happier lives than he despite his dogged pursuit of happiness. The 'paradox' is pragmatic, not logical, but it looks deep none the less: the hedonist, it would appear, ought not to be a hedonist. It seems, then, as if we have come across a second case in which mediating one's relations to people or projects by a particular point of view—in this case, a hedonistic point of view—may prevent one from attaining the fullest possible realization of sought-after values.

However, it is important to notice that even though adopting a hedonistic life project may tend to interfere with realizing that very project, there is no such natural exclusion between acting for the sake of another or a cause as such and recognizing how important this is to one's happiness. A

---

[10] This is a 'paradox' for individual, egoistic hedonists. Other forms the 'paradox of hedonism' may take are social in character: a society of egoistic hedonists might arguably achieve less total happiness than a society of more benevolent beings; or, taking happiness as the sole social goal might lead to a less happy society overall than could exist if a wider range of goals were pursued.

spouse who acts for the sake of his mate may know full well that this is a source of deep satisfaction for him—in addition to providing him with reasons for acting internal to it, the relationship may also promote the external goal of achieving happiness. Moreover, while the pursuit of happiness may not be the reason he entered or sustains the relationship, he may also recognize that if it had not seemed likely to make him happy he would not have entered it, and that if it proved over time to be inconsistent with his happiness he would consider ending it.

It might be objected that one cannot really regard a person or a project as an end as such if one's commitment is in this way contingent or overridable. But were this so, we would be able to have very few commitments to ends as such. For example, one could not be committed to both one's spouse and one's child as ends as such, since at most one of these commitments could be overriding in cases of conflict. It is easy to confuse the notion of a commitment to an end *as such* (or *for its own sake*) with that of an *overriding* commitment, but strength is not the same as structure. To be committed to an end as such is a matter of (among other things) whether it furnishes one with reasons for acting that are not mediated by other concerns. It does not follow that these reasons must always outweigh whatever opposing reasons one may have, or that one may not at the same time have other, mediating reasons that also incline one to act on behalf of that end.

Actual commitments to ends as such, even when very strong, are subject to various qualifications and contingencies.[11] If a friend grows too predictable or moves off to a different part of the world, or if a planned life project proves less engaging or practical than one had imagined, commitments and affections naturally change. If a relationship were highly vulnerable to the least change, it would be strained to speak of genuine affection rather than, say, infatuation. But if members of a relationship came to believe that they would be better off without it, this ordinarily would be a non-trivial change, and it is not difficult to imagine that their commitment to the relationship might be contingent in this way but none the less real. Of course, a relationship involves a shared history and shared expectations as well as momentary experiences, and it is unusual that affection or concern can be changed overnight, or relationships begun or ended at will. Moreover, the sorts of affections and commitments that can play a decisive role in shaping one's life and in making possible the deeper sorts of satisfactions are not those that are easily overridden or subject to constant reassessment or second-guessing. Thus a sensible hedonist would not

---

[11] This is not to deny that there are indexical components to commitments.

forever be subjecting his affections or commitments to egoistic calculation, nor would he attempt to break off a relationship or commitment merely because it might seem to him at a given moment that some other arrange- ment would make him happier. Commitments to others or to causes as such may be very closely linked to the self, and a hedonist who knows what he's about will not be one who turns on his self at the slightest provocation. Contingency is not expendability, and while some commit- ments are remarkably non-contingent—such as those of parent to child or patriot to country—it cannot be said that commitments of a more contin- gent sort are never genuine, or never conduce to the profounder sorts of happiness.[12]

Following these observations, we may reduce the force of the 'paradox of hedonism' if we distinguish two forms of hedonism. *Subjective hedonism* is the view that one should adopt the hedonistic point of view in action, that is, that one should whenever possible attempt to determine which act seems most likely to contribute optimally to one's happiness, and behave accordingly. *Objective hedonism* is the view that one should follow that course of action which would in fact most contribute to one's happiness, even when this would involve *not* adopting the hedonistic point of view in action. An act will be called *subjectively hedonistic* if it is done from a hedonistic point of view; an act is *objectively hedonistic* if it is that act, of those available to the agent, which would most contribute to his happi- ness.[13] Let us call someone a *sophisticated hedonist* if he aims to lead an objectively hedonistic life (that is, the happiest life available to him in the

---

[12] It does seem likely to matter just what the commitment is contingent upon as well as just how contingent it is. I think it is an open question whether commitments contingent upon the satisfaction of egoistic hedonist criteria are of the sort that might figure in the happiest sorts of lives ordinarily available. We will return to this problem presently.

Those who have had close relationships often develop a sense of *duty* to one another that may outlast affection or emotional commitment, that is, they may have a sense of obligation to one another that is less contingent than affection or emotional commitment, and that should not simply be confused with them. If such a sense of obligation is in conflict with self-interest, and if it is a normal part of the most satisfying sorts of close relationships, then this may pose a problem for the egoistic hedonist.

[13] A few remarks are needed. First, I will say that an act is available to an agent if he would succeed in performing it if he tried. Second, here and elsewhere in this article I mean to include quite 'thick' descriptions of actions, so that it may be part of an action that one perform it with a certain intention or goal. In the short run (but not so much the long run) intentions, goals, motives, and the like are usually less subject to our deliberate control than overt behaviour—it is easier to say 'I'm sorry' than to say it and mean it. This, however, is a fact about the relative availability of acts to the agent at a given time, and should not dictate what is to count as an act. Third, here and elsewhere I ignore for simplicity's sake the possibility that more than one course of action may be maximally valuable. And fourth, for reasons I will not enter into here, I have formulated objective hedonism in terms of actual outcomes rather than expected values (rela- tive to the information available to the agent). One could make virtually the same argument using an expected value formulation.

circumstances) and yet is not committed to subjective hedonism. Thus, within the limits of what is psychologically possible, a sophisticated hedonist is prepared to eschew the hedonistic point of view whenever taking this point of view conflicts with following an objectively hedonistic course of action. The so-called paradox of hedonism shows that there will be such conflicts: certain acts or courses of action may be objectively hedonistic only if not subjectively hedonistic. When things are put this way, it seems that the sophisticated hedonist faces a problem rather than a paradox: how to act in order to achieve maximum possible happiness if this is at times—or even often—*not* a matter of carrying out hedonistic deliberations.

The answer in any particular case will be complex and contextual—it seems unlikely that any one method of decision-making would always promote thought and action most conducive to one's happiness. A sophisticated hedonist might proceed precisely by looking at the complex and contextual: observing the actual modes of thought and action of those people who are in some ways like himself and who seem most happy. If our assumptions are right, he will find that few such individuals are subjective hedonists; instead, they act for the sake of a variety of ends as such. He may then set out to develop in himself the traits of character, ways of thought, types of commitment, and so on, that seem common in happy lives. For example, if he notes that the happiest people often have strong loyalties to friends, he must ask how he can become a more loyal friend—not merely how he can seem to be a loyal friend (since those he has observed are not happy because they merely seem loyal)—but how he can in fact be one.

Could one really make such changes if one had as a goal leading an optimally happy life? The answer seems to me a qualified *yes*, but let us first look at a simpler case. A highly competitive tennis-player comes to realize that his obsession with winning is keeping him from playing his best. A pro tells him that if he wants to win he must devote himself more to the game and its play as such and think less about his performance. In the commitment and concentration made possible by this devotion, he is told, lies the secret of successful tennis. So he spends a good deal of time developing an enduring devotion to many aspects of the activity, and finds it peculiarly satisfying to become so absorbed in it. He plays better, and would have given up the programme of change if he did not, but he now finds that he plays tennis more for its own sake, enjoying greater internal as well as external rewards from the sport. Such a person would not keep thinking—on or off the court—'No matter how I play, the only thing I really care about is whether I win!' He would recognize such thoughts as self-defeating, as evidence that his old, unhelpful way of looking at things was returning. Nor would such a person be self-deceiving. He need not hide from himself his goal of winning, for this goal is consistent with his increased devotion to the game. His commitment to the activity is not eclipsed by, but made more vivid by, his desire to succeed at it.

The same sort of story might be told about a sophisticated hedonist and friendship. An individual could realize that his instrumental attitude toward his friends prevents him from achieving the fullest happiness friendship affords. He could then attempt to focus more on his friends as such, doing this somewhat deliberately, perhaps, until it comes more naturally. He might then find his friendships improved and himself happier. If he found instead that his relationships were deteriorating or his happiness declining, he would reconsider the idea. None of this need be hidden from himself: the external goal of happiness reinforces the internal goals of his relationships. The sophisticated hedonist's motivational structure should therefore meet a *counterfactual condition*: he need not always act for the sake of happiness, since he may do various things for their own sake or for the sake of others, but he would not act as he does if it were not compatible with his leading an objectively hedonistic life. Of course, a sophisticated hedonist cannot guarantee that he will meet this counterfactual condition, but only attempt to meet it as fully as possible.

Success at tennis is a relatively circumscribed goal, leaving much else about one's life undefined. Maximizing one's happiness, by contrast, seems all-consuming. Could commitments to other ends survive alongside it? Consider an analogy. Ned needs to make a living. More than that, he needs to make as much money as he can—he has expensive tastes, a second marriage, and children reaching college age, and he does not have extensive means. He sets out to invest his money and his labour in ways he thinks will maximize return. Yet it does not follow that he acts as he does solely for the sake of earning as much as possible.[14] Although it is obviously true that he does what he does because he believes that it will maximize return, this does not preclude his doing it for other reasons as well, for example, for the sake of living well or taking care of his children. This may continue to be the case even if Ned comes to want money for its own sake, that is, if he comes to see the accumulation of wealth as intrinsically as well as extrinsically attractive.[15] Similarly, the stricture that one seek the object

[14] Michael Stocker considers related cases in 'Morally Good Intentions', *Monist*, 54 (1970) 124–41. I am much indebted to his discussion.

[15] There may be a parallelism of sorts between Ned's coming to seek money for its own sake and a certain pattern of moral development: what is originally sought in order to live up to familial or social expectations may come to be an end in itself.

It might be objected that the goal of earning as much money as possible is quite unlike the goal of being as happy as possible, since money is plainly instrumentally valuable even when it

ively hedonistic life certainly provides one with considerable guidance, but it does not supply the whole of one's motives and goals in action.

My claim that the sophisticated hedonist can escape the paradox of hedonism was, however, qualified. It still seems possible that the happiest sorts of lives ordinarily attainable are those led by people who would reject even sophisticated hedonism, people whose character is such that if they were presented with a choice between two entire lives, one of which contains less total happiness but none the less realizes some other values more fully, they might well knowingly choose against maximal happiness. If this were so, it would show that a sophisticated hedonist might have reason for changing his beliefs so that he no longer accepts hedonism in any form. This still would not refute objective hedonism as an account of the (rational, prudential, or moral) *criterion* one's acts should meet, for it would be precisely in order to meet this criterion that the sophisticated hedonist would change his beliefs.[16]

V. THE PLACE OF NON-ALIENATION
AMONG HUMAN VALUES

Before discussing the applicability of what has been said about hedonism to morality, we should notice that alienation is not always a bad thing, that we may not want to overcome all forms of alienation, and that other values, which may conflict with non-alienation in particular cases, may at times have a greater claim on us. Let us look at a few such cases.

It has often been argued that a morality of duties and obligations may appropriately come into play in familial or friendly relationships when the relevant sentiments have given out, for instance, when one is exasperated with a friend, when love is tried, and so on.[17] 'Ought' implies 'can' (or, at least, 'could'), and while it may be better in human terms when we do what we ought to do at least in part out of feelings of love, friendship, or sympathy, there are times when we simply cannot muster these sentiments, and the right thing to do is to act as love or friendship or sympathy would have directed rather than refuse to perform any act done merely from a sense of duty.

---

s sought for its own sake. But happiness, too, is instrumentally valuable, for it may contribute to realizing such goals as being a likeable or successful person.

[16] An important objection to the claim that objective hedonism may serve as the *moral* criterion one's acts should meet, even if this means not believing in hedonism, is that moral principles must meet a *publicity* condition. I will discuss this objection in Sect. VI.

[17] See, for example, Stocker, 'The Schizophrenia of Modern Ethical Theories'.

But we should add a further role for unspontaneous, morally motivated action: even when love or concern is strong, it is often desirable that people achieve some distance from their sentiments or one another. A spouse may act toward his mate in a grossly over-protective way; a friend may indulge another's ultimately destructive tendencies; a parent may favour one child inordinately. Strong and immediate affection may overwhelm one's ability to see what another person actually needs or deserves. In such cases a certain distance between people or between an individual and his sentiments, and an intrusion of moral considerations into the gap thus created, may be a good thing, and part of genuine affection or commitment. The opposite view, that no such mediation is desirable as long as affection is strong, seems to me a piece of romanticism. Concern over alienation therefore ought not to take the form of a cult of 'authenticity at any price'.

Moreover, there will occur regular conflicts between avoiding alienation and achieving other important individual goals. One such goal is autonomy. Bernard Williams has emphasized that many of us have developed certain 'ground projects' that give shape and meaning to our lives, and has drawn attention to the damage an individual may suffer if he is alienated from his ground projects by being forced to look at them as potentially overridable by moral considerations.[18] But against this it may be urged that it is crucial for autonomy that one hold one's commitments up for inspection—even one's ground projects. Our ground projects are often formed in our youth, in a particular family, class, or cultural background. It may be alienating and even disorienting to call these into question, but to fail to do so is to lose autonomy. Of course, autonomy could not sensibly require that we question all of our values and commitments at once, nor need it require us to be forever detached from what we are doing. It is quite possible to submit basic aspects of one's life to scrutiny and arrive at a set of autonomously chosen commitments that form the basis of an integrated life. Indeed, psychological conflicts and practical obstacles give us occasion for re-examining our basic commitments rather more often than we'd like.

At the same time, the tension between autonomy and non-alienation should not be exaggerated. Part of avoiding exaggeration is giving up the Kantian notion that autonomy is a matter of escaping determination by any contingency whatsoever. Part, too, is refusing to conflate autonomy with sheer independence from others. Both Rousseau and Marx emphasized that achieving control over one's own life requires participation in

[18] Williams, 'A Critique of Utilitarianism'.

certain sorts of social relations—in fact, relations in which various kinds of alienation have been minimized.

Autonomy is but one value that may enter into complex trade-offs with non-alienation. Alienation and inauthenticity do have their uses. The alienation of some individuals or groups from their milieu may at times be necessary for fundamental social criticism or cultural innovation. And without some degree of inauthenticity, it is doubtful whether civil relations among people could long be maintained. It would take little ingenuity, but too much of the reader's patience, to construct here examples involving troubling conflicts between non-alienation and virtually any other worthy goal.

VI. REDUCING ALIENATION IN MORALITY

Let us now move to morality proper. To do this with any definiteness, we must have a particular morality in mind. For various reasons, I think that the most plausible sort of morality is consequentialist in form, assessing rightness in terms of contribution to the good. In attempting to sketch how we might reduce alienation in moral theory and practice, therefore, I will work within a consequentialist framework (although a number of the arguments I will make could be made, *mutatis mutandis*, by a deontologist).

Of course, one has adopted no morality in particular even in adopting consequentialism unless one says what the good is. Let us, then, dwell briefly on axiology. One mistake of dominant consequentialist theories, I believe, is their failure to see that things other than subjective states can have intrinsic value. Allied to this is a tendency to reduce all intrinsic values to one—happiness. Both of these features of classical utilitarianism reflect forms of alienation. First, in divorcing subjective states from their objective counterparts, and claiming that we seek the latter exclusively for the sake of the former, utilitarianism cuts us off from the world in a way made graphic by examples such as that of the experience machine, a hypothetical device that can be programmed to provide one with whatever subjective states he may desire. The experience machine affords us decisive subjective advantages over actual life: few, if any, in actual life think they have achieved all that they could want, but the machine makes possible for each an existence that he cannot distinguish from such a happy state of affairs.[19] Despite this striking advantage, most rebel at the notion of the experience machine. As Robert Nozick and others have pointed out,

---

[19] At least one qualification is needed: the subjective states must be psychologically possible. Perhaps some of us desire what are, in effect, psychologically impossible states.

it seems to matter to us what we actually *do* and *are* as well as how life *appears* to us.[20] We see the point of our lives as bound up with the world and other people in ways not captured by subjectivism, and our sense of loss in contemplating a life tied to an experience machine, quite literally alienated from the surrounding world, suggests where subjectivism has gone astray. Second, the reduction of all goals to the purely abstract goal of happiness or pleasure, as in hedonistic utilitarianism, treats all other goals instrumentally. Knowledge or friendship may promote happiness, but is it a fair characterization of our commitment to these goals to say that this is the only sense in which they are ultimately valuable? Doesn't the insistence that there is an abstract and uniform goal lying behind all of our ends bespeak an alienation from these particular ends?

Rather than pursue these questions further here, let me suggest an approach to the good that seems to me less hopeless as a way of capturing human value: a pluralistic approach in which several goods are viewed as intrinsically, non-morally valuable—such as happiness, knowledge, purposeful activity, autonomy, solidarity, respect, and beauty.[21] These good

---

[20] Robert Nozick, *Anarchy, State, and Utopia* (New York: Basic Books, 1974), 42 ff.

[21] To my knowledge, the best-developed method for justifying claims about intrinsic value involves thought experiments of a familiar sort, in which, for example, we imagine two lives, or two worlds, alike in all but one respect, and then attempt to determine whether rational, well-informed, widely experienced individuals would (when vividly aware of both alternatives) be indifferent between the two or have a settled preference for one over the other. Since no one is ideally rational, fully informed, or infinitely experienced, the best we can do is to take more seriously the judgements of those who come nearer to approximating these conditions. Worse yet: the best we can do is to take more seriously the judgements of those we *think* better approximate these conditions. (I am not supposing that facts or experience somehow entail values, but that in rational agents, beliefs and values show a marked mutual influence and coherence.) We may overcome some narrowness if we look at behaviour and preferences in other societies and other epochs, but even here we must rely upon interpretations coloured by our own beliefs and values. Within the confines of this article I must leave unanswered a host of deep and troubling questions about the nature of values and value judgements. Suffice it to say that there is no reason to think that we are in a position to give anything but a tentative list of intrinsic goods.

It becomes a complex matter to describe the psychology of intrinsic value. For example, should we say that one values a relationship of solidarity, say, a friendship, *because it is a* friendship? That makes it sound as if it were somehow instrumental to the realization of some abstract value, friendship. Surely this is a misdescription. We may be able to get a clearer idea of what is involved by considering the case of happiness. We certainly do not value a particular bit of experienced happiness because it is instrumental in the realization of the abstract goal, happiness—we value the experience for its own sake because it is a happy experience. Similarly, a friendship is itself the valued thing, the thing of a valued kind. Of course, one can say that one values friendship and therefore seeks friends, just as one can say one values happiness and therefore seeks happy experiences. But this locution must be contrasted with what is being said when, for example, one talks of seeking *things that make one happy*. Friends are not 'things that make one achieve friendship'—they partially constitute friendships, just as particular happy experiences partially constitute happiness for an individual. Thus taking friendship as an intrinsic value does not entail viewing particular friendships instrumentally.

need not be ranked lexically, but may be attributed weights, and the criterion of rightness for an act would be that it most contribute to the weighted sum of these values in the long run. This creates the possibility of trade-offs among values of the kinds discussed in the previous section. However, I will not stop here to develop or defend such an account of the good and the right, since our task is to show how certain problems of alienation that arise in moral contexts might be dealt with if morality is assumed to have such a basis.

Consider, then, Juan, who, like John, has always seemed a model husband. When a friend remarks on the extraordinary concern he shows for his wife, Juan characteristically responds: 'I love Linda. I even *like* her. So it means a lot to me to do things for her. After all we've been through, it's almost a part of me to do it.' But his friend knows that Juan is a principled individual, and asks Juan how his marriage fits into that larger scheme. After all, he asks, it's fine for Juan and his wife to have such a close relationship, but what about all the other, needier people Juan could help if he broadened his horizon still further? Juan replies, 'Look, it's a better world when people can have a relationship like ours—and nobody could if everyone were always asking themselves who's got the most need. It's not easy to make things work in this world, and one of the best things that happens to people is to have a close relationship like ours. You'd make things worse in a hurry if you broke up those close relationships for the sake of some higher goal. Anyhow, I know that you can't always put family first. The world isn't such a wonderful place that it's OK just to retreat into your own little circle. But still, you need that little circle. People get burned out, or lose touch, if they try to save the world by themselves. The ones who can stick with it and do a good job of making things better are usually the ones who can make that fit into a life that does not make them miserable. I haven't met any real saints lately, and I don't trust people who think they are saints.'

If we contrast Juan with John, we do not find that the one allows moral considerations to enter his personal life while the other does not. Nor do we find that one is less serious in his moral concern. Rather, what Juan recognizes to be morally required is not by its nature incompatible with acting directly for the sake of another. It is important to Juan to subject his life to moral scrutiny—he is not merely stumped when asked for a defence of his acts above a personal level, he does not *just* say 'Of course I take care of her, she's my wife!' or 'It's Linda' and refuse to listen to the more impersonal considerations raised by his friend. It is consistent with what he says to imagine that his motivational structure has a form akin to that of

the sophisticated hedonist, that is, his motivational structure meets a
counterfactual condition: while he ordinarily does not do what he does
simply for the sake of doing what's right, he would seek to lead a different
sort of life if he did not think his were morally defensible. His love is not
a romantic submersion in the other to the exclusion of worldly responsibilities, and to that extent it may be said to involve a degree of alienation
from Linda. But this does not seem to drain human value from their
relationship. Nor need one imagine that Linda would be saddened to hear
Juan's words the way Anne might have been saddened to overhear the
remarks of John.[22]

Moreover, because of his very willingness to question his life morally,
Juan avoids a sort of alienation not sufficiently discussed—alienation from
others, beyond one's intimate ties. Individuals who will not or cannot allow
questions to arise about what they are doing from a broader perspective
are in an important way cut off from their society and the larger world.
They may not be troubled by this in any very direct way, but even so they
may fail to experience that powerful sense of purpose and meaning that
comes from seeing oneself as part of something larger and more enduring
than oneself or one's intimate circle. The search for such a sense of purpose and meaning seems to me ubiquitous—surely much of the impulse to
religion, to ethnic or regional identification (most strikingly, in the 'redis-
covery' of such identities), or to institutional loyalty stems from this desire
to see ourselves as part of a more general, lasting, and worthwhile scheme
of things.[23] This presumably is part of what is meant by saying that
secularization has led to a sense of meaninglessness, or that the decline of
traditional communities and societies has meant an increase in anomie.
(The sophisticated hedonist, too, should take note: one way to gain a
firmer sense that one's life is worth while, a sense that may be important to

---

[22] If one objects that Juan's commitment to Linda is lacking because it is contingent in some
ways, the objector must show that the *kinds* of contingencies involved would destroy his
relationship with Linda, especially since moral character often figures in commitments—the
character of the other, or the compatibility of a commitment with one's having the sort of
character one values—and the contingencies in Juan's case are due to his moral character.

[23] I do not mean to suggest that such identities are always matters of choice for individuals.
Quite the reverse, identities often arise through socialization, prejudice, and similar influences.
The point rather is that there is a very general phenomenon of identification, badly in need of
explanation, that to an important extent underlies such phenomena as socialization and prejudice, and that suggests the existence of certain needs in virtually all members of society—needs
to which identification with entities beyond the self answers.

Many of us who resist raising questions about our lives from broader perspectives do so, I
fear, not out of a sense that it would be difficult or impossible to lead a meaningful life if one
entertained such perspectives, but rather out of a sense that our lives would not stand up to
much scrutiny therefrom, so that leading a life that *would* seem meaningful from such perspectives would require us to change in some significant way.

realizing various values in one's own life, is to overcome alienation from others.)

Drawing upon our earlier discussion of two kinds of hedonism, let us now distinguish two kinds of consequentialism. *Subjective consequentialism* is the view that whenever one faces a choice of actions, one should attempt to determine which act of those available would most promote the good, and should then try to act accordingly. One is behaving as subjective consequentialism requires—that is, leading a *subjectively consequentialist life*—to the extent that one uses and follows a distinctively consequentialist mode of decision-making, consciously aiming at the overall good and conscientiously using the best available information with the greatest possible rigour. *Objective consequentialism* is the view that the criterion of the rightness of an act or course of action is whether it in fact would most promote the good of those acts available to the agent. Subjective consequentialism, like subjective hedonism, is a view that prescribes following a particular mode of deliberation in action; objective consequentialism, like objective hedonism, concerns the outcomes actually brought about, and thus deals with the question of deliberation only in terms of the tendencies of certain forms of decision-making to promote appropriate outcomes. Let us reserve the expression *objectively consequentialist act (or life)* for those acts (or that life) of those available to the agent that would bring about the best outcomes.[24] To complete the parallel, let us say that a *sophisticated consequentialist* is someone who has a standing commitment to leading an objectively consequentialist life, but who need not set special stock in any particular form of decision-making and therefore does not necessarily seek to lead a subjectively consequentialist life. Juan, it might be argued (if the details were filled in), is a sophisticated consequentialist, since he seems to believe he should act for the best but does not seem to feel it appropriate to bring a consequentialist calculus to bear on his every act.

Is it bizarre, or contradictory, that being a sophisticated consequentialist

[24] Although the language here is causal—'promoting' and 'bringing about'—it should be said that the relation of an act to the good need not always be causal. An act of learning may non-causally involve coming to have knowledge (an intrinsic good by my reckoning) as well as contributing causally to later realizations of intrinsic value. Causal consequences as such do not have a privileged status. As in the case of objective hedonism, I have formulated objective consequentialism in terms of actual outcomes (so-called 'objective duty') rather than expected values relative to what is rational for the agent to believe ('subjective duty'). The main arguments of this article could be made using expected value, since the course of action with highest expected value need not in general be the subjectively consequentialist one. See also nn. 13 and 21.

Are there any subjective consequentialists? Well, various theorists have claimed that a consequentialist must be a subjective consequentialist in order to be genuine—see Williams, 'A Critique of Utilitarianism', 135, and Rawls, *A Theory of Justice*, 182.

may involve rejecting subjective consequentialism? After all, doesn't an adherent of subjective consequentialism also seek to lead an objectively consequentialist life? He may, but then he is mistaken in thinking that this means he should always undertake a distinctively consequentialist deliberation when faced with a choice. To see his mistake, we need only consider some examples.

It is well known that in certain emergencies, the best outcome requires action so swift as to preclude consequentialist deliberation. Thus a sophisticated consequentialist has reason to inculcate in himself certain dispositions to act rapidly in obvious emergencies. The disposition is not a mere reflex, but a developed pattern of action deliberately acquired. A simple example, but it should dispel the air of paradox.

Many decisions are too insignificant to warrant consequentialist deliberation ('Which shoe-lace should I do up first?') or too predictable in outcome ('Should I meet my morning class today as scheduled or should I linger over the newspaper?'). A famous old conundrum for consequentialism falls into a similar category: before I deliberate about an act, it seems I must decide how much time would be optimal to allocate for this deliberation; but then I must first decide how much time would be optimal to allocate for this time allocation decision; but before that I must decide how much time would be optimal to allocate for *that* decision; and so on. The sophisticated consequentialist can block this paralysing regress by noting that often the best thing to do is not to ask questions about time allocation at all; instead, he may develop standing dispositions to give more or less time to decisions depending upon their perceived importance, the amount of information available, the predictability of his choice, and so on. I think we all have dispositions of this sort, which account for our patience with some prolonged deliberations but not others.

There are somewhat more intriguing examples that have more to do with psychological interference than mere time efficiency: the timid, put-upon employee who knows that if he deliberates about whether to ask for a raise he will succumb to his timidity and fail to demand what he actually deserves; the self-conscious man who knows that if, at social gatherings, he is forever wondering how he should act, his behaviour will be awkward and unnatural, contrary to his goal of acting naturally and appropriately; the tightrope-walker who knows he must not reflect on the value of keeping his concentration; and so on. People can learn to avoid certain characteristically self-defeating lines of thought—just as the tennis-player in an earlier example learned to avoid thinking constantly about winning—and the sophisticated consequentialist may learn that consequentialist deliberation is in a variety of cases self-defeating, so that other habits of thought should be cultivated.

The sophisticated consequentialist need not be deceiving himself or acting in bad faith when he avoids consequentialist reasoning. He can fully recognize that he is developing the dispositions he does because they are necessary for promoting the good. Of course, he cannot be preoccupied with this fact all the while, but then one cannot be *preoccupied* with anything without this interfering with normal or appropriate patterns of thought and action.

To the list of cases of interference we may add John, whose all-purpose willingness to look at things by subjective consequentialist lights prevents the realization in him and in his relationships with others of values that he would recognize to be crucially important.

Bernard Williams has said that it shows consequentialism to be in grave trouble that it may have to usher itself from the scene as a mode of decision-making in a number of important areas of life.[25] Though I think he has exaggerated the extent to which we would have to exclude consequentialist considerations from our lives in order to avoid disastrous results, it is fair to ask: If maximizing the good were in fact to require that consequentialist reasoning be *wholly* excluded, would this refute consequentialism? Imagine an all-knowing demon who controls the fate of the world and who visits unspeakable punishment upon man to the extent that he does not employ a Kantian morality. (Obviously, the demon is not himself a Kantian.) If such a demon existed, sophisticated consequentialists would have reason to convert to Kantianism, perhaps even to make whatever provisions could be made to erase consequentialism from the human memory and prevent any resurgence of it.

Does this possibility show that objective consequentialism is self-defeating? On the contrary, it shows that objective consequentialism has the virtue of not blurring the distinction between the *truth-conditions* of an ethical theory and its *acceptance-conditions* in particular contexts, a distinction philosophers have generally recognized for theories concerning other subject-matters. It might be objected that, unlike other theories, ethical theories must meet a condition of publicity, roughly to the effect that it must be possible under all circumstances for us to recognize a true ethical theory as such and to promulgate it publicly without thereby violating that theory itself.[26] Such a condition might be thought to follow from

---

[25] Williams, 'A Critique of Utilitarianism', 135.

[26] For discussion of a publicity condition, see Rawls, *A Theory of Justice*, 133, 177–82, 582. The question whether a publicity condition can be justified is a difficult one, deserving fuller discussion than I am able to give it here.

the social nature of morality. But any such condition would be question-begging against consequentialist theories, since it would require that one class of actions—acts of adopting or promulgating an ethical theory—*not* be assessed in terms of their consequences. Moreover, I fail to see how such a condition could emanate from the social character of morality. To prescribe the adoption and promulgation of a mode of decision-making regardless of its consequences seems to me radically detached from human concerns, social or otherwise. If it is argued that an ethical theory that fails to meet the publicity requirement could under certain conditions endorse a course of action leading to the abuse and manipulation of man by man, we need only reflect that no psychologically possible decision procedure can guarantee that its widespread adoption could never have such a result. A 'consequentialist demon' might increase the amount of abuse and manipulation in the world in direct proportion to the extent that people act according to the categorical imperative. Objective consequentialism (unlike certain deontological theories) has valuable flexibility in permitting us to take consequences into account in assessing the appropriateness of certain modes of decision-making, thereby avoiding any sort of self-defeating decision procedure worship.

A further objection is that the lack of any direct link between objective consequentialism and a particular mode of decision-making leaves the view too vague to provide adequate guidance in practice. On the contrary, objective consequentialism sets a definite and distinctive criterion of right action, and it becomes an empirical question (though not an easy one) which modes of decision-making should be employed and when. It would be a mistake for an objective consequentialist to attempt to tighten the connection between his criterion of rightness and any particular mode of decision-making: someone who recommended a particular mode of decision-making regardless of consequences would not be a hard-nosed, non-evasive objective consequentialist, but a self-contradicting one.

VII. CONTRASTING APPROACHES

The seeming 'indirectness' of objective consequentialism may invite its confusion with familiar indirect consequentialist theories, such as rule-consequentialism. In fact, the subjective–objective distinction cuts across the rule–act distinction, and there are subjective and objective forms of both rule- and act-based theories. Thus far, we have dealt only with subjective and objective forms of act-consequentialism. By contrast, a *subjective rule*-consequentialist holds (roughly) that in deliberation we should always attempt to determine which act, of those available, conforms to that set of rules general acceptance of which would most promote the good; we then should attempt to perform this act. An *objective rule-*consequentialist sets actual conformity to the rules with the highest acceptance value as his criterion of right action, recognizing the possibility that the best set of rules might in some cases—or even always—recommend that one not perform rule-consequentialist deliberation.

Because I believe this last possibility must be taken seriously, I find the objective form of rule-consequentialism more plausible. Ultimately, however, I suspect that rule-consequentialism is untenable in either form, for it could recommend acts that (subjectively or objectively) accord with the best set of rules even when these rules are *not* in fact generally accepted, and when as a result these acts would have devastatingly bad consequences. 'Let the rules with greatest acceptance utility be followed, though the heavens fall!' is no more plausible than 'Fiat justitia, ruat coelum!'—and a good bit less ringing. Hence, the arguments in this article are based entirely upon act-consequentialism.

Indeed, once the subjective–objective distinction has been drawn, an act-consequentialist can capture some of the intuitions that have made rule- or trait-consequentialism appealing.[27] Surely part of the attraction of these indirect consequentialisms is the idea that one should have certain traits of character, or commitments to persons or principles, that are sturdy enough that one would at least sometimes refuse to forsake them even when this refusal is known to conflict with making some gain—perhaps small—in total utility. Unlike his subjective counterpart, the objective act-consequentialist is able to endorse characters and commitments that are sturdy in just this sense.

To see why, let us first return briefly to one of the simple examples of Section VI. A sophisticated act-consequentialist may recognize that if he were to develop a standing disposition to render prompt assistance in emergencies without going through elaborate act-consequentialist deliberation, there would almost certainly be cases in which he would perform acts worse than those he would have performed had he stopped to deliberate, for example, when his prompt action is misguided in a way he would have noticed had he thought the matter through. It may still be right for him to develop this disposition, for without it he would act rightly in emergencies still less often—a quick response is appropriate much more often than not, and it is not practically possible to develop a disposition

[27] For an example of trait-consequentialism, see Robert M. Adams, 'Motive Utilitarianism', *Journal of Philosophy*, 73 (1976), 467–81.

that would lead one to respond promptly in exactly those cases where this would have the best results. While one can attempt to cultivate dispositions that are responsive to various factors which might indicate whether promptness is of greater importance than further thought, such refinements have their own costs and, given the limits of human resources, even the best cultivated dispositions will sometimes lead one astray. The objective act-consequentialist would thus recommend cultivating dispositions that will sometimes lead him to violate his own criterion of right action. Still, he will not, as a trait-consequentialist would, shift his criterion and say that an act is right if it stems from the traits it would be best overall to have (given the limits of what is humanly achievable, the balance of costs and benefits, and so on). Instead, he continues to believe that an act may stem from the dispositions it would be best to have, and yet be wrong (because it would produce worse consequences than other acts available to the agent in the circumstances).[28]

This line of argument can be extended to patterns of motivation, traits of character, and rules. A sophisticated act-consequentialist should realize that certain goods are reliably attainable—or attainable at all—only if people have well-developed characters; that the human psyche is capable of only so much self-regulation and refinement; and that human perception and reasoning are liable to a host of biases and errors. Therefore, individuals may be more likely to act rightly if they possess certain enduring motivational patterns, character traits, or prima-facie commitments to rules in addition to whatever commitment they have to act for the best. Because such individuals would not consider consequences in all cases, they would miss a number of opportunities to maximize the good; but if they were instead always to attempt to assess outcomes, the overall result would be worse, for they would act correctly less often.[29]

---

[28] By way of contrast, when Robert Adams considers application of a motive-utilitarian view to the ethics of actions, he suggests 'conscience utilitarianism', the view that 'we have a *moral duty* to do an act, if and only if it would be demanded of us by the most useful kind of conscience we could have' ('Motive Utilitarianism', 479). Presumably, this means that it would be morally wrong to perform an act contrary to the demands of the most useful sort of conscience. I have resisted this sort of redefinition of rightness for actions, since I believe that the most useful sort of conscience may on occasion demand of us an act that does not have the best overall consequences of those available, and that performing this act would be wrong.

Of course, some difficulties attend the interpretation of this last sentence. I have assumed throughout that an act is available to an agent if he would succeed in performing it if he tried. I have also taken a rather simple view of the complex matter of attaching outcomes to specific acts. In those rare cases in which the performance of even one exceptional (purportedly optimizing) act would completely undermine the agent's standing (optimal) disposition, it might not be possible after all to say that the exceptional act would be the right one to perform in the circumstances. (This question will arise again shortly.)

[29] One conclusion of this discussion is that we cannot realistically expect people's behaviour to be in strict compliance with the counterfactual condition even if they are committed sophis-

We may now strengthen the argument to show that the objective act-consequentialist can approve of dispositions, characters, or commitments to rules that are sturdy in the sense mentioned above, that is, that do not merely supplement a commitment to act for the best, but sometimes override it, so that one knowingly does what is contrary to maximizing the good. Consider again Juan and Linda, whom we imagine to have a commuting marriage. They normally get together only every other week, but one week she seems a bit depressed and harried, and so he decides to take an extra trip in order to be with her. If he did not travel, he would save a fairly large sum that he could send Oxfam to dig a well in a drought-stricken village. Even reckoning in Linda's uninterrupted malaise, Juan's guilt, and any ill effects on their relationship, it may be that for Juan to contribute the fare to Oxfam would produce better consequences overall than the unscheduled trip. Let us suppose that Juan knows this, and that he could stay home and write the cheque if he tried. Still, given Juan's character, he in fact will not try to perform this more beneficial act but will travel to see Linda instead. The objective act-consequentialist will say that Juan performed the wrong act on this occasion. Yet he may also say that if Juan had had a character that would have led him to perform the better act (or made him more inclined to do so), he would have had to have been less devoted to Linda. Given the ways Juan can affect the world, it may be that if he were less devoted to Linda his overall contribution to human well-being would be less in the end, perhaps because he would become more cynical and self-centred. Thus it may be that Juan should have (should develop, encourage, and so on) a character such that he sometimes knowingly and deliberately acts contrary to his objective consequentialist duty. Any other character, of those actually available to him, would lead him to depart still further from an objectively consequentialist life. The issue is not whether staying home would *change* Juan's character—for we may suppose that it would not—but whether he would in fact decide to stay home if he had that character, of those available, that would lead him to perform the most beneficial overall sequence of acts. In some cases, then, there will exist an objective act-consequentialist argument for developing

---

icated consequentialists. At best, a sophisticated consequentialist tries to meet this condition. But it should be no surprise that in practice we are unlikely to be morally ideal. Imperfections in information alone are enough to make it very improbable that individuals will lead objectively onsequentialist lives. Whether or when to *blame* people for real or apparent failures to behave ideally is, of course, another matter.

Note that we must take into account not just the frequency with which right acts are performed, but the actual balance of gains and losses to overall well-being that results. Relative frequency of right action will settle the matter only in the (unusual) case where the amount of good at stake in each act of a given kind—for example, each emergency one comes across—is he same.

and sustaining characters of a kind Sidgwick and others have thought an act-consequentialist must condemn.[30]

VIII. DEMANDS AND DISRUPTIONS

Before ending this discussion of consequentialism, let me mention one other large problem involving alienation that has seemed uniquely troubling for consequentialist theories and that shows how coming to terms with problems of alienation may be a social matter as well as a matter of individual psychology. Because consequentialist criteria of rightness are linked to maximal contribution to the good, whenever one does not perform the very best act one can, one is 'negatively responsible' for any shortfall in total well-being that results. Bernard Williams has argued that to accept such a burden of responsibility would force most of us to abandon or be prepared to abandon many of our most basic individual commitments, alienating ourselves from the very things that mean the most to us.[31]

To be sure, objective act-consequentialism of the sort considered here is a demanding and potentially disruptive morality, even after allowances have been made for the psychological phenomena thus far discussed and for the difference between saying an act is wrong and saying that the agent ought to be blamed for it. But just *how* demanding or disruptive it would

---

[30] In *The Methods of Ethics* (1874; 7th edn. New York: Dover, 1966). IV. v. 4, Sidgwick discusses 'the Ideal of character and conduct' that a utilitarian should recognize as 'the sum of excellences or Perfections', and writes that 'a Utilitarian must hold that it is always wrong for a man knowingly to do anything other than what he believes to be most conducive to Universal Happiness' (p. 492). Here Sidgwick is uncharacteristically confused—and in two ways. First, considering act-by-act evaluation, an objective utilitarian can hold that an agent may simply be wrong in believing that a given course of action is most conducive to universal happiness, and therefore it may be right for him knowingly to do something other than this. Second, following Sidgwick's concern in this passage and looking at enduring traits of character rather than isolated acts, and even assuming the agent's belief to be correct, an objective utilitarian can hold that the ideal character for an individual, or for people in general, may involve a willingness knowingly to act contrary to maximal happiness when this is done for the sake of certain deep personal commitments. See ibid.

It might be thought counter-intuitive to say, in the example given, that it is not right for Juan to travel to see Linda. But it must be kept in mind that for an act-consequentialist to say that an action is not right is not to say that it is without merit, only that it is not the very best act available to the agent. And an intuitive sense of the rightness of visiting Linda may be due less to an evaluation of the act itself than to a reaction to the sort of character a person would have to have in order to stay home and write a check to Oxfam under the circumstances. Perhaps he would have to be too distant or righteous to have much appeal to us—especially in view of the fact that it is his spouse's anguish that is at stake. We have already seen how an act-consequentialist may share this sort of character assessment.

[31] Williams, 'A Critique of Utilitarianism', sect. 3.

be for an individual is a function—as it arguably should be—of how bad the state of the world is, how others typically act, what institutions exist, and how much that individual is capable of doing. If wealth were more equitably distributed, if political systems were less repressive and more responsive to the needs of their citizens, and if people were more generally prepared to accept certain responsibilities, then individuals' everyday lives would not have to be constantly disrupted for the sake of the good.

For example, in a society where there are no organized forms of disaster relief, it may be the case that if disaster were to strike a particular region, people all over the country would be obliged to make a special effort to provide aid. If, on the other hand, an adequate system of publicly financed disaster relief existed, then it probably would be a very poor idea for people to interrupt their normal lives and attempt to help—their efforts would probably be unco-ordinated, ill-informed, an interference with skilled relief work, and economically disruptive (perhaps even damaging to the society's ability to pay for the relief effort).

By altering social and political arrangements we can lessen the disruptiveness of moral demands on our lives, and in the long run achieve better results than free-lance good-doing. A consequentialist theory is therefore likely to recommend that accepting negative responsibility is more a matter of supporting certain social and political arrangements (or rearrangements) than of setting out individually to save the world. Moreover, it is clear that such social and political changes cannot be made unless the lives of individuals are psychologically supportable in the meanwhile, and this provides substantial reason for rejecting the notion that we should abandon all that matters to us as individuals and devote ourselves solely to net social welfare. Finally, in many cases what matters most is *perceived* rather than actual demandingness or disruptiveness, and this will be a relative matter, depending upon normal expectations. If certain social or political arrangements encourage higher contribution as a matter of course, individuals may not sense these moral demands as excessively intrusive.

To speak of social and political changes is, of course, to suggest eliminating the social and political pre-conditions for a number of existing projects and relationships, and such changes are likely to produce some degree of alienation in those whose lives have been disrupted. To an extent such people may be able to find new projects and relationships as well as maintain a number of old projects and relationships, and thereby avoid intolerable alienation. But not all will escape serious alienation. We thus have a case in which alienation will exist whichever course of action we follow—either the alienation of those who find the loss of the old order disorienting, or the continuing alienation of those who under the present order cannot lead lives expressive of their individuality or goals. It would seem that to follow the logic of Williams's position would have the unduly conservative result of favouring those less alienated in the present state of affairs over those who might lead more satisfactory lives if certain changes were to occur. Such conservativism could hardly be warranted by a concern about alienation if the changes in question would bring about social and political pre-conditions for a more widespread enjoyment of meaningful lives. For example, it is disruptive of the ground projects of many men that women have begun to demand and receive greater equality in social and personal spheres, but such disruption may be offset by the opening of more avenues of self-development to a greater number of people.

In responding to Williams's objection regarding negative responsibility, I have focused more on the problem of disruptiveness than the problem of demandingness, and more on the social than the personal level. More would need to be said than I am able to say here to come fully to terms with his objection, although some very general remarks may be in order. The consequentialist starts out from the relatively simple idea that certain things seem to matter to people above all else. His root conception of moral rightness is therefore that it should matter above all else whether people, in so far as possible, actually realize these ends.[32] Consequentialist moralities of the sort considered here undeniably set a demanding standard, calling upon us to do more for one another than is now the practice. But this standard plainly does not require that most people lead intolerable lives for the sake of some greater good: the greater good is empirically equivalent to the best possible lives for the largest possible number of people.[33] Objective consequentialism gives full expression to this root in-

---

[32] I appealed to this 'root conception' in rejecting rule-consequentialism in Sect. VII. Although consequentialism is often condemned for failing to provide an account of morality consistent with respect for persons, this root conception provides the basis for a highly plausible notion of such respect. I doubt, however, that any fundamental ethical dispute between consequentialists and deontologists can be resolved by appeal to the idea of respect for persons. The deontologist has his notion of respect—e.g. that we not use people in certain ways—and the consequentialist has *his*—e.g. that the good of every person has an equal claim upon us, a claim unmediated by any notion of right or contract, so that we should do the most possible to bring about outcomes that actually advance the good of persons. For every consequentially justified act of manipulation to which the deontologist can point with alarm there is a deontologically justified act that fails to promote the well-being of some person(s) as fully as possible to which the consequentialist can point, appalled. Which notion takes 'respect for persons' more seriously? There may be no non-question-begging answer, especially once the consequentialist has recognized such things as autonomy or respect as intrinsically valuable.

[33] The qualification 'empirically equivalent to' is needed because in certain empirically unrealistic cases, such as utility monsters, the injunction 'Maximize overall realization of human value' cannot be met by improving the lives of as large a proportion of the population as possible. However, under plausible assumptions about this world (including diminishing marginal value) the equivalence holds.

tuition by setting as the criterion of rightness actual contribution to the realization of human value, allowing practices and forms of reasoning to take whatever shape this requires. It is thus not equivalent to requiring a certain, alienated way of thinking about ourselves, our commitments, or how to act.

Samuel Scheffler has recently suggested that one response to the problems Williams raises about the impersonality and demandingness of consequentialism could be to depart from consequentialism at least far enough to recognize as a fundamental moral principle an agent-centred prerogative, roughly to the effect that one is not always obliged to maximize the good, although one is always permitted to do so if one wishes. This prerogative would make room for agents to give special attention to personal projects and commitments. However, the argument of this article, if successful, shows there to be a firm place in moral practice for prerogatives that afford such room even if one accepts a fully consequentialist fundamental moral theory.[34]

IX. ALIENATION FROM MORALITY

By way of conclusion, I would like to turn to alienation from morality itself, the experience (conscious or unconscious) of morality as an external set of demands not rooted in our lives or accommodating to our perspectives. Giving a convincing answer to the question 'Why should I be moral?' must involve diminishing the extent that morality appears alien.

Part of constructing such an answer is a matter of showing that abiding by morality need not alienate us from the particular commitments that make life worth while, and in the previous sections we have begun to see how this might be possible within an objective act-consequentialist account of what morality requires. We saw how in general various sorts of projects or relationships can continue to be a source of intrinsic value even though one recognizes that they might have to undergo changes if they could not be defended in their present form on moral grounds. And again, knowing that a commitment is morally defensible may well deepen its value for us, and may also make it possible for us to feel part of a larger world in a way that is itself of great value. If our commitments are regarded by others as responsible and valuable (or if we have reason to think that others should

---

[34] For Scheffler's view, see *The Rejection of Consequentialism: A Philosophical Investigation of the Considerations Underlying Rival Moral Conceptions* (Oxford: Clarendon Press, 1982). The consequentialist may also argue that at least some of the debate set in motion by Williams is more properly concerned with the question of the relation between moral imperatives and imperatives of rationality than with the content of moral imperatives as such. (See n. 42.)

so regard them), this may enhance the meaning or value they have for ourselves, while if they are regarded by others as irresponsible or worthless (especially, if we suspect that others regard them so justly), this may make it more difficult for us to identify with them or find purpose or value in them. Our almost universal urge to rationalize our acts and lives attests our wish to see what we do as defensible from a more general point of view. I do not deny that bringing a more general perspective to bear on one's life may be costly to the self—it may cause re-evaluations that lower self-esteem, produce guilt, alienation, and even problems of identity. But I do want to challenge the simple story often told in which there is a personal point of view from which we glimpse meanings which then vanish into insignificance when we adopt a more general perspective. In thought and action we shuttle back and forth from more personal to less personal standpoints, and both play an important role in the process whereby purpose, meaning, and identity are generated and sustained.[35] Moreover, it may be part of mature commitments, even of the most intimate sort, that a measure of perspective beyond the personal be maintained.

These remarks about the role of general perspectives in individual lives lead us to what I think is an equally important part of answering the question 'Why should I be moral?': reconceptualization of the terms of the discussion to avoid starting off in an alienated fashion and ending up with the result that morality still seems alien. Before pursuing this idea, let us quickly glance at two existing approaches to the question.

Morality may be conceived of as in essence selfless, impartial, impersonal. To act morally is to subordinate the self and all contingencies concerning the self's relations with others or the world to a set of imperatives binding on us solely as rational beings. We should be moral, in this view, because it is ideally rational. However, morality thus conceived seems bound to appear as alien in daily life. 'Purity of heart' in Rawls's sense would be essential to acting morally, and the moral way of life would appear well removed from our actual existence, enmeshed as we are in a web of 'particularistic' commitments—which happen to supply our *raisons d'être*.

A common alternative conception of morality is not as an elevated purity of heart but as a good strategy for the self. Hobbesian atomic individuals are posited and appeal is made to game theory to show that pay-offs to such individuals may be greater in certain conflict situations—

---

[35] For example, posterity may figure in our thinking in ways we seldom articulate. Thus, nihilism has seemed to some an appropriate response to the idea that mankind will soon destroy itself. 'Everything would lose its point' is a reaction quite distinct from 'Then we should enjoy ourselves as much as possible in the meantime', and perhaps equally comprehensible.